THE ALCHEMY PRESS
BOOK OF THE DEAD 2020

Cover of The Little People by John Christopher (Avon Books, 1968) by artist Hector Garrido (1928–2020).

THE ALCHEMY PRESS BOOK OF THE DEAD 2020

Compiled by
STEPHEN JONES

The Alchemy Press

Copyright © Stephen Jones 2021

First Edition

10 9 8 7 6 5 4 3 2 1

ISBN 978-1-911034-12-4

All rights reserved by Stephen Jones. The right of Stephen Jones to be identified as the Author of this Work has been asserted by him in accordance with the Copyright, Designs and Patents Act 1988.

With thanks to Peter Coleborn, David Barraclough, Mandy Slater, Andrew I. Porter, Amanda Foubister, Jo Fletcher, Jean-Daniel Brèque, Fran Weighell and Michael Marshall Smith for all their help and support.

Special thanks are also due to *Classic Images*, *Ansible*, *Locus*, *Entertainment Weekly* and other sources that were used for reference.

Cover design by Smith & Jones

About the cover

Detail from the cover of *Mysterious Adventures* No.18 (Story Comics, Inc., 1954) by Hy Fleishman (1927–2020). This issue of the pre-code horror comic was cited as an example of "depraved violence" by the 1954-55 Senate Investigation into Comic Books and Juvenile Delinquency.

The Alchemy Press
Staffordshire, England

Published in England

Visit our website at www.alchemypress.co.uk
Visit the author's website at www.stephenjoneseditor.com

Contents

Introduction	13
Derek Acorah	15
Joseph Adler	15
Raymond Allen	15
Bruce Allpress	15
Joseph Altairac	17
Charles Alverson	17
Nando Angelini	17
Michael Angelis	18
Brice Armstrong	18
Neda Arnerić	18
Sean Arnold	20
Kelly Asbury	20
David Ashford	20
Sei Ashina	21
Baby Peggy	21
Chuck Bail	22
Pip Baker	22
Dick Balduzzi	22
Brian N. Ball	23
John Bangsund	23
Dana Baratta	23
Harry Basch	24
Orson Bean	24
Alex Beaton	24
Jay Benedict	25
John Benfield	25
Ed Benguiat	25
Julie Bennett	26
Ronald Bergan	26
Warren Berlinger	26
Steve Bing	27
Merv Binns	27
Honor Blackman	28
Robert Blanche	28
William Blinn	28
Brian Blume	29
William Bogert	29
Thomas "Doc" Boguski	29
Frank W. Bolle	30
Claude Bolling	30
Roscoe Born	30
Lucia Bosè	31
Chadwick Boseman	31
Ben Bova	31
Gregory Tyree Boyce	32
Charly Bravo	32
Richard Bright	32
Wilford Brimley	34
David Britton	34
Tim Brooke-Taylor	35
Pat Brymer	35
Jeremy Bulloch	35
Jack Burns	36
Kevin Burns	36
Cindy Butler	37
Edd Byrnes	37
Elisa Cabrera	37
Steven Cagan	38
Rachel Caine	38
R.D. Call	39
John Callahan	39
Earl Cameron	39
Jason Scott Campbell	40
Raymundo Capetillo	40
Pierre Cardin	40
Lewis John Carlino	40
Chris Carnel	41
Brent Carver	41
David S. Cass	42
Marge Champion	42
Michael Chapman	42
Heather Chasen	43
Mary Higgins Clark	43
Harry Clein	43
Ron Cobb	44
Robert Cobert	44
Daisy Coleman	46
Raphaël Coleman	46
David Collings	46

Forrest Compton	47	James Drury	65
Sean Connery	47	George Dugdale	65
Robert Conrad	49	Cheryl Wheeler Duncan	67
Kevin Conway	49	Marj Dusay	67
Wendy Cooling	49	Hilary Dwyer	68
Ben Cooper	49	Gene Dynarski	68
Richard Corben	50	Robert Eighteen-Bisang	68
Nick Cordero	50	Phyllis Eisenstein	70
Cis Corman	52	Susan Ellison	71
Stuart Cornfeld	52	John Ericson	71
Dale Crain	52	Mort Fallick	71
Doug Crane	52	Sergio Fantoni	72
Gary William Crawford	53	Melinda Fee	72
Linda Cristal	53	Edward S. Feldman	72
Denise Cronenberg	53	Andrew J. Fenady	73
Ben Cross	54	Mike Fenton	73
Frances Cuka	54	Giancarlo Ferrando	74
Julian Curry	55	Conchata Ferrell	74
Clive Cussler	55	Keith Ferrell	74
Nick Cuti	55	Lee Fierro	75
Abby Dalton	56	Alison Fiske	75
Wally K. Daly	56	Hy Fleishman	75
Sonia Darrin	56	Rhonda Fleming	76
Allen Daviau	57	Ronald Forfar	76
Matteo De Cosmo	57	M.A. Foster	76
Richard De Croce	57	Derek Fowlds	76
Olivia de Havilland	58	Samantha Fox	77
Gianni Dei	58	John Fraser	77
Gene Deitch	58	Janet Freer	79
Dorothy Dells	59	Bruce Jay Friedman	79
Brian Dennehy	59	Nikki Fritz	79
Dimitri Diatchenko	59	Bob Fujitani	80
Dena Dietrich	60	Carl Gafford	80
Arthur Dignam	60	David Galanter	82
Vasilis Dimitriou	60	Janet Ann Gallow	82
Malcolm Dixon	61	Gerald Gardner	82
Kevin Dobson	61	Allen Garfield	84
Mario Donatone	62	Robert Garland	84
Kirk Douglas	62	Hector Garrido	84
Shirley Douglas	62	Jill Gascoine	85
Kaye Dowd	64	Leslie Hamilton Gearren	85
Debra Doyle	64	David Geiser	85
Mort Drucker	64	Thomas Gianni	86

Rob Gibbs	86	Danny Hicks	105
David Giler	88	Michael Z. Hobson	105
Juan Giménez	88	Jim Holloway	105
Mark Glamack	88	Ian Holm	106
Milton Glaser	89	Sandy Holt	106
Mary Pat Gleason	89	Walter Hooper	107
Rolf Gohs	90	Silvio Horta	107
Billy Goldenberg	90	Robert Hossein	107
Danny Goldman	90	Roy Hudd	108
Terry Goodkind	91	Peter H. Hunt	108
Charles Gordon	91	Grant Imahara	108
Joyce Gordon	91	Dean Ing	109
Stuart Gordon	91	Andrew Jack	109
Victor Gorelick	93	Jael	110
Galyn Görg	93	Anthony James	110
Graydon Gould	94	Jim Janes	110
John Grant	94	Barbara Jefford	111
Juliette Gréco	95	Rafer Johnson	111
Cliff Green	95	Ken Jones	112
Michael Greene	95	Terry Jones	112
Terence Greer	96	Patrick Jordan	112
Arv Greywal	96	Eizo Kaimai	113
P.M. Griffin	96	Joe Kane	113
Jerome Guardino	97	John Karlen	115
James E. Gunn	97	Al Kasha	115
Ron Haddrick	97	Hisashi Katsuda	116
Chanin Hale	99	James Keast	116
William Hale	99	Hugh Keays-Byrne	116
Parnell Hall	99	Michael P. Keenan	117
Paul Hammond	100	Jack Kehoe	117
Terry Hands	100	Paula Kelly	117
Robert Harper	100	Earl Kemp	117
Alan Harris	101	Johnny Kevorkian	118
Dee Hartford	101	Irrfan Khan	118
Margot Hartman	101	Gary B. Kibbe	120
Ronald Harwood	102	Stan Kirsch	120
Eddie Hassell	102	Shirô Kishibe	120
David Hemblen	102	G. Howard Klar	120
James Henerson	103	Douglas Knapp	121
Buck Henry	103	Paul Knight	121
Richard Herd	104	Rosalind Knight	121
Aarón Hernán	104	Shirley Knight	122
Jery Hewitt	104	Pamela Kosh	122

Tsugunobu Kotani	122	Penny McCarthy	140
John Lafia	123	Kay McCauley	140
Len Lakofka	123	Martin McKenna	140
Peter Lamont	123	Frank McLaughlin	141
David Lander	124	Armelia McQueen	141
Charles Lanyer	124	Michael Medwin	142
David Larkin	124	Francis Megahy	142
Dieter Laser	125	Andree Melly	142
Philip Latham	125	Jiří Menzel	144
Moonyeenn Lee	125	Monique Mercure	144
Stevie Lee	127	Hans Meyer	144
Johnny Leeze	127	Norma Michaels	144
Silvia Legrand	127	Clark Middleton	145
Robert Lesser	128	George Mikell	145
Gerry Lewis	128	Thomas L. Miller	145
Anita Linda	128	Fabrizio Mioni	145
William Link	128	Kurt Mitchell	146
Charles M. Lippincott	129	Haruma Miura	146
Tommy "Tiny" Lister	129	Marvin Mondlin	147
Little Richard	130	"Morgus"	147
Sam Lloyd	130	Ennio Morricone	147
Michael Lonsdale	130	Kirby Morrow	148
Xavier Loyá	131	Basil Moss	148
Rebecca Luker	131	Jean-Pierre Moumon	149
Richard A. Lupoff	131	Becky Mullen	149
Alison Lurie	133	Jerrold Mundis	149
Ann Lynn	133	Bruce Myers	150
John Mahon	133	Kellye Nakahara	150
Louis Mahoney	135	Lori Nelson	150
Johnny Mandel	135	Claudette Nevins	152
Dr. Colin Manlove	136	Ted Newsom	152
Bob March	136	Jeremy Newson	153
Rafael R. Marchent	136	Brian Nickels	153
Vincent Marezello	137	Daria Nicolodi	153
Detto Mariano	137	Sue Nicols	154
Malcolm Marmorstein	137	Lennie Niehaus	154
Gillian Martell	138	Margaret Nolan	156
Henry Martin	138	Nobuhiko Ôbayashi	156
Philip Martin	138	George Ogilvie	156
Robert Martin	138	Michael O'Hear	157
Tom Maschler	139	Denny O'Neil	157
Phil May	139	Ernie Orsatti	158
Helen McCabe	139	James Otis	158

Name	Page
Ulf Ôtsuki	159
Geoffrey Palmer	159
Alan Parker	159
Nicholas Parsons	161
Martin Pasko	161
Ivan Passer	162
Alan Pattillo	162
Pilar Pellicer	162
Krzysztof Penderecki	162
Regis Philbin	163
Michel Piccoli	163
Hayford Pierce	163
Tom Pollock	164
Wu Pong-fong	164
Leslie A. Pope	164
Peggy Pope	165
Lovelady Powell	165
Taryn Power	165
Kelly Preston	166
Dave Prowse	166
André Ptaszynski	168
Joseph S. Pulver, Sr.	168
Tommy Rall	168
Rebecca Ramsey	169
James Randi	169
Elsa Raven	169
Marguerite Ray	170
Helen Reddy	170
Marge Redmond	170
Joel M. Reed	171
Carl Reiner	171
Barbara Remington	171
Mike Resnick	173
Ramon Revilla	173
Gene Reynolds	173
Allan Rich	174
Diana Rigg	174
Naya Rivera	175
Maurice Roëves	175
Joel Rogosin	175
"Ronald"	176
Suzanne Roquette	176
Elyse Rosenstein	176
Annie Ross	176
D.J. Rowe	177
Joe Ruby	177
Osvaldo Ruggieri	178
Barbara Rütting	178
José Montalbán Saiz	178
Evelyn Sakash	180
Richard Sala	180
Robert Sampson	180
Reni Santoni	182
Charles R. Saunders	182
Nancy Saunders	183
John Saxon	183
Tony Scannell	185
Joel Schumacher	185
Ronald L. Schwary	185
Esther Scott	186
Jacqueline Scott	186
Carol Serling	186
John Sessions	187
Lynn Shelton	187
Keith Short	187
John Shrapnel	188
Geno Silva	188
Fred Silverman	188
Lisa Simone	189
Joe Sinnott	189
Susan Sizemore	190
Jan Skopecek	190
Guy N. Smith	190
Lance Smith	191
Herbert F. Solow	191
Phyllis Somerville	191
Ken Spears	193
Norm Spencer	193
Jackie Stallone	193
Sirry Steffen	194
Monica Stephens	194
Steve Stiles	194
Jerry Stiller	194
Anton Strout	195
Héctor Suárez	195
Ann Sullivan	195

"Superhost"	196	Dawn Wells	206
Carol Sutton	196	Tim White	206
Yûko Takeuchi	196	Stuart Whitman	207
Tony Tanner	197	David Whorf	207
Gianrico Tedeschi	197	Fred Willard	207
Marilyn J. Tenser	197	Logan Williams	208
Dyanne Thorne	198	Mark S Williams	208
Patrick Tilley	198	Barbara Ker Wilson	208
Ann E. Todd	198	Barbara Windsor	209
Christopher Tolkien	200	Frank Windsor	209
Nicholas Tucci	200	Mel Winkler	211
Marshall B. Tymn	200	Jimmy Winston	211
Albert Uderzo	201	David Wise	211
Shôzô Uehara	201	Charles Wood	212
Manuel "Loco" Valdés	201	Arthur Wooster	212
Dan van Husen	202	Ned Wynn	213
Monique van Vooren	202	Merritt Yohnka	213
Max von Sydow	204	Carlos Ruiz Zafón	213
Philip Voss	204	Nazzareno Zamperla	214
Lyle Waggoner	205	Jerry Zeitman	214
Kent L. Wakeford	205	Terri Zimmern	216
Lee Wallace	205	Index by Date	217
Ron Weighell	205	About the Author	225

Commemorating the passing of writers, artists, performers and technicians who, during their lifetimes, made significant contributions to the horror, science fiction and fantasy genres (or left their mark on popular culture in other, often fascinating, ways) . . .

A portrait of Stephen Jones and friends by British artist Martin McKenna (1969–2020), originally published in Dark Horizons *No. 36 (1995).*

Introduction

FOR THE PAST thirty years or so, Kim Newman and I (with the help of numerous correspondents around the world) had been contributing an annual "Necrology" to my "years best" anthology series, *Best New Horror*.

These lists, as stated in the introductory paragraph, were compiled to mark "The passing of writers, artists, performers and technicians who, during their lifetimes, made significant contributions to the horror, science fiction and fantasy genres (or left their mark on popular culture and music in other, often fascinating, ways) . . ."

As reference sources became more easily available, these yearly lists steadily grew from a handful of pages to more than 100 in the latter volumes. The "Necrology" became a huge amount of work — from the time-consuming research to just simply pulling all the information together for each year it covered.

Which is why, when I finally ended *Best New Horror* after a record-breaking thirty-one volumes, I was not unhappy to stop collecting obituaries. The final year covered by the anthology is 2019, and for the first couple of months of 2020 I was free to get on with other things.

And then, in March, COVID-19 happened.

With hundreds, then soon thousands of people dying from coronavirus around the world, it quickly became apparent to me that many of those genre names who we were also losing during this period were simply being overlooked amongst the greater tragedy unfolding all over the planet.

With the death of Roy Hudd in mid-March, I doubted that the many tributes in the press and media would note that the British actor and comedian had made a memorable cameo appearance alongside Peter Cushing in the 1968 film *The Blood Beast Terror* (aka *The Vampire-Beast Craves Blood*).

So I decided to revive the obituaries again on Facebook — this time with the added bonus of photographs, allowing the reader to put a face to the name (especially for the more obscure entries). Before I knew it, I was back keeping a weekly record of the passing of those personalities — both famous and uncelebrated — who had made "significant contributions" to the horror, science fiction and fantasy genres.

And so it has continued.

But then something unexpected happened. Peter Coleborn, the perceptive publisher of the award-winning British independent imprint The Alchemy Press, contacted me and asked me if I had ever considered compiling these electronic obituaries into book form. I admitted that I hadn't — the online format was already different from the way it would appear in print, plus I was doubtful that anyone would even be interested in such a volume.

Although Peter conceded that I might have a point, he also maintained that these mini-tributes were an important record of our genre and should be preserved in some form as an annual volume.

I could see it involving me in a lot more work again. But then, the more I considered it, the more I realised how we could just make it happen. Especially with the addition of photographs and illustrations. And so I got to work — re-formatting and updating those obituaries that I had already posted on Facebook, adding new entries that I had missed first time around, and researching the visuals to accompany the written material.

The book you hold in your hand is the result of that work. We've put a lot of thought into the design and format, and I am more than delighted with the way this first (of hopefully further) volumes has turned out. It stands as a record of those genre figures that we lost during one of the most traumatic years any of us has ever lived through.

There are more than 460 mini-biographies in this volume, including a trio of Hollywood legends . . . possibly the last star of silent pictures . . . the screen's best James Bond . . . a pair of British actresses who were both "Bond girls" *and* Avengers . . . two British actors who played — but did not voice — iconic *Star Wars* characters . . . an author who did for crustaceans what James Herbert did for rodents . . . a forgotten pioneer of "sword and soul" fantasy . . . and, once again, far too many friends and colleagues . . .

However, despite all that, I'm still not sure who is going to be interested in reading this . . . except perhaps for Peter and me.

And, of course, *you*.

Stephen Jones
London, England
April 2021

Derek Acorah

Self-styled British "spiritual medium" Derek Acorah (Derek Francis Johnson) died after a short illness on January 3, aged 69. The former professional football player starred in his own reality TV shows, *Most Haunted* (2002–05), *Derek Acorah's Ghost Towns* (2005–06) and *Derek Acorah* (2009), and he also turned up in the 2017 horror movie *Crispy's Curse* and an episode of *Doctor Who* ('Army of Ghosts').

Joseph Adler

Joseph Adler, who directed, edited and produced the regional low budget movie *Scream Baby Scream* (aka *House of Mutant Women*, 1969), scripted by Larry Cohen, died on April 16, aged 79.

Raymond Allen

American character actor Raymond Allen (Raymond Gilmore Allen, Sr.), who played "Uncle Woodrow 'Woody' Anderson" on TV's *Sanford and Son* (1974–77), died of a non-COVID-related respiratory illness on August 10, aged 91. He had been living at a long-term care facility in California. Allen made his screen debut in the "All Colored" horror-comedy *Fight That Ghost* in 1946 and went on to appear in a number of TV shows during the 1970s, including having a recurring role in *Starsky and Hutch*.

Bruce Allpress

New Zealand actor Bruce [Robert] Allpress, who starred in the family fantasy *The Water Horse* (2007), died of complications of Lou Gehrig's disease (ALS) on April 23, aged 89. His other credits include *The Lord of the Rings: The Two Towers* (as "Aldor") and episodes of TV's *The Ray Bradbury Theatre*,

Raymond Allen (1929–2020) made his screen debut in
Fight That Ghost (1946).

Hercules: The Legendary Journeys and *Power Rangers Jungle Fury*.

Joseph Altairac

One of the leading French scholars of science fiction, Joseph Altairac, died on November 9, aged 63. Affectionately known as "Uncle Joe", he was a critic, essayist and writer whose books include *Les Terres Creuses: Commented Bibliography of Imaginary Underground Worlds* (Encrage/Les Belles lettres, 2006) with Guy Costes, along with volumes on H.G. Wells and A.E. Van Vogt. Altairac launched the fanzine *Lovecraftian Studies* in the 1990s before curating the "Cahiers d'études lovecraftiennes" series at Encrage editions. He founded the Elder Rosny Prize in 1980, awarded each summer at the national science fiction convention, and himself received the Prix spécial Imaginaire Award for the two-volume study *Rétrofictions: Encyclopedia of Rational Romantic Conjecture* (Les Belles Lettres, 2019), again with Costes.

Charles Alverson

American scriptwriter and author Charles Alverson died in Serbia on January 10, aged 84. He co-scripted the 1977 film *Jabberwocky* and wrote the first draft of *Brazil* (1985), both for director Terry Gilliam.

Nando Angelini

Italian character actor Nando Angelini (Ferdinando Angelini) died on August 7, aged 86. He appeared in such *peplums* as *Ulysses Against Hercules*, *Colossus of the Stone Age*, *Hercules and the Masked Rider* and *Hercules Samson & Ulysses*. Angelini's other film credits include Riccardo Freda's *The Giants of*

Thessaly, Ape Man of the Jungle, The Seventh Grave, Bloody Pit of Horror (billed as "Nick Angel"), *The War of the Planets, Ypotron – Final Countdown, Star Pilot, Operation Kid Brother* and Antonio Margheriti's *The Young the Evil and the Savage* (which he was also second assistant director on). He retired from the screen in the late 1960s.

Michael Angelis

British actor [Nicholas] Michael Angelis, best known as the voice of the "Narrator" for TV's *Thomas the Tank Engine & Friends* (1991-2012) and various spin-off shows, died of a heart attack on May 30, aged 68. Angelis also starred as "Merlin" in the 1992 children's series *Wail of the Banshee*.

Brice Armstrong

Prolific American voice actor Brice [Weeks] Armstrong [Jr.] died on January 10, aged 84. Best known for his work on the English versions of the "Dragon Ball Z" and "Lupin III" series, he also contributed voices to many other Funimation *anime* series and video games, including *Yu Yu Hakusho: Ghost Files*, *Detective Conan* and *Samurai 7*. Armstrong was also the voice of "Miss Etta Kette" on the children's TV show *Barney & Friends* (1997-2000).

Neda Arnerić

Serbian actress Neda Arnerić, who co-starred in Peter Sykes' 1971 film *Venom* (aka *The Legend of Spider Forest*), died on

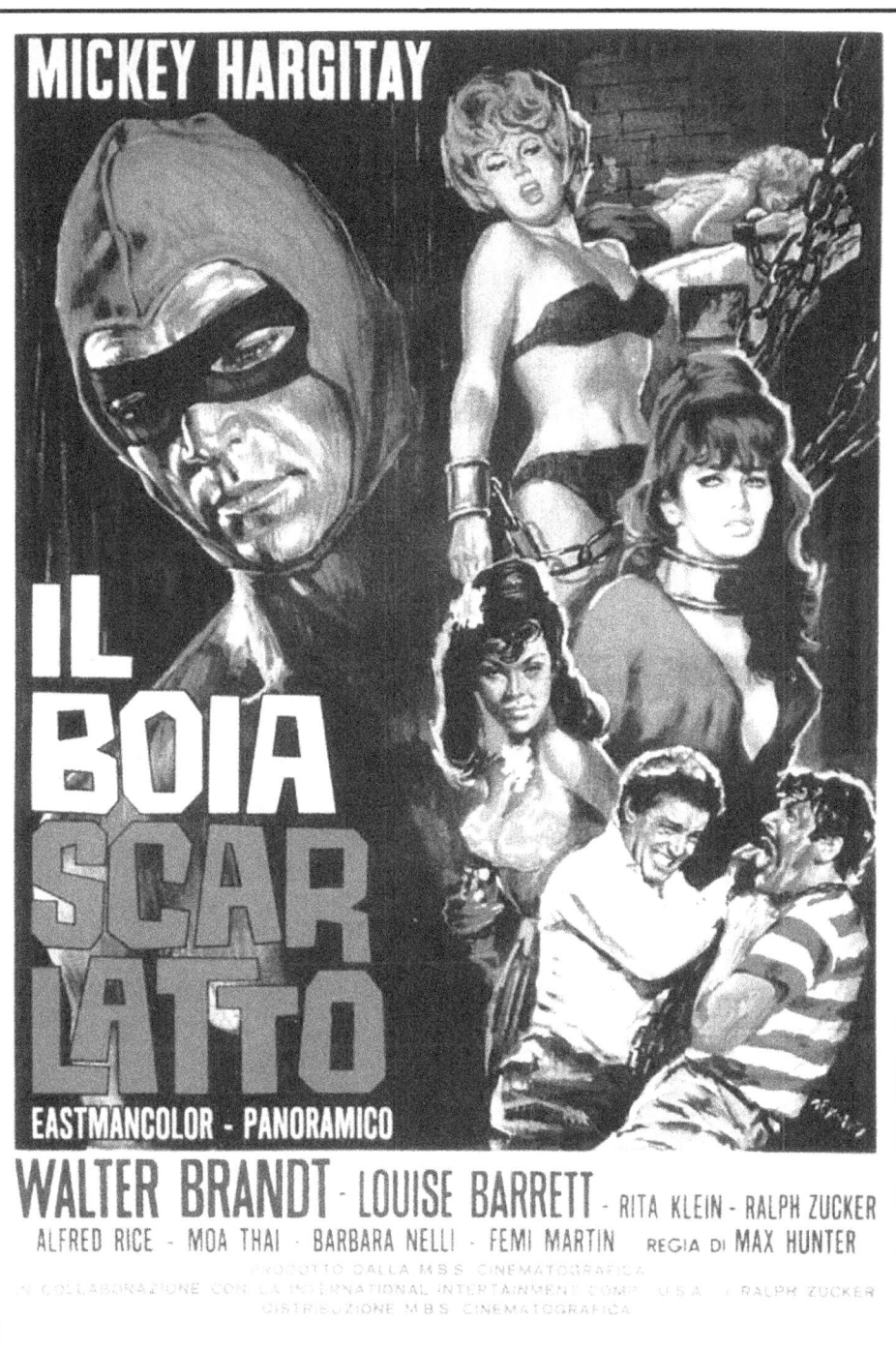

Nando Angelini (1933–2020) had a supporting role in
Bloody Pit of Horror *(1965).*

January 10, aged 66. She was also in another horror movie, *Dark Echoes* (1977).

Sean Arnold

British character actor and practising psychotherapist Sean Arnold died after a long illness in the Channel Islands on April 15, aged 78. He was in *Haunters of the Deep* and *Speaking of the Devil*, along with episodes of TV's *Out of the Unknown* and *Bugs*.

Kelly Asbury

American animation director Kelly [Adam] Asbury died after a long battle with cancer on June 26, aged 60. He started his career at Walt Disney Feature Animation in 1983 – where he was mentored by legendary Warner Bros. animator Chuck Jones – and contributed storyboards and character designs to such movies as *The Black Cauldron*, *The Little Mermaid*, *Rescuers Down Under*, *Beauty and the Beast* (1991), *The Nightmare Before Christmas*, *Toy Story*, *James and the Giant Peach*, *Shrek*, *Frozen* and *Sherlock Gnomes*, going on to co-direct the Oscar-nominated *Shrek 2* and direct *Gnomeo & Juliet*, *Smurfs: The Lost Village* and *Uglydolls*. More recently, he was the story consultant for *The Addams Family* (2019). Absury also wrote and illustrated twelve children's books, while his non-fiction study *Dummy Days* focused on such ventriloquists as Jeff Dunham, Shari Lewis, Jimmy Nelson, Edgar Bergen and Paul Winchell.

David Ashford

British actor, author and artist David [John] Ashford died of pneumonia on December 17, aged 79. He had been diagnosed with terminal cancer some months earlier. As an actor, he appeared in *A Midsummer Night's Dream* (1968) and episodes of TV's *Quatermass* (aka *The Quatermass Conclusion*) and *Doctor Who* ('The Greatest Show in the Galaxy'). A contributor to such magazines as *Golden Fun*, *Illustrated Comics Journal*, *Antiquarian Book Monthly*, *Book and Magazine Collector*, *Rare Book Review* and *Illustrators*, Ashford wrote *The Comic Art of Roy Wilson* (with Alan Clark, *The Art of Denis McLoughlin* and, in collaboration with Norman Wright, *Sexton Blake: A Celebration of the Great Detective*, *Lightning Swords! Smoking Pistols!*, *The Thriller Comics Companion* and *Masters of Fun & Thrills*. He was also in the 1965–66 stage play *The Curse of the Daleks*, which ran for a month at London's Wyndham Theatre.

Sei Ashina

Japanese actress Sei Ashina (Aya Igarashi) committed suicide on September 14, aged 36. Best known for her starring role in *Silk* (2007), Ashina also appeared in the superhero TV series *Kamen Rider Hibiki* and the spin-off move *Kamen Rider Hibiki & the Seven Fighting Demons*. Her other credits include *Kamogawa Horumo: Battle League in Kyoto*, *Nanase: The Psychic Wanderers* and *AI Amok*, along with episodes of TV's *Kaidan Horror Classics*, *The Ancient Dogoo Girls* and *Suzuki Kôji: Real Horror*.

Baby Peggy

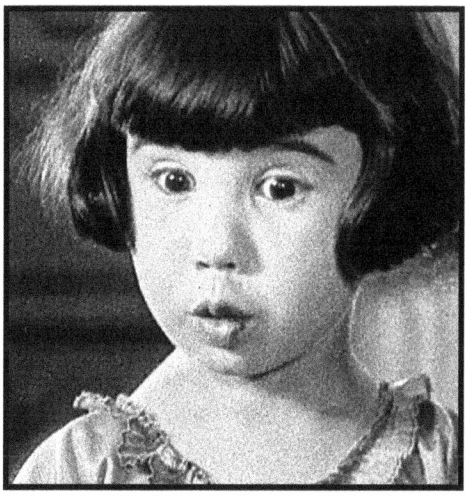

Possibly the last surviving silent film star, Baby Peggy (Peggy-Jean Montgomery), died on February 24, aged 101. Between 1921–23 she appeared in nearly 150 shorts and nine feature films. Her credits include *Little Red Riding Hood* (1922), *Hansel and Gretel* (1923) and *Jack and the Beanstalk* (1924). Unfortunately, her career was over by the age of eight, and relatives depleted most of her estimated $2 million fortune. She later appeared (uncredited) in the first chapter of the 1934 serial *The Return of Chandu*, starring Bela Lugosi, but retired from the screen four years later. Having suffered from nervous breakdowns and lived in near-poverty for many years, she reinvented herself in the mid-1970s as a publisher and writer of Hollywood histories under the pen name "Diana Serra Cary". Her autobiography, *Whatever Happened to Baby Peggy?*, was published in 1996.

Chuck Bail

American stunt actor and director Chuck Bail (Charles Bail) died of COVID-19 on November 25, aged 85. He had underlying heart and gall bladder issues. Bail did stunts and/or appeared in *Werewolves on Wheels*, *The House of Seven Corpses* (with John Carradine) and episodes of *Thriller* ('Well of Doom' as a stunt double for Richard Kiel), *Batman* (1966-67) and *The Man from U.N.C.L.E.* As a director Bail's credits include the blaxploitation *Cleopatra Jones and the Casino of Gold* and episodes of TV's *Manimal* and *Knight Rider*. He was also a second-unit director on *The Beastmaster* and an action and effects director on the 1997-98 TV series *Conan*.

Pip Baker

British scriptwriter Pip Baker (Philip Baker) died on April 14, aged 91. He had been ill for some time, following a fall. With his wife Jane (who died in 2014) he wrote the 1969 film *Captain Nemo and the Underwater City* (starring Robert Ryan as Jules Verne's anti-hero) and contributed additional scenes to Terence Fisher's *Night of the Big Heat* (aka *Island of the Burning Damned*) co-starring Christopher Lee and Peter Cushing. On TV, the writing team scripted an episode of *Space: 1999* and three 1980s series of *Doctor Who*, creating Kate O'Mara's renegade Time Lady, "The Rani". They also created the 1991-92 family SF sitcom *Watt on Earth* for the BBC. The Bakers wrote the *Doctor Who* Target tie-ins *The Mark of the Rani*, *Terror of the Vervoids*, *Time and the Rani* and *The Ultimate Foe*, along with the game book *Make Your Own Adventure with Doctor Who: Race Against Time*.

Dick Balduzzi

Italian-American character actor Dick Balduzzi (Richard Kenneth Balduzzi) died on January 27, aged 91. He was in

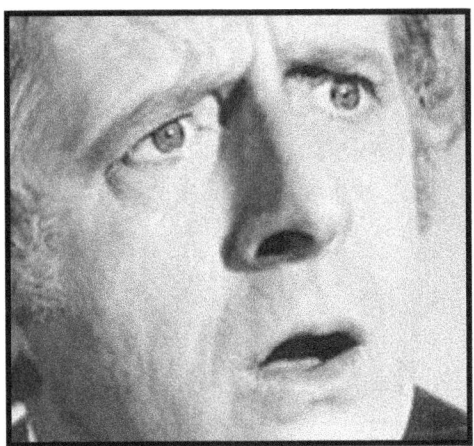

Coma (1978), *Zapped!* and episodes of TV's *I Dream of Jeannie*, *Bewitched*, *It's About Time*, *The Flying Nun*, *The Girl with Something Extra*, *The Invisible Man* (1975), *Holmes and Yoyo*, *The Bionic Woman*, *The Amazing Spider-Man*, *Darkroom* and *Amazing Stories*. Balduzzi retired from the screen in 1990.

Brian N. Ball

British author Brian N. (Neville) Ball died of cancer on July 23, aged 88. He began his writing career in 1962, selling stories to such magazines as *New Worlds Science Fiction* and *Science Fantasy*. Ball's SF and horror novels include *Sundog*, *Lesson for the Damned*, *Devil's Peak*, *The Regiments of Night* (aka *Night of the Robots*), *Singularity Station*, *The Venomous Serpent*, *The Mark of the Beast*, *The Evil at Monteine*, *The Starbuggy*, *The Doomship of Drax*, *Malice of the Soul* and the *Space: 1999* tie-in *The Space Guardians*.

John Bangsund

Australian SF fan John Bangsund died of COVID-19 on August 22, aged 81. He edited and published *Australian Science Fiction Review* (1966–69) and *Scythrop* (1969–73), and wrote the 1974 study *John W. Campbell: An Australian Tribute*.

Dana Baratta

American TV writer and producer Dana Baratta died of ovarian cancer on October 18, aged 59. She was a co-producer and scriptwriter on *Warehouse 13*, *The Secret Circle* and *Jessica Jones*, amongst a number of other successful shows.

Harry Basch

American TV actor Harry Basch (Harry Leo Basch III), who guest-starred in the original *Star Trek* episode 'What Are Little Girls Made Of?' (scripted by Robert Bloch), died on June 23, aged 94. He also appeared in episodes of *Get Smart*, *Holmes and Yoyo* and *The Wizard*, along with the movie *Coma* (1978) and the mini-series *World War III*. Basch retired from the screen in the late 1980s and wrote a couple of very successful travel books with his late wife, the actress Shirley Slater.

Orson Bean

91-year-old American actor, comedian and TV personality Orson Bean (Dallas Frederick Burrows) died after being struck by two cars while walking near Venice Boulevard, Los Angeles, on

February 7. He was in *Miracle on 34th Street* (1959), *Innerspace*, *Being John Malkovich* and *Alien Autopsy*, along with episodes of *The Twilight Zone*, *The Fall Guy* ('October the 31st', with Elvira, John Carradine and his sons David, Keith and Robert) and *Monsters* (Dan Simmons' 'The Offering'). Bean played the voice of "Bilbo Baggins" in the animated 1977 TV movie of *The Hobbit*, and "Bilbo" and "Frodo Baggins" in the 1980 sequel, *The Return of the King*. He was a founding member of Sons of the Desert, an organization dedicated to the memory and films of comedy team Stan Laurel and Oliver Hardy.

Alex Beaton

American producer Alex Beaton, whose credits include such TV series as *Kung Fu* (1973-75), *The Greatest American Hero* (1981) and *Otherworld* (1985), died on January 10, aged 86. Beaton also produced *Midnight Offerings*, *Nightmares* (1983) and the TV movies *Dr. Scorpion*, *Dr. Strange* (1978), *The Night Rider*, *Annihilator*, *Knight Rider 2010*, *The Man Who Wouldn't Die* and the failed 1996 American re-boot of *Doctor Who*.

Jay Benedict

American character actor Jay Benedict, who appeared (uncredited) as Newt's father in *Aliens* (1986), died of complications from COVID-19 on April 4, aged 68. Benedict worked for many years in the UK and Europe, and his other credits include *Mansquito*, *The Dark Knight Rises*, *Scarefest* and episode of TV's *Lexx* and *Jonathan Creek*.

John Benfield

British tough-guy character actor John Benfield (John Turner), best known for playing DCI Tennison's boss, Chief Superintendent Kernan, in the various *Prime Suspect* series on TV (1991-95), died of a rare cancer on June 16, aged 68. He also appeared in *The Sign of Four* (1983), *Whoops Apocalypse*, Disney's *101 Dalmatians* (1996), *An Angel for May*, *Evilenko*, *Flood* (2007), *Speed Racer*, *Cold Skin* and episodes of TV's *The Day of the Triffids* (1981), *Tales from the Crypt* and *Lucky Man*.

Ed Benguiat

American graphic designer, typographer and lettering artist Ed Benguiat (Ephram Edward Benguiat) died on October 15, aged 92. A former "cleavage retoucher" for movies, he created the logotypes for many famous magazines, along with the distinctive title design for *Planet of the Apes* (1968). Benguiat also created more than 600 typeface designs, including Tiffany, ITC Bookman, Panache, Souvenir, Edwardian Script, and the eponymous ITC Benguiat and Benguiat Gothic. The Benguiat style was used on Stephen King's books throughout the 1980s, the main credits in *Star Trek: Generations* and *Star Trek: First Contact*, and the logo and opening credits of Netflix's *Stranger Things*.

Julie Bennett

American actress Julie Bennett died complications from COVID-19 on March 31, aged 88. She appeared in episodes of TV's *Lights Out*, *Adventures of Superman* and *Get Smart*, along with the 1981 mini-series *Goliath Awaits* (with Christopher Lee and John Carradine). From 1960 onwards she also worked on TV as a prolific voice actor, most notably as "Cindy Bear" in various *Yogi Bear* cartoons. Bennett also contributed to such cartoon series as *The Superman/Aquaman Hour of Adventure* (as "Lois Lane"), *Funky Phantom*, *Jeannie*, *Captain Caveman and the Teen Angels*, *The Mighty Orbots*, *The Real Ghostbusters* and *Spider-Man: The Animated Series* (as "Aunt May Parker"), along with the classic 1963 Warner Bros. short *Transylvania 6-5000*. The actress also dubbed all the female voices for the English-language version of *King Kong Escapes* (1967).

Ronald Bergan

South African-born British film scholar journalist, author and critic Ronald Bergan (Ronald Ginsberg) died of urosepsis on July 23, aged 82. He wrote numerous film studies and biographies, including *Haunted Life: Anthony Perkins*, *Francis Ford Coppola Close-Up: The Making of His Movies* and *The Film Book: A Complete Guide to the World of Film*. From 1989 onwards Bergan also contributed obituaries to *The Guardian* newspaper.

Warren Berlinger

American character actor Warren Berlinger, the nephew of comic Milton Berle, died on December 2, aged 83.

His credits include Disney's *The Shaggy D.A.* and *Ten Little Indians* (1989), along with episodes of TV's *My Brother the Angel*, *Gemini Man*, *Herbie the Love Bug*, *Misfits of Science* and *Blacke's Magic* ('Wax Poetic' with Vincent Price).

Steve Bing

55-year-old American movie producer and philanthropist Steve [Leo] Bing committed suicide by jumping from his twenty-seventh-floor Los Angeles apartment on June 22. He had been suffering from depression due to "lack of human contact" during the coronavirus lockdown. Reportedly having inherited a $600 million fortune from his grandfather, Leo S. Bing, when he was eighteen, he was best known for being the former boyfriend of actress Liz Hurley, with whom he fathered a son. Bing invested nearly $80 million into the budget of *The Polar Express* (2004), covering roughly half the cost of the Robert Zemeckis motion-capture movie.

Merv Binns

Melbourne's "Mr. Science Fiction", Merv Binns (Mervyn Russell Binns), died of heart problems on April 7 after a long illness. He was 85. In 1952 Binns was one of a small group of Australian teenagers who co-founded the Melbourne Science Fiction Group (later the Melbourne Science Fiction Club), which became the focal point for the city's SF fandom. During the late 1950s and '60s he edited *Australian Science Fiction Newsletter*, and he later revived the fanzine as *Australian SF News*. In 1971, with help from Lee Harding, Paul Stevens and Sydney fan Ron Graham, Binns established Space Age Books in the centre of Melbourne. The store finally closed in 1985, just a few months after

Aussiecon II. Merv Binns received four lifetime achievement awards – the Forrest J Ackerman Big Heart Award, the Australian SF Foundation A. Bertram Chandler Award, the Peter MacNamara Award and the Eternity Award).

Honor Blackman

British leading lady Honor Blackman, who co-starred as the leather-clad "Cathy Gale" alongside Patrick Macnee's "John Steed" in two seasons of TV's *The Avengers* (1962-64), died on April 6, aged 94. She also appeared in the films *Daughter of Darkness, So Long at the Fair, Jason and the Argonauts, Goldfinger* (as "Pussy Galore"), *Fright*, Hammer's *To the Devil a Daughter* (with Christopher Lee), *The Cat and the Canary* (1978), *Tale of the Mummy, The Sight, Jack and the Beanstalk: The Real Story* and *Cockneys vs Zombies*. On TV, Blackman's credits include episodes of *The New Adventures of Charlie Chan, Hour of Mystery, The Invisible Man* (1958), *Doctor Who* ('The Trial of the Time Lord') and *Dr. Terrible's House of Horrible* ('Vampire Lesbian Lovers of Lust'). Her second husband (1961-75) was actor Maurice Kaufmann.

Robert Blanche

American character actor Robert [Clinton] Blanche, who played "Sergeant Franco" in the NBC-TV series *Grimm* (2012-17), died of complications following lung transplant surgery on January 3, aged 57. He had been suffering from hypersensitivity pneumonitis (a progressive fibrotic lung disease). Often cast as policemen, Blanche's other credits include *Total Reality, Zombie Apocalypse* (2011), *Something Wicked, Bermuda Tentacles, Stormageddon* and *The Brain That Wouldn't Die* (2020), along with episodes of *Nowhere Man, Medium, Ghost Whisperer, Z Nation* and the 2002 mini-series *Rose Red* (scripted by Stephen King). He also co-created and produced *Jason Rising: A Friday the 13th Fanfilm* (2021).

William Blinn

American TV screenwriter and producer William [Frederick] Blinn,

who created the series *Starsky and Hutch* (1975-79) and *Heaven Help Us* (1994), died on October 22, aged 82. He wrote *Heaven Only Knows* (1979) and contributed scripts to such shows as *My Favorite Martian* and *The Invaders*. Blinn was also executive story consultant on the 1977 TV movie *The Possessed*.

Brian Blume

American game designer Brian Blume, a former business partner of Gary Gygax in *Dungeons & Dragons* publisher TSR and co-writer with Gygax of the 1976 game supplement *Eldritch Wizardry*, died on March 31 aged 70.

William Bogert

American character actor William Bogert (William Russell Bogert III) died on January 12, aged 83. He was in *The Sentinel* (uncredited), *Heaven Can Wait* (1978), *A Fire in the Sky*, *Hero at Large* and *WarGames*, along with episodes of TV's *Project U.F.O.*, *Salvage 1*, *The Incredible Hulk*, *Fantasy Island*, *3rd Rock from the Sun* and *The Greatest American Hero*.

Thomas "Doc" Boguski

American production assistant and coordinator Thomas "Doc" Boguski died on February 27, aged 58. He worked on the James Bond film *A View to a Kill*, *Mannequin*, Roger Corman's *Frankenstein Unbound* (based on the novel by Brian W. Aldiss), *The Prophecy*, *12 Monkeys*, *Children of the Corn: The Gathering*, *Jack Frost*, *Fallen*, *Beloved*, *Tuck Everlasting* and M. Night Shyamalan's *The Sixth Sense*, *Unbreakable*, *Signs* and *The Village*.

Frank W. Bolle

Italian-born American comics artist Frank W. Bolle died on May 12, aged 95. He immigrated to the US in 1929 to join his mother in Brooklyn, New York City. Bolle began illustrating for Timely Comics around 1943 and, following World War II, worked for such companies as Fawcett, Magazine Enterprises, DC Comics, Atlas, Gold Key, Dell, Tower, Marvel and Charlton. Amongst the many titles he contributed to were *Mystic*, *Marvel Tales*, *Mystical Tales*, *Strange Tales*, *Journey Into Mystery*, *Sherlock Holmes*, *Buck Rogers*, *Flash Gordon*, *The Phantom*, *The Twilight Zone*, *Doctor Solar Man of the Atom*, *Grimm's Ghost Stories*, *Boris Karloff's Tales of Mystery*, *Creepy*, *Vampirella*, *House of Secrets*, *Adventures Into Fear*, *Werewolf by Night* and *Shroud of Mystery*. Three strips Bolle did for the 1966 paperback anthology *Christopher Lee's Treasury of Terror* were reprinted in Warren Publications' *Eerie*, and he also illustrated numerous newspaper strips (including "ghosting" such titles as *Rip Kirby*, *Tarzan* and *Prince Valiant*).

Claude Bolling

French jazz composer Claude [Jean Harry] Bolling died on December 29, aged 90. A former child prodigy, his many film scores include *The Hands of Orlac* (1960) and *The Awakening* (1980).

Roscoe Born

American soap opera actor Roscoe [Conklin] Born committed suicide on March 3, aged 69. He had long suffered from bipolar disorder. Born appeared in *End of the World* (with Christopher Lee), *The Haunting of Sarah Hardy* and an episode of TV's *The Incredible Hulk*.

Lucia Bosè

Italian-born actress Lucia Bosè (Lucia Boriani), who starred as the vampiric "Erzebeth Bathory" in Jorge Grau's *The Legend of Blood Castle* (1973), died of pneumonia in Spain on March 23, aged 89. A former Miss Italy in 1947, her other films include *Testament of Orpheus*, *Nocturne 29*, *Sotto il segno dello scorpione*, *Fellini Satyricon*, *Something Creeping in the Dark*, *Arcana*, *Blood Stains in a New Car* and *Moon Child* (1989).

Chadwick Boseman

American actor and playwright Chadwick Boseman, who portrayed Marvel Comics hero "T'Challa"/

"Black Panther" in *Black Panther*, *Captain America: Civil War*, *Avengers: Infinity War* and *Avengers: Endgame*, died after a four-year battle with colon cancer on August 28, aged 42. His other movie credits include *Gods of Egypt*, and he appeared in an episode of TV's *Fringe*.

Ben Bova

American science fiction writer and editor Ben Bova (Benjamin William Bova) died of COVID-19-related pneumonia and a stroke on November 29, aged 88. A six-time Hugo Award winner and a former editor of *Analog Science Fiction & Fact* (1972-78) and

Omni (1978–82), he was also president of the Science Fiction Writers of America (SFWA, 1990–92). Bova's early SF stories appeared in *Amazing Stories*, *Analog*, *Galaxy* and other digest magazines of the 1960s. He wrote more than 120 books, including the novels *THX 1138* (the novelisation of the George Lucas movie), *The Winds of Altair*, *Gremlins Go Home!* (with Gordon R. Dickson), and the "Exiles", "Kinsman", "Voyagers", "Orion" and "Grand Tour" series. His short fiction was collected in *Forward in Time*, *Maxwell's Demons*, *Escape Plus*, *Future Crimes*, *My Favorites* and other titles, and he edited the anthologies *The Many Worlds of Science Fiction*, *The Best of the Nebulas* and the *Analog*, *Omni* and *Science Fiction Hall of Fame* series. Bova also worked as a science advisor on the 1973 TV series *The Starlost*, a frustrating experience that he loosely fictionalised in his 1975 novel *The Starcrossed*. He also scripted an episode of *Land of the Lost* and worked as a consultant on both *Repo Man* and *Altered Carbon*.

Gregory Tyree Boyce

30-year-old American actor Gregory Tyree Boyce, who played "Tyler" in *Twilight* (2008), died of a cocaine and fentanyl overdose in Las Vegas, Nevada, on May 13.

Charly Bravo

Morocco-born Spanish character actor Charly Bravo (Ramón Carlos Mirón Bravo, aka "Charlie Bravo" and "Carlos Bravo") died in the hotel where he had lived for the past thirty years on June 23, aged 73. Best known for his supporting roles in numerous "Spaghetti Westerns" during the 1960s and '70s, he also appeared in *Night of the Werewolf*, *Panic Beats* and *The Beast and the Magic Sword* (all with Paul Naschy), *The Cannibal Man*, *Conan the Barbarian*, *Tunka el guerrero*, *Monster Dog*, *The Sea Serpent* (with Ray Milland), *Tex and the Lord of the Deep* and *Eliminators*.

Richard Bright

British TV producer Richard Bright committed suicide in late July, after

First paperback of The Starcrossed *(Pyramid, 1976) by Ben Bova (1932–2020).*

suffering a breakdown. He was 51. Bright's credits include the 2018 BBC docu-drama *Angela Carter: Of Wolves & Women* and the TV series *Mark Kermode's Secrets of Cinema*, co-scripted by Kim Newman.

Wilford Brimley

American character actor [Anthony] Wilford Brimley (aka "A. Wilford Brimley") died on August 1, aged 85. A former rodeo rider and bodyguard to Howard Hughes, his movie credits include *The China Syndrome*, *The Wild Wild West Revisited*, John Carpenter's *The Thing*, *10 to Midnight*, *The Natural*, *Cocoon* and *Cocoon: The Return*, *Murder in Space*, *Remo Williams: The Adventure Begins* (aka *Remo Williams: Unarmed and Dangerous*), *Ewoks: The Battle for Endor*, *Eternity*, *Hard Target*, *Heaven Sent*, *Mutant Species*, *Progeny* and *I Believe*. On TV, Brimley was a regular on *The Waltons* (1974-77) and appeared in an episode of *Kung Fu* ('One Step to Darkness').

David Britton

British writer, artist and publisher David Britton died of complications from diabetes on December 29, aged 75. Best known as the creator of the anarchic "Lord Horror" and "Meng and Ecker" books and comics for his and Michael Butterworth's controversial Savoy Books imprint, he edited issues of *Weird Fantasy*, *Crucified Toad* and *New Worlds*, along with *The Savoy Book* and *Savoy Dreams: The Secret Life of Savoy Books* (both with Butterworth). Britton's novels include *Lord Horror* (the last publication to be banned under the UK's Obscene Publications Act), *Motherfuckers: The*

Auschwitz of Oz, *Baptised in the Blood of Millions*, *La Squab: The Black Rose of Auschwitz*, *Invictus Horror* and *Razor King*.

Tim Brooke-Taylor

British comedy actor and writer Tim Brooke-Taylor OBE (Timothy Julian Brooke-Taylor) died of complications from COVID-19 on April 12, aged 79. Best known as one of the founding members of the surreal comedy group *The Goodies* (along with Graeme Garden and Bill Oddie), which ran on BBC-TV from 1970-82, he also turned up in *Willy Wonka & the Chocolate Factory* (uncredited), *Under the Bed*, *Torn up Tales* and a creepy episode of *Shades of Greene* ('The Overnight Bag').

Pat Brymer

American puppeteer Pat Brymer (James Patrick Brymer) died of cardiomyopathy on April 12, aged 70. He worked on *Short Circuit*, *My Stepmother Is an Alien*, *So I Married an*

Axe Murderer, *Team America: World Police* and *The Last Day of Summer*.

Jeremy Bulloch

British character actor Jeremy Bulloch, who was inside the "Boba Fett" Mandalorian warrior and bounty-hunter suit for both *Star Wars: The Empire Strikes Back* and *Star Wars: Return of the Jedi* (the character was voiced by Jason Wingreen), died of Parkinson's disease on December 17, aged 75. A former child actor, he also had small roles in the James Bond films *The Spy Who Loved Me*, *For Your Eyes Only* and *Octopussy*. Bulloch also appeared in *O Lucky Man!*, *The Final Conflict*, *Star Wars Episode III: Revenge of the Sith* and episodes of TV's *Doctor Who* ('The Time Warriors'), *Thriller* (1974), *Chocky* and *Chocky's Children* (created by John Wyndham), *Robin of Sherwood* (in the recurring role of "Edward of Wickham") and *Starhyke*.

Jack Burns

American comedy actor, scriptwriter and producer Jack Burns (John Francis Burns), a member of Chicago's Second City comedy troupe and former stand-up partner of George Carlin and, later, Avery Schreiber, died of respiratory failure on January 27, aged 86. He appeared in episodes of *The Ghost & Mrs. Muir* and *The Pitts* ('Squarewolves'), co-adapted the 1976 TV movie of *Peter Pan*, co-scripted *The Muppet Movie* (1979), and worked as a producer on *The Muppet Show* (1976-77) and *Sesame Street* (1979).

Kevin Burns

American TV executive Kevin Burns died of cardiac arrest on September 27,

aged 65. In 1993, he co-founded Foxstar Productions, a TV movie production unit at 20th Century Fox Television, where he executive produced the first three *Alien Nation* TV movies: *Alien Nation: Dark Horizon*, *Alien Nation: Body and Soul* and *Alien Nation: Millennium*. He then formed Van Ness Films, Inc. the following year, executive producing (and also occasionally writing and directing) documentaries for such networks as A&E (*Biography*), AMC, The Sci-Fi Channel, Fox Family Channel and USA Network. These included *The Fantasy Worlds of Irwin Allen*, *To the Galaxy and Beyond with Mark Hamill*, *Monster Mania*, *Behind the Planet of the Apes*, *Lost in Space Forever* and *Attack of the 50 Foot Monster Mania*. In 1999, Burns retired from Foxstar to form Prometheus Entertainment, and he continued to make documentaries such as *The Fly Papers: The Buzz on Hollywood's Scariest Insect*, *Bride of Monster Mania*, *The Omen Legacy*, *The Alien Saga*, *Halloween: A Cut Above the Rest*, *Empire of Dreams: The Story of the Star Wars Trilogy*, *Monsterama: A Tribute to Horror Hosts*, *Ultimate Super Heroes*

Vixens & Villains, Look Up in the Sky! The Amazing story of Superman, The Science of Superman, Star Wars: The Legacy Revealed, Star Wars: Star Warriors, Indiana Jones and the Ultimate Quest, Batman Unmasked and the half-hour series *Monsterama* (2004-05), along with such "reality" shows as *In Search of Aliens, The Curse of Oak Island, In Search of Monsters, The UnXplained* and *Ancient Aliens*. Also in 1999, Burns formed Synthesis Entertainment with producer Jon Jashni to administrate and develop television and film franchises based on the works of producer Irwin Allen. This led to the unaired pilots *The Robinsons: Lost in Space* (2004) and *The Time Tunnel* (2006), and the short *Lost in Space: The Epilogue* (2015). Burns was also an executive producer on Netflix's 2018 re-boot of *Lost in Space*. His childhood idol was actor Fred Gwynne ("Herman Munster"), and Burns had the world's largest collection of *The Munsters* memorabilia.

Cindy Butler

American actress Cindy [Lu] Butler died on May 26 aged 64. She only appeared in three movies, all for writer/director Charles B. Pierce: *The Town That Dreaded Sundown* (1976), *Boggy Creek II: The Legend Continues* and the Western *Grayeagle*.

Edd Byrnes

American actor Edd Byrnes (Edward Byrne Breitenberger), who co-starred in ABC-TV's *77 Sunset Strip* (1958-63) as parking-lot attendant "Kookie", died on January 8, aged 87. He also appeared in the horror movie *Wicked, Wicked* (1973) and episodes of *The Alfred Hitchcock Hour, Thriller* (1975) and *Fantasy Island*. In 1958, Byrnes had a hit record, 'Kookie, Kookie, Lend Me Your Comb', with Connie Stevens.

Elisa Cabrera

British independent filmmaker Elisa Cabrera died of cancer on July 20, aged 49. He worked in a number of capacities on films, including producing, writing and directing *Demonsoul* and *Witchcraft X: Mistress of the Craft*. He additionally produced *Virtual Terror, Ibiza Undead* (aka *Zombie*

Spring Breakers) and *The Tombs*. Cabera had a small role in the *Fangoria* movie *I Zombie: The Chronicles of Pain*, and he also co-hosted, executive produced and directed the weekly web discussion show *Talking Who* (2011-13), about the world of *Doctor Who*, and the YouTube subscription series *Mina Murray's Journal*, inspired by *Dracula*.

Steven Cagan

American composer, conductor and songwriter Steven Cagan, whose few screen credits include Radley Metzger's 1978 version of *The Cat and the Canary*, died of chronic obstructive pulmonary disease (COPD) on February 1, his 77th birthday.

Rachel Caine

Prolific American author Rachel Caine (Roxanne Longstreet Conrad) died on November 1, aged 58. In 2018 she was diagnosed with soft tissue carcinoma. Best known for her "Morganville Vampires", "Weather Warden", "Outcast Season", "Red Letter Days" and "Revivalist" series, Caine wrote more than fifty books (some under the names "Roxanne Longstreet", "Ian Hammel" and "Roxanne Conrad"), starting with her debut novel *Stormriders* in 1991. Her other books include *The Undead*, *Red Angel*, *Cold Kiss*, *Copper Moon* and *Bridge of Shadows*. With Ann Aquirre she wrote the YA novels *Honor Among Thieves*, *Honor Bound* and *Honor Lost*. She also wrote a *Stargate* tie-in under the name "Julie Fortune". Caine produced the low budget TV show *Morganville: The Series* (2014), based on her books, and scripted an episode of *Whatever After*.

R.D. Call

American character actor R. (Roy) D. (Dana) Call died complications from back surgery on February 27, aged 70. He appeared in *Timestalkers* and *Waterworld*, along with episodes of TV's *V*, *The X Files*, *Supernatural* and the Stephen King mini-series *Golden Years* (1991).

John Callahan

American soap opera actor and TV host John [Kevin] Callahan died of a massive stroke on March 28, aged 66. He appeared in the TV movies *Bone Eater* and *Dinocroc vs. Supergator* (both directed by Jim Wynorski under different pseudonyms), and his other credits include *eCupid* and an episode of *Fantasy Island*.

Earl Cameron

Bermuda-born actor Earl Cameron CBE died in Warwickshire, England, on July 3, aged 102. He arrived in the UK in 1939 and eventually found work in the chorus line of the theatre production *Chu Chin Chow*. Cameron was one of the first black actors to star in a British film when he took a leading role in the Ealing crime film *Pool of London* (1951). His other movie credits include *Tarzan the Magnificent*, *Tarzan's Three Challenges*, the James Bond film *Thunderball*, *Battle Beneath the Earth*, *Revelation* and Christopher Nolan's *Inception*. On TV Cameron appeared in the 1966 *Doctor Who* serial 'The Tenth Planet', becoming the first black actor to ever play an astronaut, along with episodes of *The Andromeda Breakthrough*, *The Prisoner*, *The Frighteners* and Neil Gaiman's *Neverwhere* (1996). He was appointed a Commander of the Order of the British Empire (CBE) in 2009.

Jason Scott Campbell

American actor Jason Scott Campbell committed suicide on July 19, aged 43. He had suffered from bipolar disorder for more than a decade. Campbell's small number of credits include *Evil Ambitions*, *The Final Patient* and *Nightmare* (2005).

Raymundo Capetillo

Mexican leading man Raymundo [Sánchez] Capetillo died of complications from COVID-19 on July 12, aged 75. He appeared in *Santo en Anónimo mortal*, *Bestia nocturna*, *El virus del poder* (aka *Síndrome del apocalipsis*) and *A Christmas Carol* (1999), along with the 1969 TV show *De la tierra a la luna*.

Pierre Cardin

French fashion designer and icon Pierre Cardin (Piero Costante Cardin) died on December 29, aged 98. In the 1960s Cardin revolutionised the fashion industry with his "cosmic" futuristic designs and his ability to bring them into the high street. Cardin began his career as a costume- and mask-maker on Jean Cocteau's version of *La belle et la bête* (*Beauty and the Beast*, 1946), and he designed the clothes that Patrick Macnee's John Steed wore in TV's *The Avengers* (1967–69), but his influence went far beyond those couple of credits.

Lewis John Carlino

Oscar-nominated American screenwriter and playwright Lewis John Carlino, who created *The Mechanic* franchise back in 1972, died of the blood disease myelodysplastic syndrome on July 17, aged 88. His credits include John Frankenheimer's *Seconds* (1966), *A Reflection of Fear*, the TV movie *Where Have All the People Gone?*, *The Sailor Who Fell from Grace with the Sea* (which he also directed), *Resurrection* (1980 and 1999 versions) and *Haunted Summer*.

Chris Carnel

57-year-old American stunt actor and fight choreographer Chris Carnel (Christopher Paul Carnel) died on October 5 when he lost control of his Harley-Davidson as he attempted to pass a turning car, and was pinned under the motorcycle as it caught fire. Carnel's numerous credits include *Project Viper*, *Spider-Man* (2002), *Scorcher*, *Out for Blood*, *The Island*, *The Devil's Rejects*, *Hatchet*, *Spider-Man 3*, *Iron Man*, *My Bloody Valentine* (2009), *Friday the 13th* (2009), *The Crazies* (2010), *Hatchet II*, *Gulliver's Travels* (2010), *Transformers: Dark of the Moon*, *The Lone Ranger* (2013), *Captain America: The Winter Soldier*, *Guardians of the Galaxy*, *Bone Tomahawk*, *Ominous*, *Sharknado: the 4th Awakens*, *Heaven Sent*, *The Veil* (2017), *The Tank*, *Destruction Los Angeles*, *Monster Party*, *Shangri-La: Near Extinction*, *Palm Springs* and episodes of TV's *Grimm*, *Fight of the Living Dead*, *The Core*, *Westworld*, *Z Nation*, *Fear the Walking Dead* and *Penny Dreadful: City of Angels*.

Brent Carver

Canadian actor Brent Carver (Christopher Carver) died on August 4, aged 68. The Tony Award-winning musical Broadway star (for *Kiss of the Spider Woman*) also appeared in *Shadow Dancing*, *Millennium*, *The Legend of Sleepy Hollow* (as "Ichabod Crane", 1999), *Deeply* and episodes of TV's *The Twilight Zone* (1989), *War of the Worlds* (1989), *The Hidden Room* and *Twice in a Lifetime*. Carver also starred as "Gandalf" in the three-and-a-half-hour stage production of *The Lord of the Rings* that premiered in Toronto in 2005.

David S. Cass

Actor-stuntman David S. Cass [Sr.] died of complications from cancer on August 28, aged 78. He appeared in supporting roles in *Black Noon, Enter the Devil, The Boy Who Cried Werewolf, Earthquake, The Island of Dr. Moreau* (1977), *Captain America II: Death Too Soon, More Wild Wild West, TRON, Endangered Species* and *My Demon Lover*. A familiar face on TV — usually playing henchmen or thugs — he appeared in episodes of *The Wild Wild West, The Six Million Dollar Man, The Bionic Woman, Wonder Woman, Buck Rogers in the 25th Century, The Greatest American Hero, Voyagers!, Fantasy Island, Knight Rider, Misfits of Science* and *Highway to Heaven*. Cass was also a stunt coordinator and director (*Monster Makers*).

Marge Champion

American stage and movie dancer and choreographer Marge Champion (Marjorie Celeste Belcher), who worked on a number of MGM musicals during the 1950s, died on October 21, aged 101. Her first husband (1937-41) was

Walt Disney animator Art Babbitt, who used her as a performance or movement model on *Snow White and the Seven Dwarfs* (as "Snow White"), *Pinocchio* (as the "Blue Fairy") and *Fantasia* (as "Hyacinth the Hippo" in the 'Dance of the Hours' sequence, which she also helped choreograph). Champion's other husbands were (1947-73) actor and director Gower Champion and (1977-81) director Boris Sagal.

Michael Chapman

American cinematographer Michael [Crawford] Chapman died of congestive heart failure on September 20, aged 84. His credits include *Taxi Driver*, *Invasion of the Body Snatchers* (1978), *The Man with Two Brains*, *The Lost Boys*, *Scrooged*, *Ghostbusters II*, *Space Jam*, *The Watcher*, *Evolution* and *Bridge to Terabithia*. Chapman was also the camera operator on Steven Spielberg's *Jaws*. He directed *Clan of the Cave Bear* and *Annihilator*, and had small acting roles in a number of the movies he worked on, along with *The Abyss*.

Heather Chasen

Singapore-born British actress Heather [Jean] Chasen, best known for her role as "Valerie Pollard" in the soap opera *Crossroads* (1982–86), died on May 22, aged 92. She made her screen debut in 1949 and went on to appear in *The Deadly Females* and *The Toybox*, plus episodes of TV's *A Traveller in Time*, *Young Sherlock: The Mystery of the Manor House*, *Shades of Darkness* (L.P. Hartley's 'Feet Foremost') and *The Case-Book of Sherlock Holmes*.

Mary Higgins Clark

American mystery author Mary Higgins Clark (Mary Theresa Eleanor Higgins Clark) died on January 31, aged 92. A former copy-editor and airline stewardess, she published her first suspense novel, *Where Are the Children?*, in 1974. She received an advance of $3,000, but the paperback rights sold for $100,000. Clark sold her next book for $1.5 million, and since then her more than fifty novels have sold over 100 million copies in the US alone. Many of her books have been filmed (often for television), including *A Stranger is Watching* (1982), *The Cradle Will Fall* (1983), *Terror Stalks the Class Reunion* (1992), *A Cry in the Night* (1992), *Let Me Call You Sweetheart* (1997) and *The Mystery Cruise* (2013).

Harry Clein

Hollywood publicist and marketing executive Harry Clein died of chronic obstructive pulmonary disease on June 18, aged 82. He created the innovative

marketing campaign for *The Blair Witch Project* (1999) and wrote the original press notes for *Star Wars* (1977).

Ron Cobb

American-born artist and production designer Ron Cobb died of complications from Lewy body dementia in Australia on September 21, his 83rd birthday. He began his career as a breakdown artist on Walt Disney's *Sleeping Beauty* (1957). Forrest J Ackerman became Cobb's agent, following the artist's tour of duty in Vietnam, and commissioned him to paint covers for *Famous Monsters of Filmland* and its companion title, *Monster World*. In the late 1960s, he became a political cartoonist for the underground newspaper *Los Angeles Free Press*. After designing the spaceship exterior for John Carpenter's *Dark Star* (1974), Cobb went on to work as a designer on such movies as *Star Wars*, *Alien*, *Raiders of the Lost Ark*, *Conan the Barbarian* (1982), *The Last Starfighter*, *Back to the Future*, *Aliens*, *Leviathan*, *Meet the Hollowheads*, *The Abyss*, *Robot Jox*, *The Rift*, *Total Recall* (1990), *Space Truckers*, *Titan A.E.* and *The 6th Day*, along with the cult tv series *firefly* (2002). He also designed the credits for NBC's *Amazing Stories* (1985-87) and co-scripted a 1987 segment of *The Twilight Zone* with his wife, Robin Love. In 1969, Cobb created the international symbol for "ecology" and released it into the public domain. The following year *Look* magazine incorporated the symbol into a flag that was eventually used by environmentalists throughout the world.

Robert Cobert

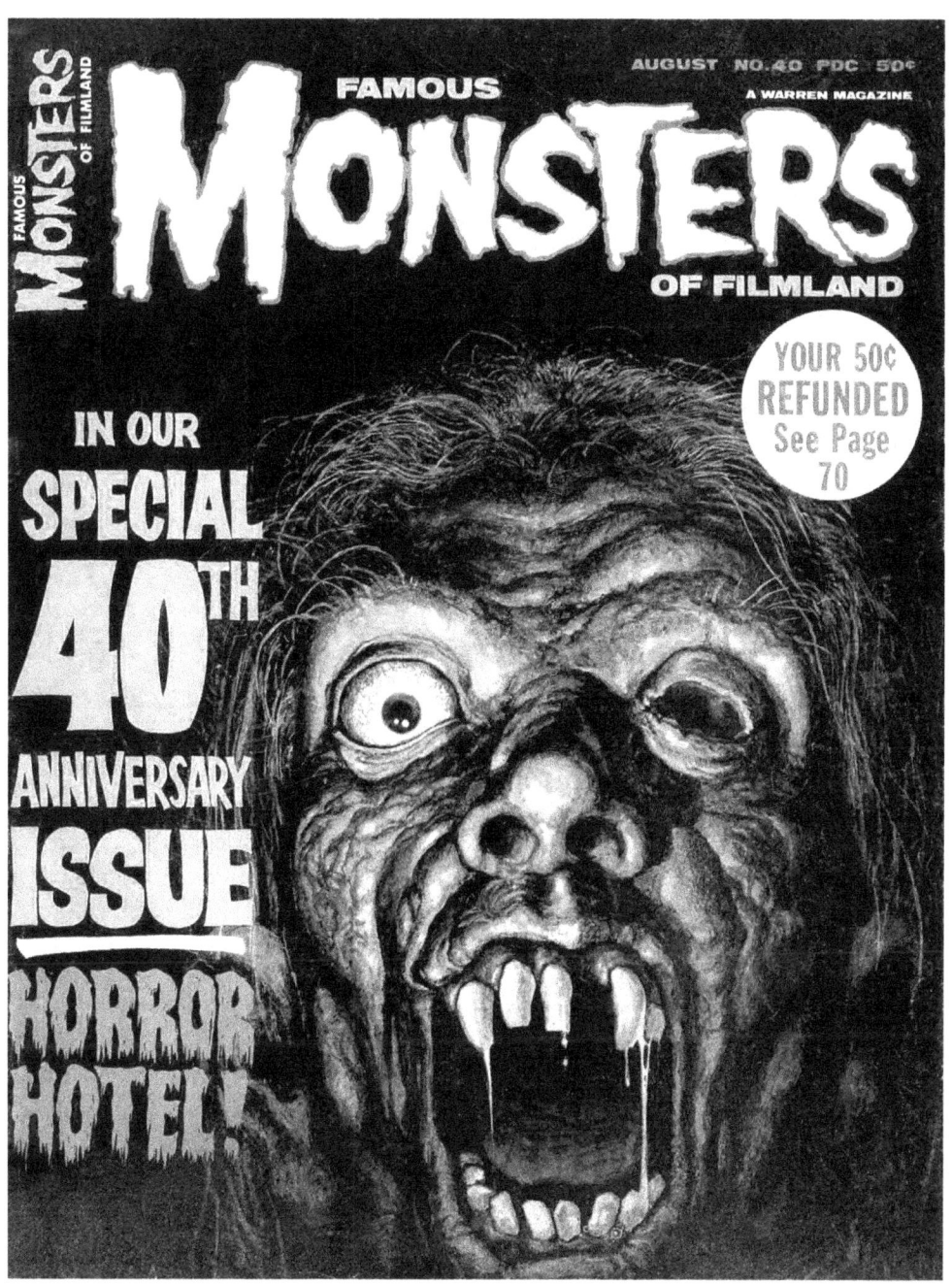

Cover of Famous Monsters of Filmland *#40 (August, 1966) by artist Ron Cobb (1937–2020).*

Veteran American composer Robert Cobert, who scored the music for both incarnations of Dan Curtis' Gothic soap opera *Dark Shadows* (1966-71 and 1991), died of pneumonia on February 19, aged 95. He continued his relationship with Curtis on *The Strange Case of Dr. Jekyll and Mr. Hyde* (1968), the failed pilot *Dead of Night: A Darkness at Blaisedon*, *House of Dark Shadows*, *Night of Dark Shadows*, *The Night Stalker*, *The Night Strangler*, *The Norliss Tapes*, *The Picture of Dorian Gray* (1973), *The Invasion of Carol Enders*, *Scream of the Wolf*, *Dracula* (1974), *The Turn of the Screw* (1974), *Frankenstein* (1973), *Trilogy of Terror*, *Burnt Offerings*, *Dead of Night* (1977), *Curse of the Black Widow* and *Trilogy of Terror II*. Cobert's other credits include *Scalpel*, the TV series *'Way Out* (1961) and *Supertrain* (1979), and episodes of *Intruders*.

Daisy Coleman

American Netflix documentary star and rape survivor [Catherine] Daisy Coleman committed suicide on August 4, aged 23. She also starred in the 2019 horror-comedy *Texas Death Trippin'* (and the re-worked *Texas Death Trippin Ax-Tended Cut* the following year).

Raphaël Coleman

British former child actor and environmental activist Raphaël [Pierre Jensen] Coleman, who played "Eric Brown" in *Nanny McPhee* (2005), died of a heart attack while out jogging on February 6, aged 25. His other credits include the 2009 remake of *It's Alive* and *The Fourth Kind*.

David Collings

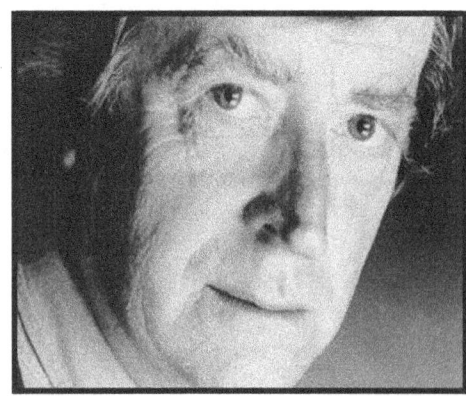

British stage and screen actor David Collings died on March 23, aged 79. He appeared in the 1970 musical *Scrooge* (as "Bob Cratchit") and on TV in episodes of *Out of the Unknown* (the J.B. Priestley-scripted 'Level Seven' and 'The Naked Sun', based on the novel by Isaac Asimov), *Mystery and Imagination* ('The Suicide Club'), *UFO*, *Dark Towers*, *Blakes 7*, *Sapphire & Steel*, *Dramarama* ('The Universe Downstairs') and three series of the BBC's *Doctor Who* ('Revenge of the Cybermen', 'The Robots of Death' and 'Mawdryn Undead'). Collings was the voice of the title character in the English version of *Monkey* (1978–80), and he also voiced an alternative version of the Doctor in the Big Finish *Doctor Who Unbound* audio drama 'Full Fathom Five'.

Forrest Compton

American supporting actor Forrest Compton, a regular on *Gomer Pyle: USMC* (1964–69), died of complications from COVID-19 on April 4, aged 94. He began his career on TV in the mid-1950s, and his credits include episodes of *The Twilight Zone* and *The Invaders*.

Sean Connery

Scottish-born film star Sir [Thomas] Sean Connery died at his home in Nassau, in the Bahamas, on October 31, aged 90. The screen's coolest James Bond in seven movies – *Dr. No* (1962), *From Russia with Love*, *Goldfinger*, *Thunderball*, *You Only Live Twice*, *Diamonds Are Forever* and *Never Say Never Again* (1983) – he also appeared in Disney's *Darby O'Gill and the Little People*, *Tarzan's Greatest Adventure*, *Macbeth* (1961), *Zardoz*, *The Man Who Would Be King* (based on the novella by Rudyard Kipling), *Meteor*, *Outland*, *Time Bandits*, *Sword of the Valiant: The Legend of Sir Gawain and the Green Knight* (with Peter Cushing), *Highlander*, *The Name of the Rose*, *Indiana Jones and the Last Crusade*, *The Hunt for Red October*, *Highlander II: The Quickening*, *The Avengers* (1998) and *The League of Extraordinary Gentlemen* (as "Allan Quatermain"). Connery was also the voice of the dragon in *Dragonheart*, and he was in a 1956 TV adaptation of Edgar Wallace's play *The Terror*.

Sean Connery (1930–2020) starred as James Bond 007 in Thunderball (1965).

Robert Conrad

American leading man Robert Conrad (Conrad Robert Norton Falk), who starred as secret agent "James 'Jim' West" in the CBS Western SF series *The Wild Wild West* (1965-69) and the spin-off movies *The Wild Wild West Revisited* and *More Wild Wild West*, died of heart failure on February 8, aged 84. He was also in the TV movies *Five Desperate Women* and *The Fifth Missile*, while his final credit was the 2002 "slasher" *Dead Above Ground*.

Kevin Conway

American character actor Kevin [John] Conway died of a heart attack on February 5, aged 77. He appeared in *Slaughterhouse-Five*, *The Lathe of Heaven* (1980, based on the novel by Ursula K. Le Guin), Tobe Hooper's *The Funhouse*, *The Elephant Man*, *Jennifer 8*, *Lawnmower Man 2: Beyond Cyberspace* and *Black Knight*. On TV, Conway appeared in episodes of *Star Trek: The Next Generation*, *Dark Angel* and *Life on Mars* (2009), and he was the "Control Voice" on the 1995-2002 seasons of *The Outer Limits*.

Wendy Cooling

British children's teacher, author and editor Wendy [Ena] Cooling MBE died on June 23, aged 78. Amongst the numerous anthologies she edited are *Bad Dreams*, *Scared Stiff*, *Simply Spooky*, *Spine Chillers*, *Time-Watch*, *Aliens to Earth*, *Weird and Wonderful*, *Out of This World: Stories of Virtual Reality*, *Stranger Than Ever* and *Mirrors*. Colling was also the founder of Bookstart, the national programme of the charity BookTrust to encourage a lifelong love of reading in babies and toddlers.

Ben Cooper

American supporting actor Ben Cooper (Benjamin Austin Cooper, Jr.) died on February 24, aged 86.

Although best known for his Western roles, he also appeared in episodes of TV's *One Step Beyond*, *The Twilight Zone* (Manly Wade Wellman's 'Still Valley') and *The Time Tunnel*. Cooper retired from the screen in 1995.

Richard Corben

Famed American comics artist and filmmaker Richard Corben died of complications from heart surgery on December 2, aged 80. He began his career in underground comics such as *Grim Wit*, *Slow Death*, *Skull*, *Fever Dreams* and his own *Fantagor*, before moving to Warren Publishing in the early 1970s, where he contributed strips and covers to *Creepy*, *Eerie*, *Vampirella* and other titles. From the mid-1970s he became a regular contributor to *Métal Hurlant/Heavy Metal* magazine (including his fantasy series 'Den'), and he adapted a Robert E. Howard story into the 1976 graphic novel *Bloodstar*. Corben went on to work at DC, Marvel, IDW and Dark Horse, creating adaptations of Edgar Allan Poe and H.P. Lovecraft for *Haunt of Horror*, William Hope Hodgson's *The House on the Borderland*, and contributing to such titles as *Hellblazer*, *Conan of Cimmeria* and *Hellboy*. Corben also worked closely with Harlan Ellison on various graphic versions of *Vic and Blood* (*A Boy and his Dog*). His own movies included the shorts *Neverwhere* (1968) and *Dagon* (1999), and *The Dark Planet*, and he scripted and designed the 'Den' episode for the animated film *Heavy Metal* (1981). Corben also designed the sleeve of Meat Loaf's album *Bat Out of Hell*, and movie posters for *Phantom of the Paradise* (1974) and *Spookies* (1986). He was the winner of the 2009 Spectrum Grand Master Award, and in 2012 was elected to the Will Eisner Award Hall of Fame.

Nick Cordero

Canadian-born Broadway star Nick Cordero (Nicholas Eduardo Alberto Cordero) died in Los Angeles of

Cover of Edgar Allan Poe (Ballantine Books, 2005) by artist Richard Corben (1940–2020).

complications from COVID-19 on July 5 aged 41. He had suffered multiple complications since contracting the virus in March, including having a leg amputated as a result of blood clots. The Tony Award-nominated musical actor made his debut in the Off-Broadway production of *The Toxic Avenger* (2008), originating the roll of "Melvin Ferd II"/"Toxie".

Cis Corman

American casting director Cis Corman died on April 27, aged 93. Her credits include *The Sentinel* (featuring John Carradine), *Eyes of Laura Mars* and *Wolfen*. She also served as president of Barbara Streisand's production company.

Stuart Cornfeld

Hollywood movie producer Stuart Cornfeld died of cancer on June 26, aged 67. Ben Stiller's producing partner in Red Hour Films, Cornfeld's credits include *The Elephant Man*, David Cronenberg's remake of *The Fly*, *The Fly II*, *Hider in the House*, *Kafka*, Guillermo del Toro's *Mimic*, *The Ruins*, *Megamind*, *Vamps* and *The Secret Life of Walter Mitty* (2013).

Dale Crain

American comics artist and archivist [Roger] Dale Crain died of a heart attack in Vietnam on April 4. He is best known as an editor, working on the Marvel Masterworks series and DC's Millennium and Archives reprint volumes. A GoFundMe page was set up by his family to repatriate his body back to the United States.

Doug Crane

American animator Doug Crane died of cancer on December 17, aged 85. He began working for Terrytoons in 1956, and his credits include such TV cartoon series as *Mighty Thor* (1966), *Spider-Man* (1968-70), *Challenge of the Superfriends* (1978), *Godzilla* (1978-79),

He-Man and the Masters of the Universe (1983-85), *She-Ra: Princess of Power* (1985) and *Bravestarr* (1987-88). At the request of Bill Hanna, Crane and Red Auguston opened and operated the Hanna-Barbera East studios in New York City. He also worked on *The Juggler of Our Lady* (featuring the voice of Boris Karloff), *Gnomes*, *Heavy Metal*, *He-Man and She-Ra: The Secret of the Sword*, *He-Man and She-Ra: A Christmas Special*, *Pinocchio and the Emperor of the Night*, *Bravestarr: The Legend* and *The Nutcracker Prince*.

Gary William Crawford

American small press poet, writer and editor Gary William Crawford died on July 9, aged 67. He founded Gothic Press in 1979, which published the critical journal *Gothic* (1979-87), the horror poetry magazine *Night Songs*, and various chapbooks. Crawford had a number of volumes of poetry published, and his short fiction is collected in *Gothic Fevers* and *Mysteries of Von Domarus and Other Stories*. He also produced studies on Ramsey Campbell, J. Sheridan Le Fanu and Robert Aickman.

Linda Cristal

Argentinean-born leading lady Linda Cristal (Marta Victoria Moya Burges), who starred as "Victoria Cannon" in the Western TV series *The High Chaparral* (1967-71), died on June 27 in Beverly Hills, aged 89. She began her movie career in Mexico in the early 1950s, before moving to Hollywood at the end of the decade. Her credits include *The Fiend Who Walked West* and the 1975 TV movie *The Dead Don't Die* (scripted by Robert Bloch), along with episodes of *Voyage to the Bottom of the Sea*, *Search* and *Fantasy Island*.

Denise Cronenberg

Canadian costume designer Denise Cronenberg died of "multiple age-

related issues" on May 22, aged 81. She began working in the wardrobe department on her younger brother David's movies *Videodrome* and *The Dead Zone*, and stepped up to full costume designer on *The Fly* (1986). She also worked with him on *Dead Ringers, Naked Lunch, Crash, eXistenZ, Spider* and other films, and her other credits include *Dracula 2000, Dawn of the Dead* (2004), *Dead Silence, The Incredible Hulk* (2008) and *Resident Evil: Afterlife*.

Ben Cross

British leading man Ben Cross (Harry Bernard Cross) died of cancer in Vienna, Austria, on August 18, aged 72. After studying acting at RADA, he went on to star in such movies as *The Unholy, Paperhouse, Nightlife, Hellfire, Temptress, 20,000 Leagues Under the Sea* (1997, as "Captain Nemo"), *The Invader, Exorcist: The Beginning, S.S. Doomtrooper, Wicked Little Things, Grendel* (2007), *Species: The Awakening, Lost City Raiders, Star Trek* (2009, as "Sarek"), *Hellhounds, Ice* (aka *Ice 2020*), *Super Tanker, Black Forest, Jack the Giant Killer* (2013), *Viking Quest* and *The Devil's Light*. On TV, Cross portrayed resurrected vampire "Barnabas Collins" in ABC's short-lived 1991 revival of *Dark Shadows*, and he appeared in episodes of the *Twilight Zone* (1986), *The Ray Bradbury Theater, Tales from the Crypt, Poltergeist: the Legacy, 12 Monkeys* and *Pandora*.

Frances Cuka

British character actress Frances Cuka died of complications from a stroke on February 16, aged 83. She appeared in the musical *Scrooge* (1970, as "Ethel Cratchit"), Disney's *The Watcher in the Woods* (1980), *Afraid of the Dark* (1991) and *Snow White: A Tale of Terror*. On TV, Cuka turned up in episodes of

Adam Adamant Lives!, *The Champions* and *Hammer House of Horror*.

Julian Curry

British character actor Julian [Burnlee] Curry, who played "Claude Erskine-Brown" on *Rumpole of the Bailey* (1978-92), died on June 27, aged 82. His credits include *Hamlet* (1970), *Baby: Secret of the Lost Legend*, *Ghost Chase*, *Loch Ness*, *Rasputin* (1996), *The Wyvern Mystery*, *Seven Days to Live* and *Sky Captain and the World of Tomorrow*. On TV, Curry also appeared in episodes of *Out of the Unknown* (Frederik Pohl's 'The Midas Plague'), *Around the World in 80 Days* (1981), *The Case-Book of Sherlock Holmes*, *Bugs*, *Stig of the Dump* (2002), *Midsomer Murders* ('Things That Go Bump in the Night') and *Truth Seekers*.

Clive Cussler

Bestselling American author Clive [Eric] Cussler died on February 24, aged 88. Best known for his 1976 novel *Raise the Titanic!* (filmed in 1980), several other volumes in his "Dirk Pitt" series have genre themes (*Night Probe!*, *Cyclops*, *Treasure*, *Atlantis Found* and *Valhalla Rising*). A number

of titles in Cussler's franchised techno-thriller series "The NUMA Files" with Graham Brown (*Zero Hour*, *Nighthawk*, *The Rising Sea* and *Sea of Greed*), and "Fargo Adventures" with Robin Burcell (*The Oracle*) also contain SF elements.

Nick Cuti

American TV animation designer Nick (Nicola) Cuti (*Defenders of Earth*, *BraveStarr*, *Gargoyles*, *RoboCop: Alpha Commando*, etc.) died on February 21, aged 75. He also scripted (with director John Lewis) the indie horror anthology movies *Tidbits of Terror* and *Tidbits of Terror II*, along with the short films *Captain Cosmos and the Gray Ghosts*,

Shock House, *The Lady Without Substance* and *Moonie and the Spider Queen* (also directing the latter two).

Abby Dalton

American actress Abby Dalton (Gladys Marlene Wasden), who played the scheming "Julia Cumson" on TV's *Falcon Crest* (1981-86), died after a long illness on November 23, aged 88. Best remembered for starring in Roger Corman's *The Saga of the Viking Women and Their Voyage to the Waters of the Great Sea Serpent* (1957), her other credits include *Roller Blade Warriors: Taken by Force*, *Cyber Tracker* and *Prank*. Dalton's daughter is actress Kathleen Kinmont.

Wally K. Daly

British scriptwriter Wally K. Daly (Walter Kevin Daly) died on April 30, aged 79. His radio plays for the BBC include *2004*, *The Children of Witchwood*, *Time Slip*, *625Y*, *Nightmare World* and the SF trilogy *Before the Screaming Begins*, *The Silent Scream* and *With a Whimper to the Grave*. Daly also wrote the *Doctor Who* novel *The Ultimate Evil*, which was based on his unproduced TV script for Colin Baker's sixth Doctor. It was finally adapted as a full-cast audio drama in 2019 for "The Lost Stories" series from BBC/Big Finish.

Sonia Darrin

American actress and dancer Sonia Darrin (Sonia Paskowitz) died of complications from a broken hip on July 19, aged 96. Best known for her role as bogus bookseller "Agnes Lozelle" opposite Humphrey Bogart's Philip Marlowe in *The Big Sleep* (1946), she also had a bit part as a villager in Universal's *Frankenstein Meets the Wolf Man* (1942). She retired from movies in 1950 and became a model.

Allen Daviau

Five-time Oscar-nominated American cinematographer [John] Allen Daviau died of complications from COVID-19 on April 15, aged 77. He was the fourth resident at the Motion Picture & Television Country House facility in Woodland Hills, California, to die from the virus after surgery in 2012 caused him to use a wheelchair for the rest of his life. Daviau collaborated with director Steven Spielberg on *Close Encounters of the Third Kind* (additional photography), *E.T. The Extra-Terrestrial*, *Twilight Zone the Movie*, *Indiana Jones and the Temple of Doom* and an episode of TV's *Amazing Stories* ('Ghost Train'). He started out creating psychedelic special effects lighting for Roger Corman's *The Trip* (1967), and his other credits include *Harry and the Hendersons*, *Congo*, *The Astronaut's Wife* and *Van Helsing*. The cousin of author Anne Rice, Daviau received lifetime achievement awards from the Art Directors Guild in 1997 and the American Society of Cinematographers in 2007.

Matteo De Cosmo

American art director Matteo De Cosmo, who worked on episodes of

Marvel's *The Punisher* (2017-19) and *Luke Cage* (2018), died of complications from COVID-19 on April 21, aged 52. His other credits also include the 2019-20 series *Emergence*.

Richard De Croce

53-year-old American TV producer Richard De Croce was killed after being struck by a freight train on October 18. For BBC America he produced the documentaries *Torchwood: Inside the Hub*, *Doctor Who: Inside the TARDIS*, *Doctor Who: The David Tennant Special*, *Doctor Who: The Ultimate Guide*, *Doctor Who: 50th Anniversary Live Pre-Show*, the four-part series *The Real History od Science Fiction* (2014) and the 2015 drama series *Tatau*.

Olivia de Havilland

The last of Hollywood's great stars of the 1930s, Japanese-British-born Dame Olivia [Mary] de Havilland, who starred in such enduring classics as *Captain Blood*, *The Charge of the Light Brigade*, *Dodge City*, *The Adventures of Robin Hood*, *The Private Lives of Elizabeth and Essex*, *Santa Fe Trail* and *They Died with Their Boots On* (all opposite Errol Flynn) and *Gone with the Wind*, died in Paris, France, on July 25, aged 104. The sister of actress Joan Fontaine, the Oscar-winning de Havilland's other credits include *A Midsummer Night's Dream* (1935), *Lady in a Cage*, *Hush . . . Hush Sweet Charlotte*, *The Screaming Woman* (based on a story by Ray Bradbury) and *The Swarm*. In 2008, at the age of 92, she received the US National Medal of Arts from George W. Bush. Two years later she was awarded the Knight Legion of Honour from French President Nicolas Sarkozy.

Gianni Dei

Italian actor Gianni Dei (Gianni Carpanelli), who portrayed the title character in *Patrick Still Lives* (1980),

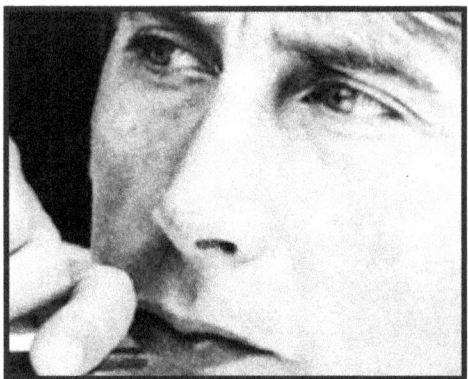

died on October 19, aged 79. His other credits include *The Seventh Grave*, *Sex of the Witch* and *Sex Demons and Death*.

Gene Deitch

Innovative American-born animation director and writer Gene Deitch (Eugene Merril Deitch) — who co-directed (with Al Kouzel) the 1958 short *The Juggler of Our Lady: A Medieval Legend*, narrated by Boris Karloff — died in Prague, Czech Republic, on April 16, aged 95. Deitch worked as an animator at UPA on projects like *Howdy Doody and His Magic Hat* before moving to Terrytoons in 1955. When he was fired in 1958, he moved to

Prague the following year, from where he directed around a dozen *Tom and Jerry* cartoons for MGM (including *Mouse Into Space*), along with the TV series *Popeye the Sailor* (1960–62) and *Krazy Kat* (1963) for King Features Syndicate. His other credits include *Alice in a New Wonderland* (aka *Alice of Wonderland in Paris*), a twelve-minute adaptation of J.R.R. Tolkien's *The Hobbit* (1966), *Strega Nona*, *Teeny-Tiny and the Witch Woman*, *Moon Man*, *The Hat* and *Sylvester and the Magic Pebble*, while Deitch's 1961 short *Munro* won an Oscar for producer William L. Snyder.

Dorothy Dells

American actress Dorothy [Emily] Dells died on April 3, aged 91. Discovered while working at a drive-in restaurant on Sunset Blvd., she was in *Space Rage* (1985) along with episodes of TV's *Future Cop*, *Supertrain* and *Highway to Heaven*.

Brian Dennehy

Reliable American supporting actor Brian [Manion] Dennehy, who often

portrayed policemen or military commanders, died of sepsis on April 15, aged 81. His movie credits include *Ants!*, *Cocoon*, *F/X* and *F/X2*, Tom Clancy's *Netforce*, *Fail Safe* (2000) and *Category 6: Day of Destruction*. He also appeared (uncredited) as the alien leader in *Cocoon: The Return*. Dennehy got his start in TV in the late 1970s, and he appeared in episodes of *Lucan*, *Darkroom*, *Faerie Tale Theatre*, *Night Visions*, *The 4400* and *Masters of Science Fiction* (Harlan Ellison's 'The Discarded').

Dimitri Diatchenko

American actor Dimitri Diatchenko died of an accidental overdose of prescription drugs on April 21, aged 52. He had not been heard from for several days, so his family asked police to do a wellness check and he was found dead in his Florida home. Although Diatchenko appeared (often cast as thugs or bodyguards) in such movies as *Indiana Jones and the Kingdom of the Skull*, *Get Smart* (2008), *Chernobyl Diaries* and *They're Watching*, along with an episode of TV's *Timecop*, he is best known for his voice work on such video games as *Quake 4*, *Iron Man*, *Wolfenstein* (2009), *Iron Man 2*, *Spider-Man: Shattered Dimensions*, *Tomb Raider* (2013), *Rise of the Tomb Raider* and *Deus Ex: Mankind Divided*, and the 2017 cartoon series *Teenage Mutant Ninja Turtles* ('The Crypt of Dracula' and 'Monsters Among Us!').

Dena Dietrich

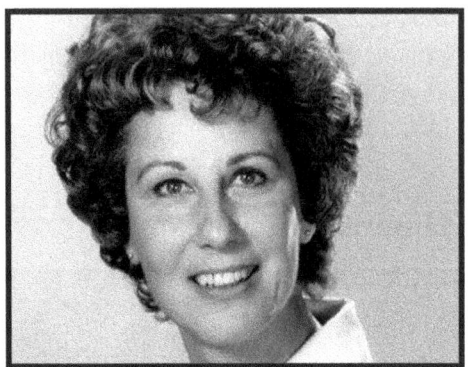

American character actress Dena Dietrich, who was best known as "Mother Nature" in a series of TV commercials for Chiffon Margarine (1972-85), died on November 21, aged 91. She appeared in the 1974 TV movie *A Strange and Deadly Occurence* and episodes of *The Ghost Busters* ('The Vampire's Apprentice'), *Space Academy*, *Turnabout*, *Out of this World*, *Harry and the Hendersons* and *The Burning Zone*.

Arthur Dignam

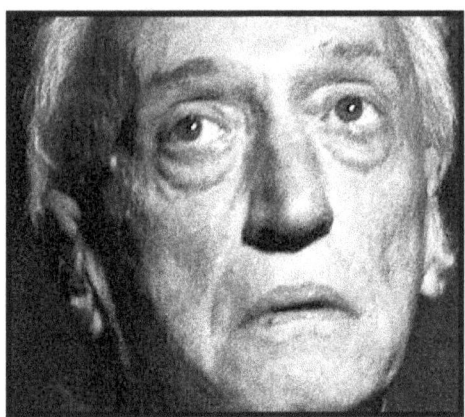

Cadaverous Australian character actor Arthur Dignam, who portrayed "Ernest Thesiger" in Bill Condon's *Gods and Monsters* (1998), died of a massive heart attack while waving to a friend during his morning walk on May 9. He was 80. Often cast as scientists (both mad and sane), Dignam's other credits include *Summer of Secrets*, *Strange Behavior* (aka *Dead Kids*), *The Return of Captain Invincible* (with Christopher Lee), *Those Dear Departed* (aka *Ghosts Can Do It*) and *The Dreaming*, plus episodes of TV's *The New Avengers*, *The Storyteller: Greek Myths* ('Perseus & the Gorgon') and *Escape from Jupiter* (1994, as regular character "Professor Ingessol").

Vasilis Dimitriou

One of the last surviving Greek movie billboard artists, Vasilis [Periklis] Dimitriou, died of Parkinson's disease on September 6, aged 84. From the

mid-1940s onwards, the self-taught artist created more than 8,000 hand-painted signs, most recently for the eight feet high and forty-two feet long billboard that adorns Athens' Athinaion movie theatre. For more than six decades he painted one or two billboards a week, using home-brewed paints mixed with glue to keep the artwork from running in the rain. He vowed to keep the craft going as long as he could lift his arms to paint. "Painting is in my blood," he said in 2014. "When I stop breathing is when I'll stop painting."

Malcolm Dixon

Four-foot, one-inch British actor Malcolm Dixon, best remembered as "Strutter" in *Time Bandits* (1981), died on April 9, aged 66. He began his career playing "Sleepy" in a 1966 BBC version of *Snow White and the Seven Dwarfs*, and he also appeared in *Willy Wonka & the Chocolate Factory* (as an uncredited "Oompa Loompa"), *Flash Gordon* (1980), *The Dark Crystal*, *Star Wars: Return of the Jedi*, *Labyrinth*, *Snow White* (1987), *Willow* and *A Witch's Way of Love*. From 1986-89 he starred in the lead role of "Bilbo Baggins" in a stage production of J.R.R. Tolkien's *The Hobbit* at the Fortune Theatre in London. His other theatre roles include productions of *Sleeping Beauty*, *Peter Pan* and *The Lion the Witch and the Wardrobe*, along with regular pantomime revivals of *Snow White and the Seven Dwarfs*.

Kevin Dobson

American actor Kevin [Patrick] Dobson, who co-starred as police detectives in the TV shows *Kojack* (1973-78) and *F/X: The Series* (1996-97), died of a heart attack on September 7, aged 77. His other credits include *Voices from the Grave* (1996), *1408* (based on the short story by Stephen King), *Portal*, *Bering Sea Beast* and episodes of *Tales of the*

Unexpected, *Touched by an Angel* and *Early Edition*.

Mario Donatone

Italian character actor [Giacinto] Mario Donatone, who was in *The Godfather: Part III* and *John Wick: Chapter 2*, died on April 14, aged 86. He also appeared in *King of Kong Island* (under the name "Dan Doney"), *Madeleine . . . anatomia di un incubo*, *La casa stregata*, Dario Argento's *Phenomena* and *Cross of the Seven Jewels*.

Kirk Douglas

Cleft-chinned Hollywood legend Kirk Douglas (Issur Herschelevitch Danielovitch) died on February 5, aged 103. The Honorary Oscar-winning actor starred in Disney's *20,000 Leagues Under the Sea* (1954) and *The Light at the Edge of the World*, *Ulysses* (1954), *The Vikings*, *Seven Days in May*, *Dr. Jekyll and Mr. Hyde* (1973), *Cat and Mouse* (aka *Mousey*), *Holocaust 2000* (aka *The Chosen*), *The Fury*, *Saturn 3* and *The Final Countdown*. On TV, Douglas also turned up in episodes of *Tales from the Crypt* (aka *Two-Fisted Tales*) and *Touched by an Angel*, and he played the Devil in Don Henley's 1995 music video for 'The Garden of Allah'. As a producer, he helped break the infamous "blacklist" in Hollywood, and in 1981 he received the Presidential Medal of Freedom (the highest civilian honour in the US) from President Jimmy Carter.

Shirley Douglas

Canadian actress and political activist Shirley [Jean] Douglas died of complications from pneumonia on April 5, aged 86. Her credits include *Really Weird Tales*, David Cronenberg's *Dead Ringers*, *Shadow Dancing* and a 1989 episode of *Alfred Hitchcock Presents*. The mother of actor Kiefer

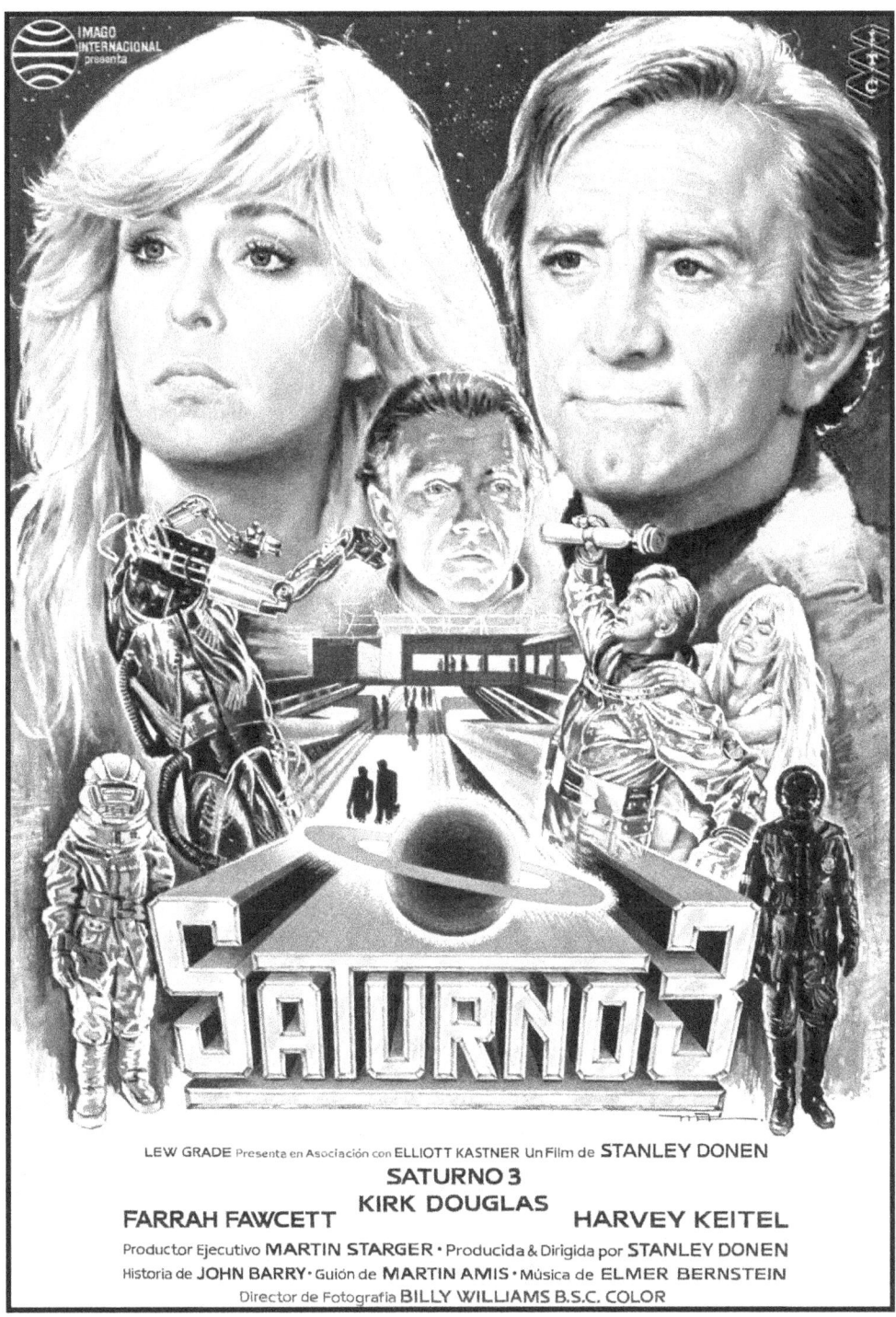

Italian foglio *for* Saturn 3 *(1980) starring Kirk Douglas (1916–2020).*

Sutherland, Douglas was married to Donald Sutherland from 1966–71.

Kaye Dowd

American actress Kaye Dowd (Catherine Marie Dowd), who starred in the 1945 fantasy movie *An Angel Comes to Brooklyn*, died on April 18, aged 96. She also had an uncredited role the same year in *I Love a Mystery*.

Debra Doyle

American author Debra Doyle died of a sudden cardiac event on October 31, aged 67. She wrote a number of novels in collaboration with her husband, James D. Macdonald, including the "Circle of Magic" series (*School of Wizardry, Tournament and Tower, City by the Sea, The Prince's Players, The Prisoners of Bell Castle, The High King's Daughter, Mystery at Wizardry School* and *Voice of the Ice*), the "Mageworlds" series (*The Price of Stars, Starpilot's Grave, By Honor Betray'd, The Gathering Flame, The Long Hunt, The Stars Asunder, A Working of Stars* and *On Suivi Point*), the "Bad Blood" trilogy (*Bad Blood, Hunters' Moon* and *Judgment Night*), *Night of Ghosts and Lightning* and *Zero-Sum Games* (as by "Robyn Tallis"), *Knight's Wyrd, Blood Brothers* and *Vampire's Kiss* (as by "Nicholas Adams"), *Groogleman, Land of Mist and Snow* and *Lincoln's Sword*. They also co-wrote tie-in books (under their own names and pseudonyms) in the "Horror High", "Robert Silverberg's Time Tours", "Tom Swift", "Daniel M. Pinkwater's Melvinge of the Megaverse", "Marvel's Spider-Man Universe" and "Gene Roddenberry's Earth: Final Conflict" franchises, and contributed short stories to such anthologies as *Werewolves* (1988), *Vampires: A Collection of Original Stories, Witch Fantastic* and many other titles.

Mort Drucker

American comics artist and caricaturist Mort Drucker (Morris Terkel) died on April 9, aged 91. In the late 1940s, following a recommendation by Will Eisner, the self-taught cartoonist began working as a teenager on comic books

and newspaper strips. During the 1950s and '60s he freelanced for Atlas/Marvel, DC Comics and other publishers on such titles as *World of Fantasy*, *World of Suspense*, *Strange Tales*, *Strange Tales of the Unusual*, *House of Secrets*, *House of Mystery*, *Tales of the Unexpected*, *Strange Adventures* and *Phantom Stranger*. Drucker joined *MAD* in 1956 and specialised in the humour magazine's satires of movies and television shows. His 1980 *Star Wars* parody 'The Empire Strikes Out' resulted in the Lucasfilm legal department sending a cease-and-desist order to the magazine, demanding that the issue be recalled. *MAD* responded with a copy of another letter they had received the previous month from director George Lucas, offering to buy the original artwork! Drucker finally retired from *MAD* in 2008. His own books include *Mort Drucker's MAD Show-Stoppers*, *Familiar Faces: The Art of Mort Drucker*, *Tomatoes from Mars* (with Arthur Yonkins) and *MAD's Greatest Artists: Mort Drucker*. In 1966 he drew the cover for Pyramid Books' *Christopher Lee's Treasury of Terror*, a collection of comic strips based on well-known horror stories, edited by Russ Jones. In 2014, Mort Drucker became the first winner of the National Society of Cartoonists' Medal of Honour for lifetime achievement.

James Drury

American actor James [Child] Drury, who starred in NBC's long-running Western series *The Virginian* (1962–71), died on April 6, aged 85. One of Drury's earliest movie roles was as a crew member in *Forbidden Planet* (1956), and he went on to appear in the TV movie *The Devil and Miss Sarah* and episodes of *Alfred Hitchcock Presents*, *Men Into Space* and *The Adventures of Brisco County Jr.*

George Dugdale

George [Michael Hallam] Dugdale, who was married to actress Caroline Munro since 1990, died on January 14, aged 65. He wrote and directed (with Mark Ezra and Peter Mackenzie Litten) the horror movies *Slaughter*

Cover for Christopher Lee's Treasury of Terror (Pyramid Books, 1966) by artist Mort Drucker (1929–2020).

High (1985, starring his future wife) and *Living Doll* (1990).

Cheryl Wheeler Duncan

59-year-old American stuntwoman and three-time World Kickboxing Champion Cheryl [Marie] Wheeler Duncan (aka "Cheryl Wheeler-Dixon") was killed, along with her husband, in a shoot-out with her former husband on February 12. No charges were filed, as the case was determined to be "justifiable homicide". Duncan did stunts on John Carpenter's *They Live* and *Ghosts of Mars*, *Cameron's Closet*, *Night Life* (aka *Grave Misdemeanours*), *Back to the Future Part II*, *Night Angel*, *Maniac Cop 2*, *976-Evil II*, *Memoirs of an Invisible Man*, *Honey I Blew Up the Kid*, *Warlock: The Armageddon*, *Sliver*, *Demolition Man*, *The Mask*, *The Relic*, *Batman & Robin* (1997), *Phantoms*, *Friday the 13th* (2009), *Thor*, *Spy Kids 4-D: All the Time in the World* and *Transformers: Age of Extinction*.

Marj Dusay

American soap opera actress Marj Dusay (Marjorie Ellen Pivonka Mahoney), who appeared as "Alexandra Spaulding" in more than 130 episodes of *Guiding Light* (1987-2009), died on January 28, aged 83. Her other credits include *A Fire in the Sky*, *Made in Heaven*, *A Chronicle of Corpses*, the 1969 TV pilot *Dead of Night: A Darkness at Blaisedon*, and episodes of *Get Smart*, *Star Trek* ('Spock's Brain'), *The Wild Wild West*, *The Immortal*, *The Bionic Woman*, *The Fantastic Journey*, *The Hardy Boys/Nancy Drew Mysteries*, *Galactica 1980*, *Tucker's Witch* and *Friday the 13th: The Series*.

Hilary Dwyer

75-year-old British actress Hilary Dwyer (aka Hilary Heath), who co-starred with Vincent Price in AIP's *Witchfinder General* (aka *The Conqueror Worm*), *The Oblong Box* and *Cry of the Banshee*, died on April 3 of complications from COVID-19. She also appeared in *The Body Stealers*, *Wuthering Heights* (1970), and episodes of TV's *The Avengers*, *The Prisoner* and *Space: 1999*. Dwyer retired from the screen in the late 1970s to run a talent agency with her husband and later became a successful film producer. "I adored Vincent," she said in 2010. "I played his mistress, his daughter and his wife. And he said, 'If you ever play my mother, I'll marry you'."

Gene Dynarski

American character actor Gene Dynarski (Eugene Dynarski) died on February 27, aged 86. Perhaps best known for his appearances in two Steven Spielberg movies — in *Duel* he was a trucker confronted in a roadside café by Dennis Weaver's character, while in *Close Encounters of the Third*

Kind he played the supervisor who sent Richard Dreyfuss out to investigate the mysterious blackouts — Dynarski's other credits include the 1974 movie *Earthquake* and episodes of TV's *Batman* (as a henchman of Vincent Price's "Egghead"), *Voyage to the Bottom of the Sea*, *Star Trek* ('Mudd's Women'), *Land of the Giants*, *The Invisible Man* (1976), *The Magical World of Disney* ('Beyond Witch Mountain'), *Star Trek: The Next Generation* and the *X Files*.

Robert Eighteen-Bisang

Canada's self-styled "world's foremost authority" on vampire literature and mythology, Robert Eighteen-Bisang, died on September 29, aged 73. He

Italian foglio for The Oblong Box (1969), which co-starred Hilary Dwyer (1945–2020).

edited the anthologies *The Vampire Stories of Sir Arthur Conan Doyle* and *Vintage Vampire Stories* (with Richard Dalby), and compiled and annotated the Lord Ruthven Award-winning *Bram Stoker's Notes for Dracula: A Facsimile Edition and Drafts of Dracula* (both with Elizabeth Miller). Eighteen-Bisang founded Transylvania Press, Inc. in 1994 with *Dracula: The Rare Text of 1901*, and went on to publish books by Sherry Gottlieb, Chelsea Quinn Yarbro, S.P. Somtow and Miller, along with his own *A Vampire Bibliography Volume One: Literature*. He claimed to have amassed the largest collection of vampiric literature in the world, containing around 2,500 books, 2,000 comics, 1,000 magazines and more than 100 movies.

Phyllis Eisenstein

Nebula and Hugo Award-nominated American SF and fantasy author Phyllis Eisenstein (Phyllis Kleinstein) died on December 7, aged 74. She had been in a coma for the past year after suffering serious neurological problems. Her first story, written in collaboration with her husband Alex, appeared in Robert Silverberg's anthology *New Dimensions #1: Fourteen Original Science Fiction Stories* (1971). She went on to publish around fifty short stories (in such magazines as *Amazing*, *Analog*, *Galaxy* and *The Magazine of Fantasy and Science Fiction*) and six novels, including the Balrog Award-winning *Born to Exile* (published by Arkham House) and its sequel *In the Red Lord's Reach* featuring "Alaric the Minstrel", *Shadow of Earth*, *In the Hands of Glory* and the "Book of Elementals" sequence (*Sorcerer's Son*, *The Crystal Palace* and *The City in Stone*). Her short fiction (in collaboration with her husband) is collected in *Night Lives: Nine Stories of the Dark Fantastic*. Eisenstein also edited two volumes of the *Spec-Lit* anthology series for Columbia College Chicago. For fifteen years she was the managing copyeditor at Leo Burnett Agency, and after assisting Roger Zelazny at the Indiana University Writers Conference in 1977, she went on to teach creative writing at the Clarion Science Fiction Writers Workshop, Oakton Community College, the Writers Digest School and Columbia College Chicago. Her 1978 short story 'Lost and Found' was adapted by George R.R. Martin for a 1986 episode of TV's *The Twilight Zone*. She is also credited with suggesting to Martin that he include dragons in his "A Song of Ice and Fire" series, and he dedicated *A Storm of Swords* to her.

Susan Ellison

Susan Ellison (Susan Toth), the British-born widow of author Harlan Ellison, died unexpectedly on August 1, aged 60. She first met Ellison at a convention in Scotland in 1985, and the couple married the following year. She was his fifth wife, but the love of his life, and they remained inseparable until Ellison's death in 2018. She had a story in *Worlds of If* in 1973, a film and television column in *Aboriginal Science Fiction* from the late 1980s to the late '90s, and edited the fanzine/newsletter *Rabbit Hole* for many years for The Harlan Ellison Record Collection. However, she will mostly be remembered for the support she gave Harlan Ellison over their thirty-two years together, and for maintaining the author's legacy after his death.

John Ericson

German-born American leading man John Ericson (Joseph Meibes), who co-starred as "Sam Bolt" in the TV series *Honey West* (1965-66) with Anne Francis, died of pneumonia in New Mexico on May 3, aged 93. He was in the movies *7 Faces of Dr. Lao* (as the

transformed Pan), *Operation Atlantis*, *The Destructors*, *The Bamboo Saucer*, Walt Disney's *Bedknobs and Broomsticks*, Charles Band's *Crash!*, *The House of the Dead* and *The Ghosts of Buxley Hall*. Ericson's many TV credits include episodes of *Out There*, *Climax!* ('The Man Who Lost His Head' with Peter Lorre), *Shirley Temple's Storybook* ('The Legend of Sleepy Hollow'), *The Invaders*, *Knight Rider*, *Automan* and *Fantasy Island*. He also appeared in the 1965 unsold sitcom pilot *Sybil and Lionel*, about a ghost that had to perform 100 good deeds.

Mort Fallick

American film editor Mort Fallick (Morton Fallick) died of kidney failure on April 22, aged 86. His credits include the Dracula spoof *Love at First*

Bite (1979) and he executive produced the 1968 SF movie *Mission to Mars*. In the 1960s Fallick launched CineMetric, a production and post-production services company for commercials, documentaries, government/corporate films, TV shows, movie trailers and electronic press kits.

Sergio Fantoni

Veteran Italian supporting actor Sergio Fantoni died on April 17, aged 89. As well as dubbing the voices of numerous American stars in post-synchronised Italian versions of their movies, Fantoni appeared in *Hercules Unchained*, *The Giant of Marathon*, *Atom Age Vampire* (aka *Seddok [Son of Satan]*), *The Fifth Missile* and the science fiction TV series *Mission: Eureka*.

Melinda Fee

American actress Melinda [Evelyn] Fee, who co-starred as "Dr. Kate Westin" in the 1975-76 TV series *The Invisible Man*, died of a stroke on March 24, aged 77. Her other credits include *The Aliens Are Coming*, *Fade to Black* and *A Nightmare on Elm Street 2: Freddy's*

Revenge. Fee was also in episodes of *My Favorite Martian*, *I Dream of Jeannie*, *Lost in Space*, *The Bionic Woman* and *Knight Rider*. She retired from the screen in the early 1990s.

Edward S. Feldman

Hollywood producer Edward S. Feldman died on October 2, aged 91. A former publicist at 20th Century Fox, is credits include *What's the Matter with Helen?*, *Moon of the Wolf*, *The Sender*, *Explorers*, *The Hitcher*, *The Golden Child*, *Near Dark*, *Honey I Blew Up the Kid*, *Forever Young*, *The Jungle Book* (1994), *The Truman Show*, and *101 Dalmatians* (1996) and *102 Dalmatians*.

Andrew J. Fenady

American supporting actor-turned-screenwriter and producer Andrew J. Fenady (aka "A.J. Fenady") died on April 16, aged 91. His credits include the supernatural Western *Black Noon*, the TV pilot *The Stranger*, the all-star horror-fests *Terror in the Wax Museum* and *Arnold* (he also wrote the lyrics for the theme song to the latter, and both were directed by his brother Georg), and the brain-swap drama *Who is Julia?*. Fenady was also a playwright and author, and his 1977 novel *The Man with Bogart's Face* won the Mystery Writers of America Edgar Award and was turned into a movie three years later.

Mike Fenton

Veteran Hollywood casting director Mike Fenton (Ronald Michael Fenton), one of the founders of the Casting Society of America (CSA), died on December 30, aged 85. His many credits include *Young Frankenstein*, *Doc Savage: The Man of Bronze*, *Damnation Alley*, *Capricorn One*, *Magic*, *The Amityville Horror* (1979), *Raiders of the*

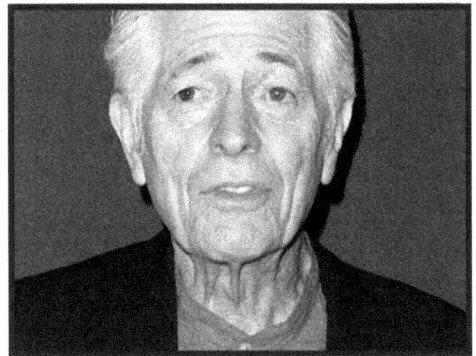

Lost Ark, *Goliath Awaits*, *Ghost Story*, *E.T. the Extra-Terrestrial*, *Poltergeist*, *Megaforce*, *Blade Runner*, *Timerider: The Adventures of Lyle Swann*, *Endangered Species*, *Superman III*, *Never Say Never Again*, *Twilight Zone: The Movie*, Michael Jackson's *Thriller*, *Indiana Jones and the Temple of Doom*, *Sheena*, *Runaway*, *The Goonies*, *Mad Max Beyond Thunderdome*, *Flesh + Blood*, *Legend*, *Return to Oz*, *Back to the Future*, *Enemy Mine*, *Short Circuit*, *Aliens*, *SpaceCamp*, *Flight of the Navigator*, *An American Tail*, *Hyper Sapien: People from Another Star*, *The Stepfather*, *Harry and the Hendersons*, *Innerspace*, *Forbidden Sun* (aka *The Bulldance*), *From the Dead of Night*, *Dream a Little Dream*, *Leviathan*, *Indiana Jones and the Last Crusade*, *Honey I Shrunk the Kids*, *Back to the Future Part II*, *Back to the Future Part III*, *Total Recall* (1990), *Arachnophobia*, *The Muppet Christmas Carol*, *Fortress*, *The NeverEnding Story III*, *Congo*, *Dr. Jekyll and Ms. Hyde*, *Toy Story*, *Crossworlds*, *Mrs. Santa Claus*, *Harvey* (1996), *Lost in Space* (1998), *Muppets from Space*, *It's a Very Merry Muppet Christmas Movie*, *Soul's Midnight*, *Weirdsville*, *Sharknado 2: The Second One* and the TV series *Amazing Stories* (1985–86), *Arabian Nights* (2000) and *Dinotopia* (2002–03).

Giancarlo Ferrando

Italian cinematographer Giancarlo Ferrando, who often collaborated with exploitation film directors Sergio Martino and Umberto Lenzi, died on August 13, aged 80. His many credits include *All the Colors of the Dark, Your Vice is a Locked Room and only I Have the Key, Torso, Slave of the Cannibal God, Screamers, The Great Alligator, The Scorpion with Two Tails, Ironmaster, 2019: After the Fall of New York, Warrior of the Lost World, Devil Fish* and *Hands of Steel* (both as "John McFerrand"), *The House of Witchcraft, House of Lost Souls, Troll 2* and Lucio Fulci's *Door to Silence* (as "John C. Fredericks"). Ferrando also worked on the miniatures and models for *Hercules* (1985).

Conchata Ferrell

77-year-old American character actress Conchata [Galen] Ferrell died of complications following cardiac arrest on October 12. A regular on such TV shows as *E/R* (1984-85), *L.A. Law* (1988-92), *Teen Angel* (1997-98) and *Two and a Half Men* (2003-15), her other credits include *Edward Scissorhands, Touch, Modern Vampires, K-Pax, Frankenweenie* (2012), *Krampus, The Axe Murders of Villisca* and *A Very Nutty Christmas*, along with episodes of *Faerie Tale Theater, Hard Times on Planet Earth, Buffy the Vampire Slayer, Touched by an Angel* and *Sabrina the Teenage Witch*.

Keith Ferrell

[Henry] Keith Ferrell, who was editor-in-chief of *Omni* magazine from 1991-96, died of heart failure while fixing his roof on April 11, aged 66. He also edited the anthology *Black Mist and*

Other Japanese Futures with Orson Scott Card, wrote the non-fiction studies *H.G. Wells: First Citizen of the Future* and *George Orwell: The Political Pen* and published a few short stories (including a collaboration with Jack Dann).

Lee Fierro

91-year-old [Elizabeth] Lee Fierro, who appeared as "Mrs. Kinter" in both *Jaws* (1975) and *Jaws: The Revenge*, died of complications from COVID-19 on April 5. She also contributed to a number of documentaries about Steven Spielberg's classic movie.

Alison Fiske

British actress Alison [Mary] Fiske died of cancer on July 26, aged 76. Although best known as a stage actress with the National Theatre and Royal Shakespeare Company, on TV she appeared in episodes of *The Frighteners* (John Burke's 'Miss Mouse') and *Tales of the Unexpected*. She retired in 2008.

Hy Fleishman

American horror comics artist of the 1950s, Hy (Herman) Fleishman, died on April 1, aged 92. He attended the Cartoonists and Illustrators School in New York and, after his service in the US Navy, he began working for numerous comic book publishers, most notably Atlas/Marvel, where he illustrated the crime and horror titles. Hyman's most notorious strip is probably 'The Vampire with Iron Teeth' in *Dark Mysteries* #15 (1953), which was blamed for the "The Gorbals Vampire" riots in Glasgow the following year. He also contributed to such comics as *Chilling Tales of Terror*, *Haunted Tales*, *Mister Mystery*, *Mysterious*

Adventures, *Mysterious Stories*, *Strange Stories of Suspense*, *Strange Tales*, *Strange Tales of the Unusual*, *Unknown Worlds*, *World of Suspense* and many other titles.

Rhonda Fleming

Flame-haired Hollywood star Rhonda Fleming (Marilyn Cheverton Louis) died on October 14, aged 97. The "Queen of Technicolor" began her screen career in the early 1940s, and her credits include Alfred Hitchcock's *Spellbound* (1945), *The Spiral Staircase* (1946), *A Connecticut Yankee in King Arthur's Court* (1948), *The Nude Bomb* and an episode of TV's *Search*.

Ronald Forfar

British character actor Ronald Forfar, a regular on the sit-com *bread* (1986-90), died on October 11, aged 81. On TV he was in episodes of *Sherlock Holmes* (with Peter Cushing), *The New Avengers* (again with Cushing) and the mini-series *The Nightmare Man*.

M.A. Foster

American author M. (Michael) A. (Anthony) Foster died on November 14, aged 81. He spent more than sixteen years as a Captain and Russian linguist in the United States Air Force before publishing the SF trilogies: "Ler" (*The Warriors of Dawn*, *The Gameplayers of Zan* and *The Day of the Klesh*) and "Transformer" (*The Morphodite*, *Transformer* and *Preserver*), both from DAW Books. The stand-alone novel *Waves* and *Owl Time: A Collection of Fictions* were also issued by the same publisher.

Derek Fowlds

British character actor Derek Fowlds, who is best remembered as straight-man to an annoying children's hand-puppet on *The Basil Brush Show* (1969-

73), died on January 17, aged 82. He also appeared in Hammer's *Frankenstein Created Woman* (with Peter Cushing), *Tower of Evil*, the 1967 TV pilot *The Solarnauts*, and episodes of *Theatre 625* (Nigel Kneale's 'The Year of the Sex Olympics') and *Thriller* (1974).

Samantha Fox

American adult movie star Samantha Fox (Stasia Therese Angela Micula) died on April 22, aged 69. She began her career in the late 1970s, and her many XXX-rated movies include *Dracula Exotica* (1980), *The Devil in Miss Jones Part II* (1982) and *Blue Voodoo* (1984). Fox also starred in Doris Wishman's 1983 horror movie *A Night to Dismember* and turned up (as "Stasia Micula") in Chuck Vincent's *Warrior Queen* (1987), opposite Sybil Danning and Donald Pleasence. She retired from the screen that same year to teach aerobics and dance.

John Fraser

Scottish-born leading man John [Alexander] Fraser died of oesophageal cancer on November 7, aged 89. A familiar face in films and on TV during the 1950s and '60s, his movie credits include *Fury at Smugglers' Bay* (with Peter Cushing), *A Midsummer Night's Dream* (1964), Roman Polanski's *Repulsion*, *A Study in Terror*, *Hans Christian Andersen* (1970, in the title role), Pete Walker's *Schizo* and the 1972 short film, *The Man and the Snake*, based on the story by Ambrose Bierce. On TV Fraser appeared in episodes of *Mystery and Imagination* (M.R. James' 'Casting the Runes'), *Journey to the Unknown* (Oliver Onions' 'The Beckoning Fair One'), *Randall and Hopkirk (Deceased)*, *The Rivals of Sherlock Holmes*, *Supernatural* (1977), *Doctor Who* and *Young Sherlock: The*

John Fraser (1931–2020) co-starred in Roman Polanski's Repulsion (1965).

Mystery of the Manor House. He retired from the screen in 1996 and moved to Tuscany, Italy, with his long-term partner, before returning to England in 2010.

Janet Freer

The death was reported in early October of Canadian-born British literary agent Janet Freer (Janet Mulvey), who made the decision to end her life through voluntary euthanasia after being diagnosed with end-stage renal disease. She was 89. Having started her publishing career in London in 1962, Freer spent a number of years in the sales department at Panther Books before joining the Scott Meredith Literary Agency. She then set up the Janet Freer Literary Agency and, during the 1960s and '70s, the Canadian-born Freer helped further careers of a number of young science fiction and fantasy writers, including Michael Moorcock, Harlan Ellison, Christopher Priest, Thomas M. Disch and others associated with the "New Wave" SF magazine *New Worlds*. She then joined MBA Literary Agents, where she represented Anne McCaffrey, Anne Perry and Ursula K. Le Guin.

Bruce Jay Friedman

American playwright, screenwriter, author and editor Bruce Jay Friedman died on June 3, aged 90. He edited *Men: The Adventure and Entertainment Magazine* in the early 1960s, and his short stories appeared in *Playboy*, *The Magazine of Fantasy and Science Fiction*, *Rod Serling's The Twilight Zone Magazine* and various anthologies. Friedman was also nominated for an Oscar for co-writing Disney's *Splash* (1984).

Nikki Fritz

American softcore erotic actress Nikki Fritz (Nikki Goldstein) died of cancer on February 25, aged 56. Her credits (often for director Fred Olen Ray under his "Nicholas Medina" alias) include *Beach Babes from Beyond*, *Dinosaur Island*, *Attack of the 60 Foot Centerfolds*, *Burial of the Rats* (based on the story by Bram Stoker), *Terminal Virus*, *Night Shade*, *Hybrid*, *The Exotic Time Machine*, *Virtual Encounters 2*, *Veronica 2030*, *The Bare Wench Project*, *The Bare Wench Project 2: Scared Topless*, *The Bare Wench Project 3: Nymphs of Mystery Mountain*, *Cheerleader Massacre*, *Space Nuts*, *Bare Wench Project: Uncensored*, *Bikini a Go Go* (aka *Curse of the Erotic Tiki*), *The Witches of Breastwick 2*, *Bare Wench: The Final Chapter* and the short *The Vampire Hunters Club*. She mostly retired from acting in 2005.

Bob Fujitani

Irish-Japanese American comics artist and writer Bob Fujitani died on September 6, aged 98. He had suffered a stroke three months earlier. Fujitani did the cover for *Eerie Comics* No.1 (1947), a one-shot from Avon Periodicals which is widely regarded as ushering in the horror comics boom of the 1950s. He also worked for Dell Comics, Harvey Comics and others, and co-created (with writer Paul S. Newman and editor Matt Murphy) *Doctor Solar, Man of the Atom* in 1962 for Gold Key Comics. Fujitani worked as a ghostwriter on the *Flash Gordon* comic book during the 1960s and illustrated the *Rip Kirby* newspaper strip in the 1990s.

Carl Gafford

American comics editor and colourist Carl Gafford died of complications from diabetes on July 13, aged 66. He started at DC Comics in 1973 as a proof-reader, later becoming assistant production manager for *The Amazing World of DC Comics* magazine. He went on to work at Marvel before returning to DC in 1981, where he became Len Wein's assistant editor on *Justice League*, *The Flash*, *Teen Titans* and *Batman* titles, and with writer Bob Rozakis revived *Challengers of the Unknown*. Gafford also scripted most of the short-lived 'Creeper' back-up series in *The Flash* and coloured *The Legion of Super-Heroes* over an unbroken seven-year run. He later freelanced for Disney Comics, Gladstone Publishing, Dark Horse Comics, Innovation,

Cover of the one-shot Eerie Comics *(Avon Periodicals, January 1947) by artist Bob Fujitani (1920–2020).*

Defiant Comics, Topps Comics and Big Bang Comics. During the late 1970s, Gafford worked in Hanna-Barbera's layout department on such animated TV shows as *Godzilla* and *Super Friends*.

David Galanter

American *Star Trek* author David Galanter died of cancer on December 12, aged 51. He wrote a number of tie-in novels in the original *Star Trek*, *Star Trek: The Next Generation*, *Star Trek: Voyager* and *Star Trek: Discovery* universes, including four collaborations with Greg Brodeur. He also contributed stories to two *Star Trek: S.C.E.* [Starfleet Corps of Engineers] anthologies and scripted an episode of the fan production *Star Trek: New Voyages*.

Janet Ann Gallow

Former child actress Janet Ann Gallow (Janet Ann Gallo), one of the last surviving cast members from Universal's 1940s horror cycle, died of leukaemia on November 13, aged 83. Although she appeared (uncredited) in

a handful of other films during the 1940s, Gallow is best remembered for her screen debut as little "Cloestine Hussman", who is kidnapped by Lon Chaney, Jr.'s Monster in *The Ghost of Frankenstein* (1942). She later said about Chaney, Jr.: "I think what I would say is that he was a gentle giant . . . That's all I can really say about him. He's a gentle giant. Very sweet, very loving and very caring."

Gerald Gardner

American TV scriptwriter Gerald Gardner died October 12, aged 91. He was script editor on NBC's *The Monkees* and wrote twenty-two episodes (1966-68, including 'I Was a Teenage Monster' and 'The Devil and Peter

Japanese poster for Universal's The Ghost of Frankenstein *(1942), which featured Janet Ann Gallow (1937–2020).*

Tork'). Gardner's other credits include episodes of *My Brother the Angel*, *Get Smart* and *The Ghost & Mrs. Muir*.

Allen Garfield

Dependable American supporting actor Allen Garfield (Allen Goorwitz) died of complications from COVID-19 on April 7, aged 80. He had been living in a long-term nursing facility after suffering a massive stroke in 2004. Garfield's many credits include *Night Visitor* (1989), *Dick Tracy* (1990), *Until the End of the World*, *Grave Images*, *Cyborg 2: Glass Shadow*, *Destiny Turns on the Radio*, *Diabolique* (1996), *The Ninth Gate* and *The Elf Who Didn't Believe*, along with episodes of TV's *Search* and *Tales from the Darkside*.

Robert Garland

Although best known for writing the scripts for such movies as *The Electric Horseman* and *No Way Out*, Robert [Warner] Garland, who died of complications from dementia on November 21, aged 83, apparently also worked uncredited on the script for

John Landis' *Twilight Zone: The Movie* (1983). He retired from screenwriting in the mid-1990s.

Hector Garrido

Argentinean-born artist Hector Garrido, best known for his covers for Warren Murphy and Richard Sapir's *The Destroyer* covers for Pinnacle Books, died in his sleep on April 19, aged 92. He emigrated to the US in the 1950s and began working professionally on numerous SF, horror and Gothic book covers, including *Black Magic: 13 Chilling Tales*, *No Blade of Grass*, *Stranger in a Strange Land*, *The Little People*, *Witch Bane*, *Barrow Sinister*, *The Devil His Due*, *Old House of*

Fear, *Night of the Vampire*, *A Stir of Echoes*, *Infernal Idol*, *The Lucifer Cult*, *The Parasite*, *Scottish Stories of Fantasy and Horror*, *Blood Farm*, *Death Angel*, *The Island*, *The Curse*, *Summer of Night*, *Children of the Night*, *Raven* and many others. Garrido was also responsible for the colourful artwork on the packaging of G.I. Joe action figures and vehicles during the 1980s.

Jill Gascoine

British-born actress Jill [Viola] Gascoine died in Los Angeles, California, of complications from Alzheimer's disease on April 28, aged 83. Best known for starring as "Detective Inspector Maggie Forbes" in the 1980s TV series *The Gentle Touch* and *C.A.T.S. Eyes*, Gascoine made an early appearance as an uncredited St. Trinian's Girl in the *Pure Hell of St. Trinian's* (1960), and she also appeared in *Peter Pan* (1976, as a grown-up Wendy) and episodes of *Virtual Murder* ('A Dream of Dracula') and *Touched by an Angel*. Her second husband was actor Alfred Molina.

Leslie Hamilton Gearren

Leslie Hamilton Gearren (aka "Leslie H. Freas"), the identical twin sister of actress Linda Hamilton, died on August 23, aged 63. She doubled for her sister in *Terminator 2: Judgment Day* (1991).

David Geiser

American abstract expressionist painter David [Montague] Geiser died on heart disease on October 14, aged 73. During the late 1960s and '70s he created a number of underground comix in San Francisco, including such titles as *Saloon*, *Demented Pervert*, *Clowns*, *Uncle Sham*, *DTs*, *Pain*, *Sloppy Seconds* and *Edge City*, and designed posters for rock concerts at the

Fillmore. From 1999, he was the partner of actress Mercedes Ruehl.

Thomas Gianni

American artist Thomas [Francis] Gianni died of complications from pneumonia on March 30, aged 60. He had been battling cancer for several years. The younger brother of artist Gary Gianni, his interest in art began with comic books and the artists who created them, such as Jack Kirby, Frank Frazetta and Steve Ditko. He attended the American Academy of Art where he studied under Fred Berger, Irving Shapiro and Howard Mueller. There he discovered Michelangelo, Rembrandt, Howard Pyle, N.C. Wyeth and J.C. Leyendecker. He worked in advertising as a storyboard artist, in animation as a background painter, in editorial and book illustration, in portraiture, and in collectible card art for *Magic: The Gathering*, *Star Wars* and the *Harry Potter* role-playing games. Since 1981, he worked as the courtroom sketch artist for the WGN, NBC and CNN television networks, and he taught illustration and graphic design at the American Academy of Art, the School of the Art Institute of Chicago and Columbia College. His pulp-influenced artwork appeared in such periodicals and books as *Amazing Stories*, *Sherlock Holmes Mystery Magazine*, *The Big Book of Sherlock Holmes Stories*, *The Art of Horror*, *The Art of Horror Movies*, *The Art of Pulp Horror*, *The Complete Adventures of Solar Pons* and his own *Mechanic Anna* series of graphic novels. Gianni also illustrated Robert E. Howard's *Fists of Iron*, *Pirate Stories* and *Western Tales* series of books for the REH Foundation. For his work on these, the Foundation awarded him the Rankin Award for Artistic Achievement. In 2012, with his friend Kathy Von Dorn Banks, he painted a 20ft x 4ft mural for the children's room in the Eisenhower Public Library in Harwood Heights, Illinois.

Rob Gibbs

American animation writer and director Rob Gibbs (Robert James Gibbs), who worked at Pixar Animation Studios for more than two decades, died on April 24, aged 55. He began his career working as a story

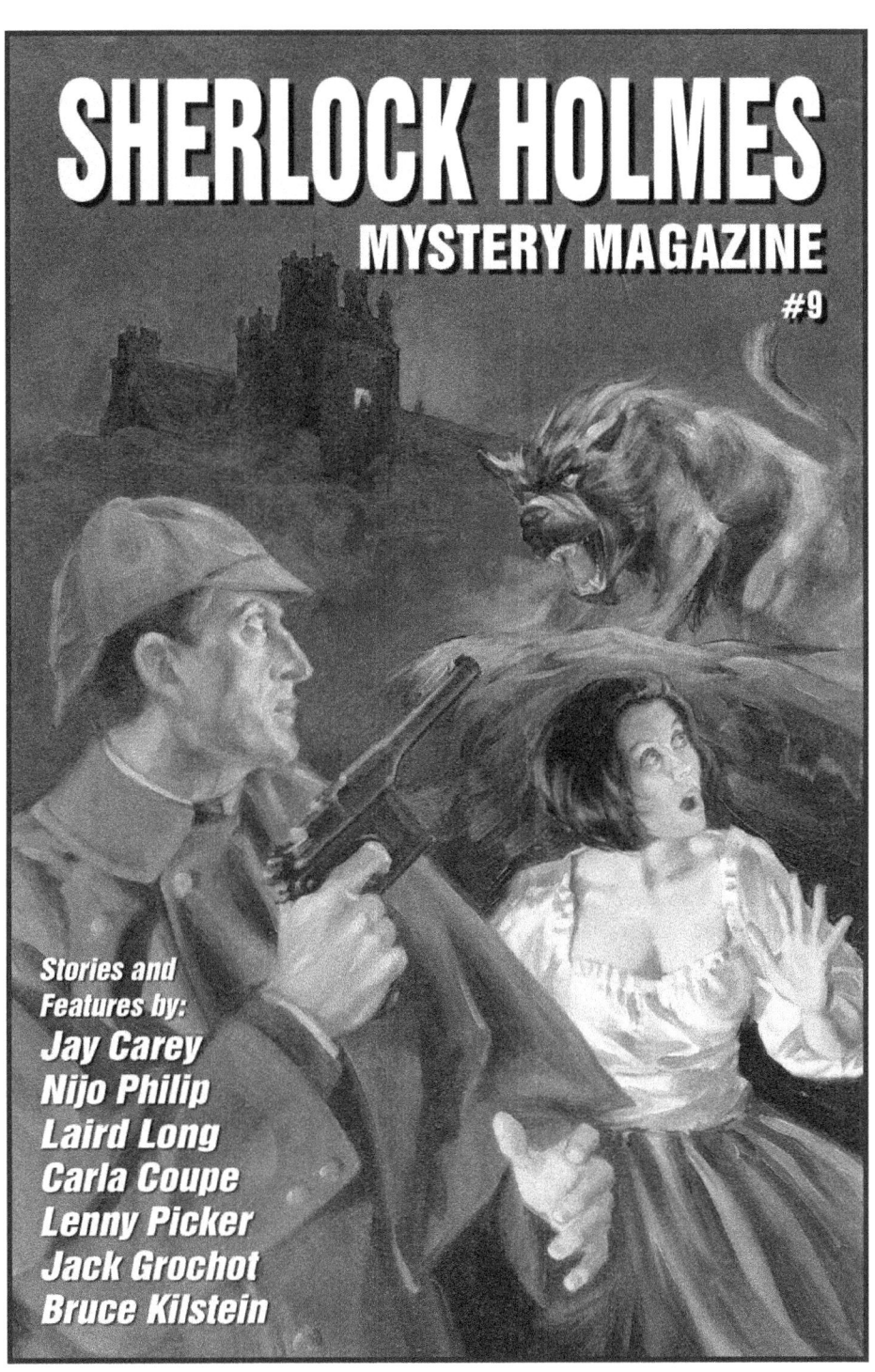

Cover of Sherlock Holmes Mystery Magazine #9 (2013) *by artist Thomas Gianni (1960–2020).*

artist on such movies as *The Brave Little Toaster Goes to Mars*, *Atlantis: The Lost Empire* and *Wall-E*, before going on to direct episodes of TV's *Mater's Tall Tales* and *Monsters at Work*.

David Giler

American screenwriter and producer David [Kevin] Giler, who controlled the *Alien* and EC comics franchises, died of cancer in Bangkok, Thailand, on December 19, aged 77. He wrote episodes of TV's *The Girl from U.N.C.L.E.* and *The Man from U.N.C.L.E.* along with *Southern Comfort* and *Alien 3*. Giler also produced the latter two movies, plus *Alien*, *Aliens*, *Two-Fisted Tales*, *Tales from the Crypt: Demon Knight*, *W.E.I.R.D. World*, *Bordello of Blood*, *Alien: Resurrection*, *Ritual*, *Alien vs. Predator*, *Alien vs. Predator: Requiem*, *Prometheus* and *Alien: Covenant*, along with such TV series as *Tales from the Crypt* (1989-96), the animated *Tales from the Cryptkeeper* (1993-94) and *Perversions of Science* (1997). From 1970-72 he was married to actress Nancy Kwan.

Juan Giménez

Having recently returned from Spain, Argentine comics artist and writer Juan [Antonio] Giménez [López] died of complications from COVID-19 on April 2, aged 76. He attended in Academy of Fine Arts in Barcelona, Spain, and he went on to work on a number of war and science fiction strips in Spain and Italy (notably the series of 'Time Paradox' SF stories). His artwork appeared in the Spanish edition of *1984*, the French *Métal hurlant* and the Italian *L'Eternauta* magazines, and has been collected in *Overload: The Art of Juan Giménez*, *l'Univers de Juan Giménez* (with Pascale Rey) and three volumes of the *Juan Giménez Sketchbook*. As a designer, Giménez contributed to the 1980s movies *Heavy Metal* (the 'Harry Canyon' segment) and *Star Knight*. With filmmaker Alejandro Jodorowsky he created *The Metabarons* fumetto series in 1992.

Mark Glamack

Emmy Award-nominated American TV animator Mark Glamack died of complications from the herbicide

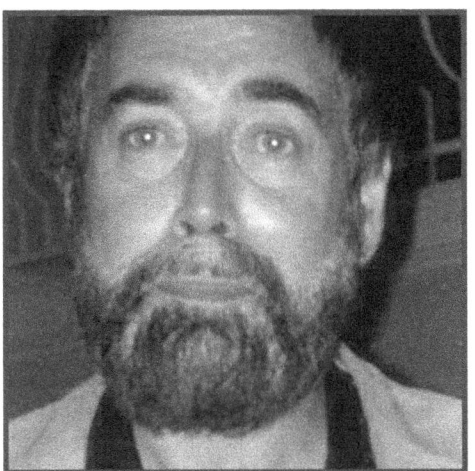

Agent Orange, which he was exposed to during service as an US Army medic in the Vietnam War, on May 29. He was 73. Glamack began his career at Walt Disney Studios, working on *The Jungle Book* (1967) and *Bedknobs and Broomsticks* (1971), followed by stints at Hanna-Barbera, Filmation, Film Roman and other companies. He worked on such cartoon shows as *The Scooby-Doo/Dynomutt Hour*, *The All-New Superfriends Hour*, *Scooby-Doo Laff-A-Lympics*, *Yogi's Space Race*, *Challenge of the Superfriends*, *The Plastic Man Comedy/Adventure Show*, *Godzilla* (1978–79), *Spider-Woman*, *He-Man and the Masters of the Universe*, *Dino Babies*, *All Dogs Go to Heaven: The Series* and many others. Glamack also directed a number of episodes of *She-Ra Princess of Power* (1985) and *Bionic Six* (1987), and produced *G.I. Joe: A Real American Hero* (1986). He served six terms as a governor of the animation branch of the Academy of Television Arts & Sciences and wrote, illustrated and published the 2009 family-friendly novel *The Littluns and the Book of Darkness*.

Milton Glaser

American graphic designer Milton Glaser died of a stroke and renal failure on June 26, his 91st birthday. He not only designed the DC Comics logo (1977–2005), but also the iconic 1966 poster for *Bob Dylan's Greatest Hits* and the 1970s "I ♥ New York" logo.

Mary Pat Gleason

American character actress Mary Pat Gleason, who was often cast as nurses, librarians and clerks, died of cancer on June 2, aged 70. She appeared in the movies *I Madman*, *The Crucible* (1996), *Evolution*, *Bruce Almighty*, *13 Going on 30*, *The Island* (2005), *Room 6*, *Earth to*

Echo and *Finders Keepers*, along with episodes of TV's *Quantum Leap*, *Highway to Heaven*, *Lois & Clark: The New Adventures of Superman*, *The Secret World of Alex Mack* and *Honey I Shrunk the Kids: The TV Show*. Gleason was also a regular on ABC Family's *The Middleman* ('The Vampiric Puppet Lamentation' and eleven other episodes, 2008), based on the graphic novels by Javier Grillo-Marxuach and Les McClaine.

Rolf Gohs

Estonian-born Swedish comics artist Rolf Gohs died on August 25, aged 86. He produced more that 900 covers for *Fantomen*, the Swedish edition of *The Phantom*.

Billy Goldenberg

American music composer, conductor and arranger Billy Goldenberg (William Leon Goldenberg) died on August 3, aged 84. His many credits include *Fear No Evil*, *Silent Night Lonely Night*, *Ritual of Evil*, Steven Spielberg's *Duel*, *Don't Be Afraid of the Dark* (1973),

The Legend of Lizzie Borden, *The UFO Incident*, *Metamorphoses*, *This House Possessed*, *Massarati and the Brain*, *Prototype*, *Frankenstein* (1986), *18 Again!* and *Sherlock Holmes and the Leading Lady*. On TV Goldenberg composed music for the pilots of *Night Gallery* (again for Spielberg), *Future Cop* and *Gemini Man*, plus episodes of *The Name of the Game* (Spielberg's 'LA 2017'), *The Sixth Sense* and *Circle of Fear* (along with the theme music for both shows), *Amazing Stories* and the 1989 mini-series *Around the World in 80 Days*. He also composed one of the themes to the Universal logo.

Danny Goldman

American character actor Danny Goldman (Daniel Goodman), who was the voice of "Brainy Smurf" in various cartoon shows, died of complications from a stroke on April 12, aged 80. He was in *Beware! The Blob*, Disney's *The World's Greatest Athlete*, *Young Frankenstein*, *It's a Bird . . . It's a Plane . . . It's Superman!*, *Beyond Death's Door*, *Wholly Moses!* and *Get Smart Again!*. On TV, Goldman appeared in episodes of *The Powers of Matthew Star* and *Sabrina the Teenage Witch*.

Field of Dreams, *The Rocketeer*, *Waterworld* and *Things That Go Bump*.

Terry Goodkind

Best-selling American epic fantasy author Terry Goodkind died on September 17, aged 72. Beginning with the 1994 novel *Wizard's First Rule*, his multi-volume "The Sword of Truth" series (and spin-offs) sold more than twenty-five million copies worldwide, was translated into twenty languages, and turned into the TV series *Legend of the Seeker* (2008-10).

Charles Gordon

American film and television producer Charles Gordon died of cancer on November 1, aged 73. His credits include *Night of the Creeps*, *Leviathan*,

Joyce Gordon

Joyce Gordon, who became the first female president of the Screen Actors Guild in 1966, died on February 28, aged 90. She dubbed Barbara Steele in Mario Bava's *Black Sunday* and Roger Corman's *The Pit and the Pendulum*, and Norma Bengell in Bava's *Planet of the Vampires*.

Stuart Gordon

American film and theatre writer and director Stuart Gordon died on March 24, aged 72. Best known for his movies based on the works of H.P. Lovecraft, including the cult classic *Re-Animator*,

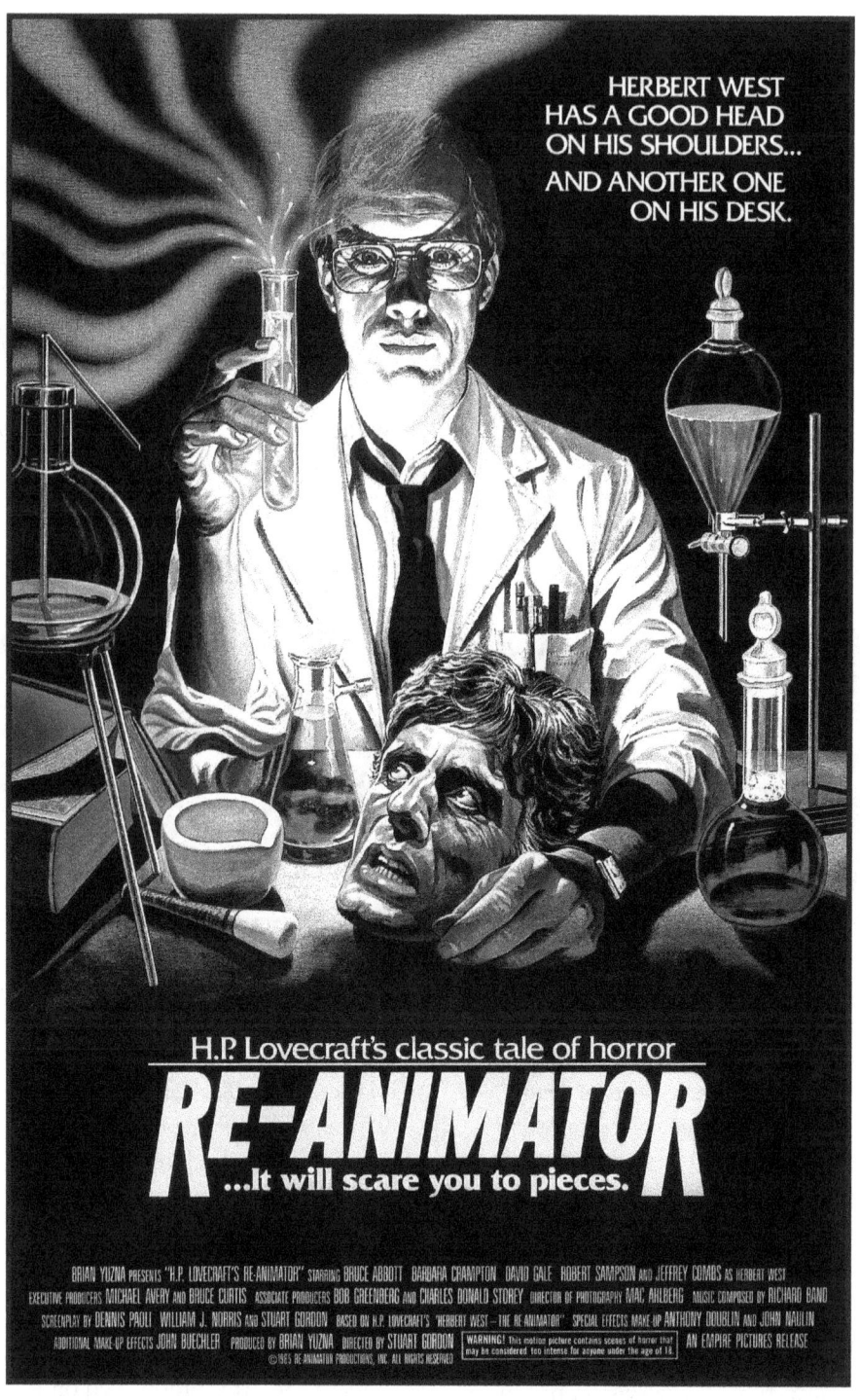

Stuart Gordon (1947–2020) directed the cult H.P. Lovecraft adaptation Re-Animator (1985).

From Beyond, *Castle Freak* and *Dagon*, his other credits include *The Dolls* (featuring Guy Rolfe), *Robot Jox*, *Daughter of Darkness* (starring Anthony Perkins), *The Pit and the Pendulum* (1991), *Fortress*, *Space Truckers* and *The Wonderful Ice Cream Suit* (1998, based on the story and play by Ray Bradbury). Gordon came up with the original stories for *Honey I Shrunk the Kids* (with Brian Yuzna and Ed Naha) and *Progeny*, and he also co-scripted *Body Snatchers* (1993, based on the novel by Jack Finney) and *The Dentist* with Dennis Paoli. On TV, he directed episodes of *Honey I Shrunk the Kids: The TV Show*, *Masters of Horror* (Lovecraft's 'Dreams in the Witch-House' and Poe's 'The Black Cat') and *Fear Itself* (Peter Crowther's 'Eater'). Gordon also had cameo roles in some of his own films, along with *The Arrival*, *Chastity Bites*, *Trophy Heads* and *Tales of Halloween* (as "Sherlock Holmes"). For the stage, he wrote the SF play *Warp!* (1980), which was later adapted into a graphic novel, and he directed productions of George Orwell's *Animal Farm*, *The Wonderful Ice Cream Suit*, *Nevermore . . . An Evening with Edgar Allan Poe* (a one-man show starring frequent collaborator Jeffrey Combs) and *Re-Animator: The Musical*. Gordon was married to actress Carolyn Purdy-Gordon, who he often killed-off in his movies.

Victor Gorelick

American comic book editor and executive Victor Gorelick died on February 8, aged 78. Starting at the age of 16, he worked in a variety of roles for Archie Comics for more 60 years, eventually rising to the position of editor-in-chief in 2007.

Galyn Görg

American actress and dancer Galyn Görg died of cancer on July 14, the day before her 56th birthday. She made her debut in the ZZ Top video for 'Sharp Dressed Man' (1983) and went on to appear in *Strangers in Paradise*, *America 3000*, *The Wizard of Speed and Time* and *RoboCop 2*. A regular on TV's *M.A.N.T.I.S.* (1994-95) as "Lt. Leora Maxwell", Görg was also in episodes of *Amazing Stories* (Michael McDowell's 'Miscalculation'), *Twin Peaks* (1990), *Star Trek: Deep Space Nine*, *Xena: Warrior Princess*, *Hercules: The Legendary Journeys*, *Star Trek: Voyager*, *Stargate SG-1*, *Lost* and *Colony*.

Graydon Gould

Canadian-born actor [Robert] Graydon Gould, the voice of "Mike Mercury" and other characters in Gerry Anderson's "Supermarionation" series *Supercar* (1961-62), died in England on February 25, aged 82. He also co-starred in the 1961 TV serial *Pathfinders to Venus*.

John Grant

Prolific Scottish-born author and editor John Grant (Paul le Page Barnett) died in America on February 3, aged 70. While a commissioning editor at Paper Tiger from 1997-2004, he edited the *Paper Tiger Fantasy Art Gallery* (2002) under his own name. His other non-fiction books include *The Book of Time* and *The Directory of Possibilities* (both with Colin Wilson), *Encyclopedia of Walt Disney's Animated Characters*, *The Encyclopedia of Fantasy and Science Fiction Art Techniques* (with Ron Tiner), *The Encyclopedia of Fantasy* (with John Clute), *Enchanted World: The Art of Anne Sudworth*, *Masters of Animation*, *Perceptualistics* (with Jael), *The Chesley Awards for Science Fiction and Fantasy Art: A Retrospective* (with Elizabeth Humphrey and Pamela D. Scoville), *Digital Art for the 21st Century: Renderosity* (with Audre Vysniauskas) and *Sci-Fi Movies: Facts, Figures and Fun*. Grant/Barnett co-wrote a number of titles in "The Legends of Lone Wolf" gamebook series with Joe Dever, a *Judge Dredd* tie-in (*The Hundredfold Problem*), and such novels as *Earthdoom!* and *Guts: A Comedy of Manners* (both with David Langford), *Strider's Galaxy*, *Strider's Universe*, *Albion*, *The World*, *The Far-Enough Window* or *The Reclaiming of Fairyland*, *Sex Secrets of Ancient Atlantis*, *The Dragons of Manhattan*, *Leaving*

Fortusa and illustrated children's editions of *Dr. Jekyll and Mr. Hyde* and *Frankenstein*. Some of his short fiction is collected in *Take No Prisoners* and *Tell No Lies*, and he edited the anthologies *Aries 1*, *Strange Pleasures 2* (with Dave Hutchinson) and *New Writings in the Fantastic*.

Juliette Gréco

and *The Steam-Driven Adventures of Riverboat Bill*, based on his own children's fantasy book.

French singer and actress Juliette Gréco died on September 23, aged 93. A muse of such French existentialists as Jean-Paul Sartre and Boris Vian, she appeared in Jean Cocteau's *Orpheus*, *The Night of the Generals* and *Belphégor: Phantom of the Louvre* (2001), along with the 1965 TV series of *Belphégor*. The second of Gréco's three husbands (1966-76) was actor Michel Piccoli, who died in May.

Cliff Green

Australian scriptwriter and author Cliff Green (Clifford Green) died on December 4, aged 85. His screen credits include *Picnic at Hanging Rock* (1975), based on the novel by Joan Lindsay,

Michael Greene

American character actor Michael [Harris] Greene died in Hawaii on January 10, aged 86. He appeared in *The Clones*, *Creator*, *White of the Eye*, *Stranded*, **batteries not included*, *Return of the Killer Tomatoes!*, *Lord of the Flies* (1990), *Eve of Destruction*, *Not of This World* and episodes of TV's *Batman* (1966), *Lost in Space*, *Kung Fu* ('The Demon God'), *The Secrets of Isis*, *Fantasy Island*, *The Twilight Zone* (1985) and *Quantum Leap*.

Terence Greer

British-born illustrator and playwright Terence Greer died in Canada on July 5, aged 90. Best known for his distinctive pen-and-ink work in the *Radio Times* during the 1950s and '60s, he also did book covers — most notably for Penguin editions by such authors as Iris Murdoch, Muriel Spark and Angus Wilson — but also the dust-jackets for the early editions of Richard Davis' anthology series *Spectre* and *Space* in the mid-1970s. Greer's first play was the musical *Ripper!: The Whitechapel Murders of 1888*, which was staged in 1973 at the original Half Moon theatre, based in a former Victorian synagogue that was just a few hundred yards from the scene of the actual murders.

Arv Greywal

American production designer and art director Arv (Arvinder) Greywal died of a heart attack on October 22. He worked on *Mimic*, *eXistenZ*, *American Psycho*, *Dawn of the Dead* (2004), *Land of the Dead*, *Survival of the Dead*, *Jennifer's Body*, *Resident Evil: Afterlife*, *Antiviral*,

Cosmopolis, the pilot for *Timeless* and the TV series *The Boys*.

P.M. Griffin

American science fiction and fantasy author P. (Pauline) M. (Margaret) Griffin died on August 10, aged 73. Between 1986 and 2004 she wrote twelve military SF novels in the "Star Commandos" series, and her other books include *Oath-Bound*, *Knowledge*, *Stand at Cornith*, *Survivor*, *Fell Conquest*, *The Purgatorio Virus*, *Haunted World*, *Bad Neighbors*, *The Elven King*, *Rebels' World* and four titles with Andre Norton: *Storms of Victory*, *Flight of Vengeance* (also with Mary H. Schaub), *Redline the Stars* and *Firehand*. Griffin's short fiction appeared in five volumes of *Catfantastic* anthologies and *Women at War*.

Jerome Guardino

American character actor [Leonard] Jerome Guardino died on January 4, aged 96. He appeared in *Octaman, Garden of the Dead, Crash!, Tarantulas: The Deadly Cargo, Victims, Dead Men Don't Die* and episodes of TV's *The Six Million Dollar Man, Fantasy Island* and *The Pretender*. In the early 1970s, Guardino worked as assistant director on the low budget horror movies *Dream No Evil* and *Grave of the Vampire*.

James E. Gunn

Hugo Award-winning SF author and scholar James E. (Edwin) Gunn died on December 23, aged 97. He made his short fiction debut in the late 1940s, with his work appearing in such pulp magazines as *Startling Stories, Thrilling Wonder Stories, Amazing Stories Quarterly, Astounding Science Fiction, Future, Science Fiction Quarterly, Planet Stories* and other publications, and his stories are collected in *Future Imperfect, The Witching Hour, Breaking Point, The Burning, Some Dreams Are Nightmares, The End of the Dreams* and *Human Voices*. Gunn's novels include *Star Bridge* (with Jack Williamson), the fix-up *The Immortals* (the basis for a 1969 TV movie and a 1970-71 ABC series which he also novelised,), *The Magicians, Kampus, The Dreamers* and *The Milennium Blues*, and he edited the anthologies *Nebula Award Stories 10, Astounding Stories: The 60th Anniversary Collection* (three volumes), *The Best of Astounding* and the six-volume *The Road to Science Fiction* series (1977-98). He won Hugo Awards for *Alternate Worlds: The Illustrated History of Science Fiction* and his 1982 study *Isaac Asimov: The Foundations of Science Fiction*, and Gunn also published such non-fiction works as *The New Encyclopedia of Science Fiction, The Science of Science-Fiction Writing* and the 2017 memoir *Star-Begotten: A Life Lived in Science Fiction*. In 2007 he received the Nebula Grand Master Award, and in 2014 he created a $1.5 million endowment for the James E. and Jane F. Gunn Professorship in Science Fiction, named after himself and his late wife.

Ron Haddrick

Australian character actor Ron Haddrick (Ronald Norman Haddrick) MBE, who starred in the 1964-65 science fiction TV series *The Stranger*, died on February 11, aged 90. His other credits include *The Tempest*

The Fall 1955 issue of Startling Stories *featured a cover story by James E. Gunn (1923–2020).*

(1963), *Shirley Thompson Versus the Aliens*, *The Haunting of Hewie Dowker* and *The Death Train*. On TV, Haddrick played the mysterious "Que" in the 1976 fantasy TV series *The Lost Islands*, and he also appeared in episodes of *The Lost World* (2000), *Farscape: The Peacekeeper Wars* and *Nightmares & Dreamscapes: From the Stories of Stephen King* ('Crouch End'). He was also the voice of "Ebenezer Scrooge" in 1969 and 1982 versions of *A Christmas Carol*, and he worked on numerous other animated TV movies, including *A Connecticut Yankee in King Arthur's Court* (1970), *Twenty Thousand Leagues Under the Sea* (1973), *The Mysterious Island* (1975), *Master of the World* (1976), *A Journey to the Center of the Earth* (1977), *Off On a Comet* (1979), *From the Earth to the Moon* (1979), *The Hunchback of Notre Dame* (1986) and a series of 1983 cartoons featuring the voice of Peter O'Toole as "Sherlock Holmes": *Sherlock Holmes and the Sign of Four*, *Sherlock Holmes and the Valley of Fear*, *Sherlock Holmes and a Study in Scarlet* and *Sherlock Holmes and the Baskerville Curse*.

Chanin Hale

American supporting actress Chanin Hale (Marilyn Victoria Haney) died on January 30, aged 91. She was in episodes of TV's *My Favorite Martian*, *The Wild Wild West* and *I Dream of Jeannie*.

William Hale

American journeyman director William Hale died on June 10, aged 88. His credits include *The Demon Murder Case* and episodes of *The Time Tunnel*, *The Invaders* and *Rod Serling's Night Gallery*.

Parnell Hall

American mystery writer Parnell Hall (aka "J.P. Hailey") died after a short illness on December 15, aged 76. He wrote the screenplay for the 1984 cult

movie *C.H.U.D.* and had a small role in the film as "Judson".

Paul Hammond

British-born surrealist artist, translator and historian Paul Hammond died of cancer in Spain on July 10, aged 72. His books include *Marvellous Méliès* (1974), the first English-language study of the pioneering French filmmaker Georges Méliès; *The Shadow and Its Shadow: Surrealists Writings on Cinema* (1978), a compilation translated from the French, and *Luis Buñuel: The Red Years* (with Román Gubern, 2009). His translations include Michel Houellebecq's *Whatever* (1998), the novelist's first appearance in English, and Borde and Chaumeton's *A Panorama of American Film Noir* (2002).

Terry Hands

British theatre director Terry Hands (Terence David Hands) CBE died on February 4, aged 79. He successfully ran the Royal Shakespeare Company for thirteen years and directed the troubled four-week try-out run of the 1988 musical production of *Carrie* (based on the novel by Stephen King) at Stratford-upon-Avon. The show transferred that same year to Broadway with an $8 million budget, where it closed after just sixteen previews and five performances.

Robert Harper

American character actor Robert [Francis] Harper died of cancer in the Netherlands on January 23, aged 68. His credits include George A. Romero's *Creepshow* ('The Crate'

segment), *Not Quite Human* and *Nick Knight*. On TV, Harper was in the unsold pilot *13 Thirteenth Avenue*, along with episodes of *Star Trek: The Next Generation* and *Picket Fences*.

Alan Harris

British supporting actor Alan Harris died on January 25, aged 81. He appeared in small (usually uncredited) bit-roles in *The Night of the Generals*, *Doppelgänger* (aka *Journey to the Far Side of the Sun*), *Scrooge* (1970), *A Clockwork Orange*, *Craze*, *The Man with the Golden Gun*, *Star Wars*, *Holocaust 2000* (aka *The Chosen*), *Superman* (1978), *The Empire Strikes Back*, *The Shining* (1980), *Flash Gordon* (1980), *Return of the Jedi*, *Morons from Outer Space*, *Eat the Rich*, *Star Wars Episode I: The Phantom Menace*, several *Carry On* films, and episodes of TV's *The Avengers*, *UFO*, *Space: 1999*, *1990* and *Doctor Who*. A former model, Harris also worked as a stand-in on Hammer's *When Dinosaurs Ruled the Earth*, *The Rocky Horror Picture Show*, *Superman II*, *The Great Muppet Caper*, *The Dark Crystal*, *Haunted Honeymoon* and Clive Barker's *Hellraiser* and *Nightbreed*.

Dee Hartford

American actress Dee Hartford (Donna Beatrice Higgins), the third wife (1953–60) of Howard Hawks, died on October 21, aged 90. The former *Vogue* model appeared on TV in episodes of *The Alfred Hitchcock Hour*, *The Outer Limits*, *The Twilight Zone*, *The Girl from U.N.C.L.E.*, *The Time Tunnel* (as "Helen of Troy"), *Batman* (1966), *Lost in Space* (along with her brother-in-law, Groucho Marx, she invested money in the series) and *Land of the Giants*. She mostly retired from the screen in the late 1960s.

Margot Hartman

American actress Margot Hartman [Tenney], the widow of low-budget producer and director Del Tenney, died on April 11, aged 86. She appeared in her husband's movies The Curse of the Living Corpse and Descendant (also contributing to the scripts for both), along with *Violent Midnight*, Peter Bogdanovich's pseudonymous *Voyage to the Planet of Prehistoric Women* and the 2001 slasher *Do You Wanna Know a Secret?* (which she co-executive produced with her husband).

Ronald Harwood

South African-born Oscar-winning playwright, novelist and scriptwriter Sir Ronald Harwood died in the UK on September 8, aged 85. He moved to London in the early 1950s and joined Sir Donald Wolfit's Shakespeare Company, becoming the actor-manager's personal dresser. Although best known for his screenplays for *A High Wind in Jamaica*, *Eyewitness* (aka *Sudden Terror*), *One Day in the Life of Ivan Denisovich* and *The Dresser* (based on his own play), the former actor also scripted Freddie Francis' *The Doctor and the Devils* and twelve episodes of TV's *Tales of the Unexpected* (1979–81).

Eddie Hassell

American actor Eddie Hassell (Ed Taylor Hassell), who had a recurring role in the short-lived NBC-TV series

Surface (2005–06), was shot to death during an attempted carjacking in Dallas, Texas, on November 1. He was 30. Hassell's other credits include *2012*, *House of Dust* and an episode of *Joan of Arcadia*. An 18-year-old man was indicted by a grand jury for the actor's murder.

David Hemblen

British-born Canadian actor David Hemblen died on November 16, aged 79. He appeared in *Short Circuit 2*, *Norman's Awesome Experience*, *TekWar: TekLords*, *Brainscan*, *Replikator*, *Rats* (2000) and *Rollerball* (2002). On TV

Hemblem portrayed "Lord Dread" in *Captain Power and the Soldiers of the Future* (1987-88) and the spin-off movie *Captain Power: The Beginning* (1991), and "Jonathan Doors" on *Earth: Final Conflict* (1997-2000). He also turned up in episodes of *Alfred Hitchcock Presents* (1988), *The Twilight Zone* (1988), *TekWar, RoboCop, Forever Knight, Goosebumps, The Outer Limits* (1997), *All Souls* and *Witchblade*. He was also the voice of "The Vultkeeper" on the cartoon TV show *Tales from the Cryptkeeper* (1993-94), and "Magneto"/"Erik Magnus Lehnsherr" in *X-Men: The Animated Series* (1992-97).

James Henerson

American scriptwriter and producer James [Stephan] Henerson died in his sleep on June 18, aged 84. He began working in TV as a story editor in the late 1950s, and his screenwriting credits include episodes of such shows as *The Flying Nun, Bewitched, I Dream of Jeannie, The Hardy Boys/Nancy Drew Mysteries* and *Starman* (which he also executive-produced with Jim Hirsch and Michael Douglas, 1986-87).

Henerson also scripted and executive-produced the two-part mini-series *The Fire Next Time* (1993) and wrote a 1998 TV movie of Shakespeare's *The Tempest*, re-set in the Mississippi bayous during the American Civil War and starring Peter Fonda.

Buck Henry

Emmy Award-winning American scriptwriter and actor Buck Henry [Zuckerman] died of a heart attack on January 8, aged 89. Henry created the TV series *Get Smart* (1965-70, with Mel Brooks), *Captain Nice* (1967) and *Quark* (1977-78), and scripted *Catch-22* (1970) and *The Day of the Dolphin*. Henry also co-directed the 1978 movie *Heaven Can Wait* with star Warren Beatty, and he appeared in *The Man Who Fell to Earth, Eating Raoul, Shakespeare's Plan 12 from Outer Space* and episodes of TV's *Alfred Hitchcock Presents* (1985) and *Tales from the Crypt*.

Richard Herd

Veteran American character actor Richard Herd (Richard Thomas Herd, Jr.) died of cancer on May 26, aged 87. Having studied Shakespeare under Claude Rains in the late 1940s, he was in *Hercules in New York*, *Dr. Scorpion*, *Terror Out of the Sky*, *Schizoid* (1980, with Klaus Kinski), *Trancers*, *The Great Los Angeles Earthquake*, *The Judas Project*, *Seduction: Three Tales from 'The Inner Sanctum'*, *Skeeter* (uncredited), *Cosmic Slop*, *The Survivor*, *I Married a Monster*, *The Cabinet of Dr. Caligari* (2005), *Inalienable* and Jordan Peele's *Get Out*. A familiar face on TV, the busy Herd also appeared in such shows as *The Greatest American Hero*, *The Powers of Matthew Star*, *V* and *V: The Final Battle* (as "John"), *Knight Rider*, *Beauty and the Beast* (1987), *Tales from the Crypt*, *Star Trek: The Next Generation*, *Quantum Leap*, *The Adventures of Brisco County Jr.*, *Seaquest 2032* (as "Admiral Noyce"), *Buffy the Vampire Slayer*, *Star Trek: Voyager* and *Star Trek: Renegades* (as "Admiral Owen Paris") and *Ghost Whisperer*.

Aarón Hernán

Busy Mexican supporting actor Aarón Hernán (Aarón Hernández Rodríguez) died on April 26, aged 88. A veteran of many "telenovelas" (including *Más allá de la muerte*), he made his movie debut in the "Lucha Libre" drama *Los tigres del ring* (1960) and went on to appear in *El planeta de las mujeres invasoras*, *Santo vs la invasión de los marcianos* (uncredited), *Rocambole contra la secta del escorpión* (also uncredited), *Apolinar*, *Presagio*, *Dulce espiritu*, *Deathstalker and the Warriors from Hell*, *Viaje directo al infierno* and *El hombre que volvió de la muerte*.

Jery Hewitt

American stunt actor and co-ordinator Jery Hewitt died on November 21, aged 71. His numerous credits include *Christmas Evil*, *The Nesting*, *Wolfen*, *The Demon Murder Case*, Disney's *Splash*, *C.H.U.D.*, *The Stuff*, *Remo Williams: The Adventure Begins*, *F/X*, *Twisted*, *My Demon Lover*, *Creepshow 2*, *A Return to Salem's Lot*, *Ghostbusters II*, *Independence*

Day, A Simple Wish, Practical Magic, In Dreams, The Bone Collector, Lost Souls, Kate & Leopold, The Manchurian Candidate (2004) and Surrogates, along with episodes of TV's 666 Park Avenue, The Tomorrow People (2013–14) and Forever.

Danny Hicks

American character actor Danny Hicks (Dan Hicks), a favourite of director Sam Raimi, died of cancer on June 30, aged 68. He co-starred in *Evil Dead II* and *Intruder*, and his other screen credits include *Maniac Cop*, *Darkman*, *The Demolitionist*, *Wishmaster*, *Spider-Man 2*, *2001 Maniacs*, *My Name is Bruce*, *Porkchop*, *Dead Season*, *Porkchop 3D*, *Oz the Great and Powerful*, *Elder Island*, *Dick Johnson & Tommygun vs. the Cannibal Cop: Based on a True Story* (which he also associated-produced) and *The Blood Hunter*.

Michael Z. Hobson

Michael Z. (Zametkin) Hobson died of heart failure on November 12, aged 83. After working as president of Scholastic's paperback book clubs, he joined Marvel Comics as executive vice president, responsible for editorial, marketing, distribution and production of Marvel's comics, magazines and graphic novels. Hobson went on to run Marvel's international business as managing director of Marvel Europe, which included companies in the UK and Italy. He later became president of Parachute Publishing, a packager of young adult books.

Jim Holloway

Self-taught American artist Jim Holloway, best known for his work related to role-playing games, died after

a long illness on June 28. His illustrations appeared in various *Dungeons and Dragons* books, along with *Dragon* and *Polyhedron* magazines. Holloway also created the cover art for *The Land Beyond the Magic Mirror*, *Dungeonland*, *Mad Monkey vs the Dragon Claw*, *Ronin Challenge*, *Tales from the Floating Vagabond* and the *Spelljammer: AD&D Adventures in Space* boxed set. He also worked on *Battle Tech* and was the original artist for the *Paranoia* RPG.

Ian Holm

British actor Sir Ian Holm [Cuthbert], who played the psychopathic cyborg "Ash" in *Alien* (1979), died of a Parkinson's-related disease on June 19, aged 88. His many credits include Peter Hall's *A Midsummer Night's Dream* (1959 and 1968, both times as "Puck"), *The Thief of Baghdad* (1978), *Time Bandits*, *Greystoke*, *Brazil*, *Dreamchild*, *Hamlet* (1990), *Kafka* (as "Doctor Murnau"), *Naked Lunch*, *Mary Shelley's Frankenstein*, *Loch Ness*, *The Fifth Element*, *Alice Through the Looking Glass* (1998), *eXistenZ*, *Simon Magus*, *From Hell* and *The Day After Tomorrow*. In 2001, Peter Jackson cast him as "Bilbo Baggins" in *The Lord of the Rings: The Fellowship of the Rings*, a role he repeated in the sequel *The Lord of the Rings: The Return of the King* and the prequels *The Hobbit: An Unexpected Journey* and *The Hobbit: The Battle of the Five Armies* (which was his last film). In fact, it wasn't Holm's first involvement with J.R.R. Tolkien's fantasy saga, having played Bilbo's nephew "Frodo" in the epic 1981 BBC Radio adaptation of *The Lord of the Rings*. On TV, the actor starred as "Pod" in the BBC series of *The Borrowers* (1992) and *The Return of the Borrowers* (1993), and he appeared in two episodes of ITV's *Mystery and Imagination* (Robert Louis Stevenson's 'The Body Snatcher' and as both creator and creation in 'Frankenstein'), *The Frighteners*, *Orson Welles Great Mysteries*, *Tales of the Unexpected* and *Chillers*.

Sandy Holt

Sandy Holt, who did ADR voice casting for movies and TV, died on February 5, aged 77. Her many credits include *The Ambulance*, *Class of 1999*, *Highlander II: The Quickening*, *Roswell*

(1994), *Star Kid*, *Antz*, *Dreamcatcher*, *Boogeyman* (2005), *Boogeyman 3*, *Race to Witch Mountain*, *Hoodwinked Too! Hood vs. Evil* and *Rattlesnake*, plus such series as *The Chronicle* (2001–02), *Revelations* (2005), *Caveman* (2007–08) and *Henry Danger* (2014 –20).

Walter Hooper

American author Walter [McGehee] Hooper, C.S. Lewis' private secretary and trustee of his literary estate, died of COVID-19 on December 7, aged 89. He wrote the non-fiction guides *C.S. Lewis: A Biography* (with Roger Lancelyn Green), *Past Watchful Dragons: The Narnian Chronicles of C.S. Lewis* and *C.S. Lewis: A Companion & Guide*. Hooper also edited a number of Lewis' collections, including *Other Worlds: Essays and Stories* (1966) and *The Dark Tower and Other Stories* (1977).

Silvio Horta

American scriptwriter and producer Silvio [Alejandro] Horta, best known for co-creating the sitcom *Ugly Betty* (2006–10) committed suicide by gunshot on January 7, aged 45. He scripted the first *Urban Legend* (1998) movie, created the TV series Jake 2.0 (2003–04), and scripted the short *Horror Movie: The Movie* and episodes of *The Chronicle*. Horta also executive produced both *The Chronicle* and *Jake 2.0*.

Robert Hossein

French leading man and director Robert Hossein (Robert Hosseinoff), who starred as "Boris Volkoff" in the Dario Argento-produced *The Wax Mask*, died of complications from COVID-19 on December 31, aged 93. He co-scripted, directed and starred in *Le Vampire de düsseldorf* (1965), based

on the same real-life killer as Fritz Lang's M (1933), and dubbed actor Ugo Tognazzi in the French version of *Barbarella* (1968). Hossein also contributed an article, 'Le film d'horreur', to the Winter 1964 issue of *Midi-Minuit Fantastique* #10–11.

Roy Hudd

British comedian and character actor Roy Hudd OBE died after a short illness on March 15, aged 83. He had a memorable cameo as the morgue attendant in Tigon's *The Blood Beast Terror* (aka *The Vampire-Beast Craves Blood*, 1968) starring Peter Cushing. His other credits include *Jack the Last Victim* and *Robot Overlords*, along with episodes of TV's *The Memoirs of Sherlock Holmes*, *Cold Lazarus*, *Randall & Hopkirk [Deceased]* (2001) and *Ashes to Ashes*. He portrayed "Max Quordlepleen", the host of the Restaurant at the End of the Universe, in the BBC radio adaptation of Douglas Adams' *The Hitchhiker's Guide to the Universe*. Hudd was also an authority on the history of music hall entertainment.

Peter H. Hunt

American director Peter H. Hunt died of complications from Parkinson's disease on April 26, aged 81. His credits include the TV movie *The Mysterious Stranger* (1982) along with episodes of *Quark*, *Lucan*, *Tucker's Witch*, *The Wizard* and *Touched by an Angel*.

Grant Imahara

American engineer and actor Grant [Masaru] Imahara, who co-hosted the Discovery Channel's science programme *Mythbusters* and Netflix's *White Rabbit Project*, died of a brain aneurysm on July 13, aged 49. He began his career at Lucasfilm's

Industrial Light & Magic, working as a model-maker on such movies as *The Lost World: Jurassic Park*, *Star Wars: Episode 1 – The Phantom Menace*, *Galaxy Quest*, *A.I. Artificial Intelligence*, *Star Wars: Episode II – Attack of the Clones*, *The Matrix Reloaded*, *Terminator 3: Rise of the Machines*, *The Matrix Revolutions*, *Van Helsing* and *Star Wars: Episode III – Revenge of the Sith*. He was one of only three people at ILM who was an official operator of the robot R2-D2. Imahara appeared in *Sharknado 3: Oh Hell No!* (2015) and turned up in episodes of TV's *The League of S.T.E.A.M.*, *Eureka* (aka *A Town Called Eureka*), *Shelf Life* and *Star Trek: Renegades*. He also portrayed "Lt. Sulu" in eleven episodes of the surprisingly well-produced, fan-made online series, *Stark Trek Continues* (2103-17).

Dean Ing

American SF author Dean [Charles] Ing died on June 21, aged 89. He made his debut in 1955 in an issue of *Astounding Science Fiction*, and his novels include *Soft Targets*, *Systemic Shock*, *Single Combat*, *Wild Country*, *Blood of Eagles*, *The Big Lifters*, *The Man-Kzin Wars* (with Poul Anderson and Larry

Niven) and *Man-Kzin Wars II* (with Niven, Pournelle and S.M. Stirling), *Silent Thunder*, *Butcher Bird* and several collaborations with Mack Reynolds: *Home Sweet Home: 2010 A.D.*, *Eternity*, *The Other Time*, *Trojan Orbit* and *Deathwish World*. Ing's short fiction is collected in *Anasazi*, *High Tension* and *Firefight 2000*.

Andrew Jack

British actor and voice coach Andrew Jack (Andrew Hutchinson), who portrayed "Major Caluan Ematt" in *Star Wars Episode VII: The Force Awakens* and *Star Wars Episode VIII: The Last Jedi*, died of complications from COVID-19 on March 31, aged 76. Jack also supplied the voice of

"Moloch" in *Solo: A Star Wars Story*. Having begun his acting career as a schoolboy on TV in 1957, he worked extensively as a dialect coach on numerous films, including *Indiana Jones and the Last Crusade*, *Loch Ness*, *Lost in Space*, *The Lord of the Rings* trilogy, *Alien vs. Predator*, *Batman Begins*, *Sunshine*, *Sherlock Holmes* (2009), *The Wolfman*, *Captain America: The First Avenger*, *Sherlock Holmes: A Game of Shadows*, *Snow White and the Huntsman*, *Hansel & Gretel: Witch Hunters*, *The World's End*, *Guardians of the Galaxy*, *The Man from U.N.C.L.E.* (2015), *Rogue One: A Star Wars Story*, *Dolittle* and *The Batman*, along with the TV mini-series *Gormenghast*, *Arabian Nights* and *Dinotopia*.

Jael

American artist Jael (Jael Brown Ruesch, nee Ashton) died on November 17, aged 83. Over a six-decade career, she produced hundreds of SF book and magazine covers for publishers such as Baen Books and DAW Books. Some of her art was collected in *Perceptualistics: Art by Jael* (2002, written by John Grant), and she was nominated for eight Chesley Awards between 1985-2002.

Anthony James

American character actor Anthony James died of cancer on May 26, aged 77. Usually cast as a creepy villain, he appeared in *High Plains Drifter*, *Burnt Offerings* (as the Chauffeur), Disney's *Return from Witch Mountain* (with Bette Davis and Christopher Lee), *Ravagers*, *Wacko*, *Blue Thunder*, *Nightmares* and *World Gone Wild*, along with episodes of TV's *Holmes and Yoyo*, *Man from Atlantis*, *Buck Rogers in the 25th Century*, *Knight Rider*, *V*, *Outlaws*, *Amazing Stories*, *Star Trek: The Next Generation* and *Beauty and the Beast* (1989). He retired from the screen in the early 1990s to become an artist.

Jim Janes

American comics artist Jim Janes died on September 1, aged 73. He began his career in 1972 in the underground comix. He went on to illustrate stories in Charlton's *The Many Ghosts of Dr. Graves* and Warren's *Rook* and *Eerie*. In

the early 1980s he was at DC Comics, illustrating *House of Mystery*, *Secrets of the Legion of Super-Heroes* and various *Superman* titles. Janes grew dissatisfied with comics, and he worked as a storyboard artist on such animated TV series as *Teenage Mutant Ninja Turtles*, *Batman: The Animated Series*, *Spider-Man: The Animated Series*, *Exosquad*, *X-Men: The Animated Series*, *The Incredible Hulk*, *Extreme Ghostbusters*, *RoboCop: Alpha Commando* and *Sherlock Holmes in the 22nd Century*. He also co-directed and appeared in Nick Cuti's movie *Captain Cosmos and the Gray Ghosts* (2007).

Barbara Jefford

British stage and screen actress Barbara [Mary] Jefford OBE, who took over the role of the vampiric "Countess Herritzen (Karnstein)" in Hammer's *Lust for a Vampire* (1970), died on September 12, aged 90. She was also in *A Midsummer Night's Dream* (1968), *The Ninth Gate* and an episode of Hammer's *Journey to the Unknown* (Charles Beaumont's 'Miss Belle'). Jefford also dubbed Bond girls Daniela Bianchi in *From Russia with Love*, Molly Peters in *Thunderball* and Caroline Munro in *The Spy Who Loved Me*. Her first husband (1953–60) was actor Terence Longdon, and she was married to actor John Turner from 1967 until her death.

Rafer Johnson

American UCLA basketball star, Olympic decathlon gold-medal winner and occasional character actor Rafer [Lewis] Johnson died on December 2, aged 86. He appeared as "Mullens" in the James Bond movie *Licence to Kill* (1989), and his other credits include *Tarzan and the Great River*, *Tarzan and the Jungle Boy* and episodes of TV's *The Alfred Hitchcock Hour*, *Tarzan* (1966) and *The Six Million Dollar Man*. In 1968, along with L.A. Rams football star Roosevelt "Rosey" Grier, he memorably tackled Robert F. Kennedy's assassin Sirhan Sirhan and secured the murder weapon, a .22 calibre revolver.

Ken Jones

American actor Ken Jones (Kenneth V. Jones), who appeared as the Morningside Cemetery's doomed caretaker in Don Coscarelli's iconic 1979 movie *Phantasm* (and in recycled footage in *Phantasm: Ravager* and *Phantasm: Extinction*), died on November 6, aged 90.

Terry Jones

Terry Jones (Terence Graham Parry Jones), the Welsh-born co-founder of the anarchic BBC comedy series *Monty Python's Flying Circus* (1969-74, with Michael Palin, Eric Idle, Graham Chapman, John Cleese and Terry Gilliam), died of complications from primary progressive aphasia (a type of dementia) on January 21, aged 77. He appeared in, and directed or co-directed, *Monty Python and the Holy Grail*, *Monty Python's Life of Brian*, *The Meaning of Life*, *Erik the Viking*, *Mr. Toad's Wild Ride*, *Absolutely Anything* and an episode of *The Young Indiana Jones Chronicles*. Jones was also in *And Now For Something Completely Different*, *Jabberwocky* and *Stranger Than Fiction*, and he co-directed an episode of *The Adventures of Young Indiana Jones*. He also scripted many of the above titles, along with *Labyrinth* and (with Michael Palin) the 1976-79 TV series *Ripping Yarns* (including 'The Curse of the Claw'). As an author, he published the novels *The Saga of Erik the Viking*, *Nicobobinus* and *Douglas Adams's Starship Titanic*, while his short fiction is collected in *Fairy Tales* and *Fantastic Stories*. Jones also collaborated with artist Brian Froud on *Lady Cottington's Pressed Fairy Book*, *The Goblins of Labyrinth*, *The Goblin Companion: A Field Guide to Goblins* and *Strange Stains and Mysterious Smells*.

Patrick Jordan

British character actor [Albert] Patrick Jordan died on January 10, aged 96. He appeared uncredited in *Behemoth the Sea Monster* (aka *The Giant Behemoth*), *Where the Bullets Fly*, *You Only Live Twice*, *Madhouse* and *Star Wars*, and was also in *Bunny Lake is Missing*, *Love Vampire Style*, *Assault* (aka *In the Devil's Garden*), *The Slipper and the Rose: The Story of Cinderella* and *The*

Pink Panther Strikes Again. On TV, Jordan turned up in episodes of TV's One Step Beyond, The Prisoner, Randall and Hopkirk (Deceased), UFO, Doomwatch, Arthur of the Britons, Thriller (1975) and the 1973 mini-series Jack the Ripper. From 1946, until her death in 2008, he was married to children's book illustrator Margery Gill.

Eizo Kaimai

Japanese kaiju suit- and model-maker Eizo Kaimai, who worked on the original Godzilla (1954) and many sequels, died of leukaemia on April 24, aged 90. Kaimai joined the production of Toho's Godzilla to help build the first Godzilla suit, working closely with Teizo Toshimitsu and the other sculptors. He then contributed to the tokusatsu sequels Godzilla Raids Again (aka Gigantis the Fire Monster), King Kong vs. Godzilla, Godzilla vs. the Thing, Ghidorah the Three-headed Monster and Invasion of the Astro-Monster, along with such other movies as Jû jin yuki otoko (aka Half Human), Rodan, The Mysterians, The H-Man, Varan the Unbelievable, Battle in Outer Space, The Secret of the Telegian, Mothra, The Last War, Gorath, Matango, Atragon, Frankenstein Conquers the World, The War of the Gargantuas, The X from Outer Space, Gappa the Triphibian Monster, Gamera vs. Guiron and Gamera vs. Jiger. In 1966 he formed his own company, Kaimai Productions, where he continued working on TV shows, including the Ultra Q and Ultraman series, until the early 1980s.

Joe Kane

American film reviewer, interviewer and columnist Joe Kane, who published under the byline "The Phantom of the Movies®", died on November 1, aged 73. He was an editor for The Monster Times during the 1970s, before working as a columnist for the New York Daily Times, under "The Phantom of the Movies" alias. Described by Entertainment Weekly as "the best movie critic in America", his writing also appeared in The National Lampoon, High Times, Maxim, The Village Voice and numerous other periodicals. Kane started publishing his

Eizo Kaimai (1929–2020) helped create the monster suit for Toho's Godzilla (1954).

cult movie fanzine/magazine *The Phantom of the Movies' Videoscope* in 1993, and many of his reviews were collected in *The Phantom's Ultimate Video Guide* (1989) and *The Phantom of the Movies' Videoscope: The Ultimate Guide to the Latest, Greatest, and Weirdest Genre Videos* (2000). He also wrote the 2010 study *Night of the Living Dead: Behind the Scenes of the Most Terrifying Zombie Movie Ever* and an autobiography-of-sorts, *Found Footage: How the Astro-Zombies Saved My Life and Other Tales of Movie Madness* (2018). One of Kane's favourite quotes was "Keep Watching the Screens!".

John Karlen

American character actor John Karlen (John Adam Karlewicz), who was best known for playing "Willie Loomis" (and other characters) in the TV Gothic soap opera *Dark Shadows* (1967-71) died of congestive heart failure on January 22, aged 86. He also supplied the opening narration for the show and recreated the "Loomis" role in the 1970 spin-off movie, *House of Dark Shadows*. His other credits include *Daughters of Darkness*, *Night of Dark Shadows*, *The Picture of Dorian Gray* (1973), *The Invasion of Carol Enders*, *Frankenstein* (1973), *The Cloning of Clifford Swimmer*, *Trilogy of Terror*, *Impulse* and *Nightmare on the 13th Floor*. On TV Karlen portrayed the husband of Tyne Daly's "Mary Beth Lacey" in *Cagney & Lacey* (1982-88) and various spin-off movies, and he also appeared in episodes of *The Sixth Sense*, *Shazam!*, *Supertrain* and *Murder She Wrote* ('Nan's Ghost'). He later reprised his role of "Willie Loomis" for four *Dark Shadows* audio dramas from Big Finish Productions.

Al Kasha

Oscar-winning American composer and songwriter Al Kasha (Alfred Kasha) died on September 14, aged 83. He contributed songs to Walt Disney's *Pete's Dragon* (1977) and composed the theme music for the TV series *Beyond Belief: Fact or Fiction*. As the former head of A&R at CBS Records, he was responsible for the signing of Aretha Franklin, Neil Diamond, Andy Williams, The Grateful Dead and Janis Joplin.

Hisashi Katsuda

Japanese voice actor Hisashi Katsuda (Hisashi Katsuta), who played "Professor Ochanomizu" in the *Astro Boy anime* TV series (1980–81), died on February 21, aged 92.

James Keast

Scottish-born costume designer James (Andrew) Keast, whose love for the screen was inspired by watching late-night horror movies on TV as a child, died on cancer on July 11, aged 63. After graduating from the Edinburgh School of Art he joined London costumiers Berman's and Nathan's as a

costume assistant, making and fitting garments on films such as *Clash of the Titans* (1981). Keast then joined the BBC on a trainee scheme, going on to work on *Truly Madly Deeply*, *The Moonstone* (1996), *The Lost World* (2001) and *The Hound of the Baskervilles* (2002). Keast's TV credits include the 1988 children's serial *Moondial*, *Five Children and It* (1991), *Screen Two* ('Midnight Movie'), *Marchlands* and the 2012 mini-series *The Mystery of Edwin Drood*.

Hugh Keays-Byrne

Indian-born Anglo-Australian actor Hugh Keays-Byrne, who played villains "Toecutter" in *Mad Max* (1979) and "Immortan Joe" in *Mad Max: Fury Road* (2015), died in Australia on December 1, aged 73. His other credits include *The Death Train*, *The Chain*

Reaction, *Lorca and the Outlaws* and *Huntsman 5.1*, the 1999 mini-series *Journey to the Center of the Earth*, episodes of *Farscape* and *Farscape: The Peacekeeper Wars*, and George Miller's post-apocalyptic TV pilot *Badlands 2005* (1988). Keays-Byrne was also cast as the "Martian Manhunter" in Miller's *Justice League: Mortal*, before the movie was abandoned.

Michael P. Keenan

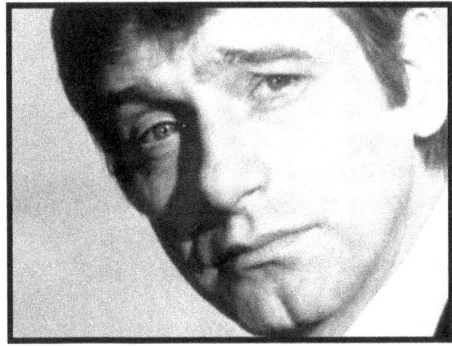

American actor Michael P. Keenan, who appeared in episodes of *Star Trek: The Next Generation*, *Star Trek: Voyager* and *Star Trek: Deep Space Nine*, died on April 30, aged 80. His other credits include *Earth vs. the Spider* (2001) and the TV shows *Starsky and Hutch* ('The Psychic'), *Lucan*, *Freddy's Nightmares*, *Picket Fences*, *Lois & Clark: The New Adventures of Superman* and *Sliders*.

Jack Kehoe

American character actor Jack Kehoe died of a stroke on January 14, aged 85. He appeared in *Dick Tracy* (1990), *Servants of Twilight* (based on the novel by Dean R. Koontz) and an episode of TV's *The Twilight Zone* (1985).

Paula Kelly

American actress, singer and dancer Paula [Alma] Kelly died of chronic obstructive pulmonary disease (COPD) on February 8, aged 77. Her credits include *The Andromeda Strain* (1971), *Soylent Green* and *Peter Pan* (1976). She retired from acting in 1999. In August 1969, Kelly was the first person in the magazine's history to show her pubic hair in *Playboy*. She was married to British director Don Chaffey from 1985 until his death in 1990.

Earl Kemp

Legendary American publisher, editor and SF fan [Finis] Earl Kemp died of a

pulmonary thromboembolism at his home in Tecate, Mexico, on February 29. He was 90. In 1956 Kemp co-founded the small press imprint Advent: Publishers with other members of the University of Chicago Science Fiction Club, he won the Hugo Award in 1961 for his amateur press fanzine *Who Killed Science Fiction*, and he chaired Chicago's 20th World Science Fiction Convention the following year. However, he is best remembered for his involvement in William Hamling's controversial publishing company Greenleaf Classics/Conrith Publications, which published erotic paperbacks. Kemp and Hamling were eventually sentenced to one year in prison for "conspiracy to mail obscene material", although both men served only the federal minimum of three months and one day. As "Jon Hanlon", he edited the anthologies *Death's Loving Arms & Other Terror Tales*, *Stories from Doctor Death and Other Terror Tales* and *The House of Living Death and Other Terror Tales*, which drew their contents from the "weird menace" pulps, and he contributed to *Sin-A-Rama: Sleaze Sex Paperbacks of the Sixties*.

Johnny Kevorkian

Cyprus-born British filmmaker Johnny Kevorkian, whose credits include *The Disappeared* and *Await Further Instructions*, died of a heart attack on November 4. He was 48.

Irrfan Khan

Indian actor Irrfan Khan (Sahabzade Irrfan Ali Khan) died of a colon infection on April 29, aged 53. He was diagnosed with a cancerous neuroendocrine tumour in 2018. Perhaps best known to Western audiences for his performance as the prehistoric park's new CEO in *Jurassic World* (a role he repeated in the Lego video game version), Khan's other

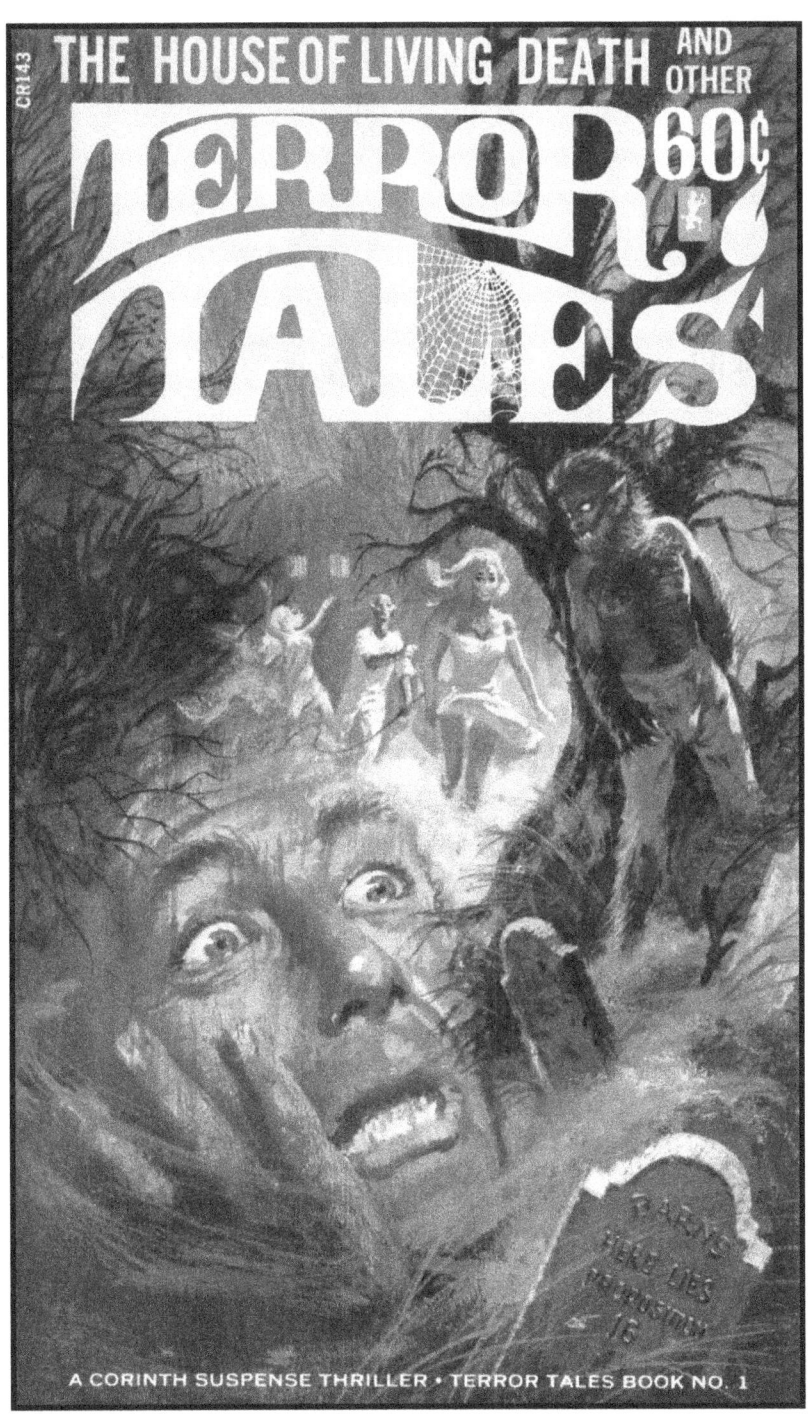

The House of Living Death and Other Terror Tales
(Conrith Publications, 1966) was edited by Earl Kemp (1929–2020)
under the pseudonym "Jon Hanlon".

credits include such Bollywood and Hollywood movies as *Dhund: The Fog*, *Hisss*, *The Amazing Spider-Man*, *Life of Pi*, *Qissa: The Tale of a Lonely Ghost* and *Inferno* (2016), along with a 1998 episode of the Indian horror TV series *X-Zone*.

Gary B. Kibbe

American cinematographer Gary B. (Brian) Kibbe died on March 9, aged 79. Best known for his collaborations with director John Carpenter (*Prince of Darkness*, *They Live*, *Body Bags*, *In the Mouth of Madness*, *Village of the Damned*, *Escape from L.A.*, *Vampires* and *Ghosts of Mars*), the former camera operator's other credits include *RoboCop 3* and an episode of TV's *Tales from the Crypt* (aka *Two-Fisted Tales*).

Stan Kirsch

51-year-old American actor Stan Kirsch (Stanley Benjamin Kirsch), who co-starred as the Immortal "Richard H. 'Richie' Ryan" in the syndicated TV show *Highlander: The Series* (1992-98), committed suicide by hanging on January 11. His other credits include *The Sky's on Fire*, *Shallow Ground*, the

animated comic *Saw Rebirth* and an episode of *Beyond Belief: Fact or Fiction*. Kirsch also worked as an uncredited acting coach on *Grimm* (2011-13).

Shirô Kishibe

Japanese actor Shirô Kishibe, who co-starred as "Sandy" in the 1978-80 TV series *Monkey*, died of dilated cardiomyopathy on August 28, aged 71.

G. Howard Klar

American supporting actor G. (Gary) Howard Klar, best remembered for his role as "Private Steel" in George A. Romero's cult classic zombie film *Day of the Dead* (1985), died on December

31, aged 73. He also had small roles in *Hero at Large*, *A Stranger is Watching* (1982) and *Big*.

Douglas Knapp

American cinematographer and camera operator Douglas H. Knapp died of pancreatic cancer on February 3, aged 70. He worked on John Carpenter's *Dark Star*, *Assault on Precinct 13* and *Escape from New York*, *Moonchild*, Russ Meyer's *Supervixens*, Tim Burton's 1984 short *Frankenweenie*, *Beetlejuice*, *Star Trek: Of Gods and Men* and episodes of *Short Story Showcase: The Fall of the House of Usher* (1976), *The Six Million Dollar Man*, *The Hardy Boys/Nancy Drew Mysteries*, *Battlestar Galactica* (1978-79), *Buck Rogers in the 25th Century*, *Star Trek: Voyager* and *Star Trek: Enterprise*.

Paul Knight

British TV producer Paul [Alexander] Knight, who collaborated with business partners Richard Carpenter and Sidney Cole on a number of successful children's shows, died on August 16, aged 76. Amongst the series he produced were *Tales of Unease* (based on the trilogy of anthologies edited by John Burke), *The Frighteners*, *Robin of Sherwood* and *Stanley's Dragon*.

Rosalind Knight

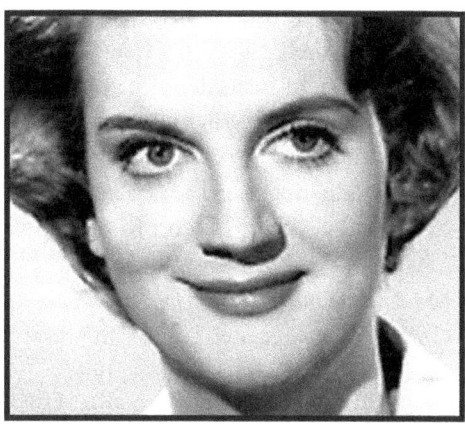

British character actress Rosalind [Marie] Knight died on December 19, aged 87. Best remembered for her roles in a few early *Carry On* and *St. Trinian's*

films, she also appeared in *Afraid of the Dark*, *Demons Never Die*, the mini-series *Jack and the Beanstalk: The True Story* and episodes of TV's *The Adventures of Sherlock Holmes* and *Sherlock* ('The Hounds of the Baskerville').

Shirley Knight

Hardworking American actress Shirley [Enola] Knight (aka "Shirley Knight Hopkins") died on April 22, aged 83. She made her screen debut in the mid-1950s and was a regular guest star on TV for more than six decades. Her many credits include *The Couch* (scripted by Robert Bloch), Roger Christian's *The Sender*, *Dad the Angel & Me*, *Diabolique* (1996), *The Uninvited* (1996), *Shadow Realm*, *Ghost Cat* (aka *Mrs. Ashboro's Cat*) and *Mercy*, plus episodes of TV's *The Outer Limits*, *The Invaders*, *Circle of Fear*, *Orson Welles Great Mysteries*, *Tales of the Unexpected*, *Hammer House of Mystery and Suspense*, *VR.5*, *Night Visions* and *Drop Dead Diva*.

Pamela Kosh

British-born American character actress Pamela Kosh died on October 21, aged 90. Her credits include episodes of TV's *Highway to Heaven*, *Star Trek: The Next Generation*, *Team Knight Rider*, *Charmed*, *Beyond Belief: Fact or Fiction* and *Pushing Daises*.

Tsugunobu Kotani

Japanese film director Tsugunobu "Tom" Kotani died on December 13, aged 84. His credits include the 1970s monster movies *The Last Dinosaur* and *The Bermuda Depths* for Rankin-Bass and Tsuburaya Productions.

John Lafia

63-year-old American movie writer and director John Lafia committed suicide by hanging on April 29. Having worked in the art departments on *Space Raiders* and *Repo Man*, he is best known as the co-creator (with John Mancini and Tom Holland) of the 1988 cult movie *Child's Play*. He is credited with coming up with the name "Chucky" and contributing the iconic line, "Hi, I'm Chucky, wanna play?". Lafia went on to direct the controversial sequel, *Child's Play 2* (1990), along with *Man's Best Friend*, *Monster!* (1999), *Chameleon 3: Dark Angel*, *The Rats*, *10.5* and the sequel *10.5: Apocalypse*, and episodes of TV's *Freddy's Nightmares*, *Babylon 5* and *The Dead Zone*. He also scripted episodes of *The Adventures of Sinbad* and *Ghost Stories* (1998).

Len Lakofka

American role-playing games designer and writer Len Lakofka died on October 23, aged around 75. As a playtester, he was influential in

developing *Dungeons & Dragons* for TSR.

Peter Lamont

Oscar-winning British art director, set decorator and production designer Peter [Curtis] Lamont died on December 18, aged 91. Best known for his work on the James Bond series, including *Goldfinger*, *Thunderball*, *You Only Live Twice*, *On Her Majesty's Secret Service*, *Diamonds Are Forever*, *Live and Let Die*, *The Man with the Golden Gun*, *The Spy Who Loved Me*, *For Your Eyes Only*, *Octopussy*, *A View to a Kill*, *The Living Daylights*, *Licence to Kill*, *Goldeneye*, *The World is Not Enough*, *Die Another Day* and *Casino Royale* (2016), Lamont's other credits include *Night of*

the Eagle (aka *Burn, Witch, Burn*), *Unearthly Stranger*, *Chitty Chitty Bang Bang*, *The Seven-Per-Cent Solution*, *The Boys from Brazil*, *Aliens*, *Eve of Destruction* and *Wing Commander*.

David Lander

American voice and character actor David [Leonard] Lander — not to be confused with the veteran British actor of the same name — died of multiple sclerosis on December 4, aged 73. He was diagnosed with the disease in 1984, but kept his illness a secret from the public for fifteen years. Best remembered for his role as "Squiggy" on the 1976-84 sit-com *Laverne & Shirley*, Lander's other credits include *Wholly Moses!*, *Pandemonium*, *Steel and Lace* and *Scary Movie*, along with episodes of TV's *Highway to Heaven*, *Monsters* (Michael Bishop's 'Their Divided Self'), *Star Trek: The Next Generation*, *Freddy's Nightmares*, *Twin Peaks* (1990-91), *Homeboys in Outer Space*, *Sabrina the Teenage Witch* and *Black Scorpion*.

Charles Lanyer

American character actor Charles [Lee] Lanyer died from complications

following surgery on February 11, aged 77. He appeared in *Alice at the Palace*, *The Stepfather* (1987) and *The Astronaut's Wife*. On TV, Lanyer's credits include episodes of *The Greatest American Hero* and *The Twilight Zone* (1986).

David Larkin

British-born editor, book designer and art director David Larkin died in upper state New York, on December 2, 2020, aged 84. Working at Panther Books (later Granada Publishing) in the late 1960s, he was the youngest art director in London. After moving to Pan Books in the early 1970s, Larkin was part of the team that created the Picador imprint and was closely involved in the development of large-format art paperbacks. Often working in collaboration with Ian and Betty Ballantine, in 1980 he moved to America to set up David Larkin Books. Titles he edited include *Fantastic Art*, *The Fantastic Kingdom*, *Kay Nielsen*, *Arthur Rackham*, *Once Upon a Time*, *The Fantastic Paintings of Charles and Heath Robinson*, *The Fantastic Creatures of Edward Julius Detmoid*, *The Unknown Paintings of Kay Nielsen*, *The Fantastic Art of Sulamith Wülfing*, *The Land of Froud*, *Brian Froud and Alan Lee's Fairies*, *Sarah Teale's Giants* and *Alan Lee's Castles*.

Dieter Laser

German actor Dieter Laser died on February 29, aged 78. Best known for his role as the evil scientist "Dr. Heiter" in the Dutch cult classic *The Human Centipede (First Sequence)*, his other credits include *The Elixirs of the Devil*, *Operation Ganymed*, *We*, *The Human Centipede (Final Sequence)* and *November*. Laser also portrayed human-insect hybrid "Mantrid" in a number of episodes of the TV series *Lexx* (1998-2000). His last stage performance, in 2019, was in a German theatre production of Franz Kafka's *The Trial*.

Philip Latham

British character actor [Charles] Philip Latham, best remembered for his performance as the Count's loyal servant "Klove" in Hammer's *Dracula, Prince of Darkness* (1966), died on June 20, aged 91. He also appeared in *Alice's Adventures in Wonderland* (1956), *The Monster of Highgate Ponds*, *Masters of Venus* and also Hammer's *The Devil-Ship Pirates* and *The Secret of Blood Island*, plus episodes of TV's *The Moonstone* (1959), *The Andromeda Breakthrough*, *The Avengers*, *UFO*, *Hammer House of Horror*, *Doctor Who* ('The Five Doctors') and *Worlds Beyond*. Latham retired from acting in the 1990s.

Moonyeenn Lee

South African casting director and talent agent Moonyeenn Lee died of complications from COVID-19 on July 18, aged 76. She worked on numerous movies, including *Curse III: Blood*

French grande affiche *for Hammer's* Dracula, Prince of Darkness *(1966), which featured Philip Latham (1929–2020).*

Sacrifice (starring Christopher Lee), *Jane and the Lost City* and *Tarzan and the Lost City*. Lee was also a casting director on the 2009 revival of AMC's *The Prisoner* and the pandemic series *The Hot Zone*.

Stevie Lee

American Midget Wrestler and bit-actor Stevie Lee [Richardson], aka "Puppet the Psycho Dwarf", died on September 9, aged 54. He turned up as a Munchkin Carriage Driver in *Oz the Great and Powerful* and was featured an episode of TV's *American Horror Story* and two video spin-off shorts. A GoFundMe was set up to help his family with funeral costs.

Johnny Leeze

British soap opera actor and stand-up comedian Johnny Leeze (John Harold Glen), who portrayed "Inspector Cox" on *The League of Gentlemen*, died of complications from COVID-19 on October 25 aged 78. His credits also include the four-part *Chimera* (1991), written by Stephen Gallagher and based on his novel, and an episode of *Life on Mars*.

Silvia Legrand

Argentinean actress Silvia Legrand (María Aurelia Paula Martínez Suárez, aka "Goldie"), the twin sister of actress and TV host Mirtha Legrand, died on May 1, aged 93. In 1970 she co-starred in the Canal 9 15-part TV series *¡Robot!*, about a scientist allowed to murder his adulterous wife if he gives his newly-invented robot over to the government.

Robert Lesser

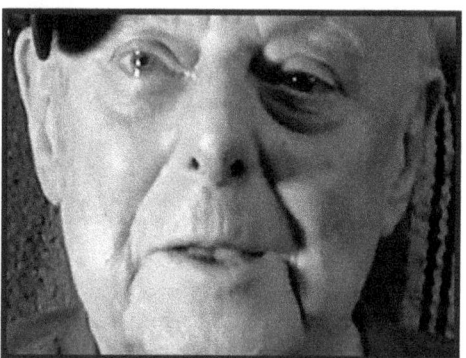

American pulp magazine historian and art collector Robert Lesser died on May 1, aged 96. A former model, physicist and salesman, he compiled the seminal 1997 volume *Pulp Art: Original Cover paintings for the Great American Pulp Magazines* for Gramercy Books. A number of institutions launched shows around The Robert Lesser Collection, and his 200 painting collection will reside with the New Britain Museum of American Art.

Gerry Lewis

British film publicist Gerry Lewis died on January 5, aged 51. He worked on Amicus' *Dr. Who and the Daleks*, *Rosemary's Baby*, *Earthquake* and Steven Spielberg's *Duel*, *Jaws*, *E.T. the Extra-Terrestrial* and *Ready Player One*.

Anita Linda

Filipino movie star turned character actress Anita Linda (Alice Lake) died on June 10, aged 95. Since making her screen debut in 1943, she appeared in more than 200 films, including *Ang sawa sa lumang simboryo*, *Magica blanca*, *The Devil's Daughter* (1974), *Lorelei*, *Voltes V*, *Kill Barbara with Panic*, *Demons* (2000), *Séance* and *Morgue*, along with an episode of the 2013 TV science fiction series *Genesis*. In October 1950, when she was the top actress at Premiere Productions, Linda's sister Mamey was murdered in a robbery attempt at the home they shared. The actress locked herself and her nieces in a bedroom and was unharmed.

William Link

American screenwriter and producer William Link (William Theodore Link, Jr.) died of congestive heart failure on December 27, aged 87. With his writing partner Richard Levinson (who

died in 1987) he created such series as *Mannix* (1967-75), *Ellery Queen* (1975-76), *Blacke's Magic* (1986), *Murder She Wrote* (1984-96) and *Columbo* (1971-2003), and wrote the TV movie *Prototype* (1983). Link went on to co-create such shows as *Probe* (1988, with Isaac Asimov) and *The Cosby Mysteries* (1994-95), and he scripted episodes of *Alfred Hitchcock Presents*, *The Alfred Hitchcock Hour* and *Darkroom*. In 1983 Levinson and Link also wrote the Tony Award-nominated book for the Broadway musical *Merlin*.

Charles M. Lippincott

Charles M. Lippincott, best remembered for his innovative merchandising campaign as marketing director for George Lucas' original *Star Wars* (1977), died of complications from COVID-19 on May 20, aged 80. He began his career as a publicist and marketing consultant, working on such movies as *Westworld* (1973), Alfred Hitchcock's *Family Plot*, *Alien* and *Flash Gordon* (1980). Lippincott went on to produce the zombie comedy *Night Life* (aka *Grave Misdemeanours*, 1989) and the 1995 movie adaptation of *Judge Dredd*, along with the ward-winning 1988 documentary *Comic Book Confidential*.

Tommy "Tiny" Lister

African-American character actor Tommy "Tiny" Lister (Thomas Duane Lister, Jr.) died on December 10, aged 62. He had been diagnosed with COVID-19 earlier in the year. A former basketball player and WWE (originally the WWF) and WCW professional wrestler (under the names "Zeus" and "ZGangsta"), Lister appeared in a number of action films during the 1980s and '90s, along with *Prison*, *Midnight*, *Universal Soldier*, *The Meteor Man*, *Hologramman*, *Barb Wire*, *The Fifth Element*, *Wishmaster 2: Evil Never Dies*, *Judgment Day*, *Little Nicky*, *Soulkeeper*, *Austin Powers in Goldmember*, *Hellborn* (aka *Asylum of the Damned*), *Dracula 3000*, *Santa's Slay*, *Vegas*

Vampires, Terra Nova, The Dark Knight, Monster Ark, Super Capers: The Origins of Ed and the Missing Bullion, The Trap Door, Heaven's Door, The Amazing Wizard of Paws, The Human Centipede III (Final Sequence), Death's Door, If I Tell You I Have to Kill You, Hauntsville, 2016, Slasher Party and *Hell Hole*. On TV, he was in episodes of *Hard Time on Planet Earth, Star Trek: Enterprise* (as "Klang", the first Klingon encountered by Starfleet) and *Saul of the Mole Men*.

Little Richard

American rock 'n' roll music legend Little Richard (Richard Wayne Penniman) died of bone cancer on May 9, aged 87. Although best known for such classic songs as 'Tutti Frutti', 'Long Tall Sally' and 'Good Golly Miss Molly', he also appeared in *Goddess of Love, Purple People Eater, Mother Goose Rock 'n' Rhyme* and *Last Action Hero*, along with episodes of TV's *Homeboys in Outer Space* and *Nightman*.

Sam Lloyd

American supporting actor Sam (Samuel) Lloyd, the nephew of actor Christopher Lloyd, died on May 1, aged 56. He had been diagnosed with an inoperable brain tumour in 2019. Best known for his work on TV, in episodes of such shows as *3rd Rock from the Sun, The Nightmare Room* and *Medium*, his movie credits include *A Bucket of Blood* (1995), *Flubber, Galaxy Quest* (as "Neru"), *Scorcher* and *Super Capers: The Origins of Ed and the Missing Bullion*.

Michael Lonsdale

Anglo-French actor Michael Lonsdale (Michael Edward Lonsdale-Crouch, aka "Michel Lonsdale"), best known for playing the James Bond villain "Sir Hugo Drax" in *Moonraker* (1979), died on September 21, aged 89. His other credits include *La redevance du fantôme*, *The Name of the Rose* and *The Mystery of the Yellow Room* (2003). The bilingual Lonsdale also dubbed himself in the French version of *Moonraker* and he voiced the role of Drax again in the 2012 video game 007 *Legends*.

Xavier Loyá

Mexican actor Xavier [Hernández] Loyá died of a myocardial infarction on September 22, aged 85. He appeared in *The Curse of the Doll People*, Luis Buñuel's *The Exterminating Angel*, *Santo vs. the Vampire Women* and *The Wailer 2*. Loya was a classmate of Marilyn Monroe when they both attended the Actor's Studio in New York during the 1950s.

Rebecca Luker

Broadway actress and singer Rebecca [Joan] Luker, who was nominated for a Tony Award for her portrayal of "Winifred Banks" in the stage

production of *Mary Poppins* (2006-10), died of Amyotrophic lateral sclerosis (ALS) on December 23, aged 59. She made her Broadway debut in 1989, stepping in for Sarah Brightman as "Christine" in a revival of *The Phantom of the Opera*, and she appeared in the 1991-93 musical *The Secret Garden* and played the fairy godmother "Marie" in *Rodgers + Hammerstein's Cinderella* (2013). Luker also appeared in a number of TV series, including an episode of *Elementary*.

Richard A. Lupoff

American author Richard A. (Allen) Lupoff died after a short illness on October 23, aged 85. Dick and his wife

Xavier Loyá (1927–2020) appeared in
The Curse of the Doll People *(1961).*

Pat, along with Bhob Stewart, edited the Hugo Award-winning SF and comics fanzine *Xero* (1960–63), and he contributed to Paul Blaisdell's early 1960s monster magazine *Fantastic Monsters of the Films*. His first non-fiction book, *Edgar Rice Burroughs: Master of Adventure* appeared in 1965, and he followed it with such scholarly studies as *All in Color for a Dime* and *The Comic-Book Book* (both with Don Thompson), *Barsoom: Edgar Rice Burroughs and the Martian Vision*, *The Great American Paperback* and the Hugo-nominated *The Best of Xero*. Dick's novels include *One Million Centuries*, *Sacred Locomotive Files*, *Into the Aether*, *The Crack in the Sky*, *Sword of the Demon*, and *Lovecraft's Book* from Arkham House. He also wrote in various other authors' universes, including TV's "Buck Rogers" with *Buck Rogers in the 25th Century* and *That Man on Beta* (both as "Addison E. Steele") and Robert E. Howard's Oriental villain in *The Return of Skull-Face*. Some of his short fiction is collected in *Before . . . 12:01 . . . and After*, *Terrors*, *Deep Space*, *Visions*, *Dreams* and *The Doom That Came to Dunwich*, while a 1973 story was filmed as a short in 1991 and turned into the TV movie *12:01* two years later.

Alison Lurie

American author Alison Lurie died on December 3, aged 94. Her short stories are collected in *Women and Ghosts*, she wrote the non-fiction books *Don't Tell the Grown-Ups* and *Boys and Girls Forever: Children's Classics from Cinderella*

to Harry Potter, and edited *The Oxford Book of Modern Fairy Tales*.

Ann Lynn

British actress [Elizabeth] Ann Lynn (aka "Anne Lynn"), who co-starred in (and stole) the 1964 horror film *The Black Torment*, died on August 30, aged 86. Her other credits include *Screamtime* and episodes of *Out of This World* (hosted by Boris Karloff), *Adam Adamant Lives!*, *The Champions* (Terry Nation's 'The Body Snatchers') and *Shadows*. Lynn was married to Anthony Newley from 1956–63.

John Mahon

American supporting actor John [Patrick] Mahon, who was often cast as

Edgar Rice Burroughs: Master of Adventure (*Ace Books, 1968*)
by Richard A. Lupoff (1935–2020).

authority figures, died on May 18, aged 82. Best known as the astronomer who first spots the world-killer asteroid in *Armageddon* (1998), his other credits include *The Exorcist*, John Carpenter's *Someone's Watching Me!*, Wes Craven's *The People Under the Stairs*, *Lifepod*, *Natural Selection* (aka *Dark Reflection*), *Austin Powers: The Spy Who Shagged Me* and *Zodiac*, along with episodes of TV's *Manimal*, *Automan*, *Misfits of Science*, *Knight Rider*, *Space Rangers*, *Roswell*, *The Pretender*, *The X Files*, *Angel*, *Touched by an Angel*, *Strange World* and *Star Trek: Enterprise*.

Louis Mahoney

Gambia-born British character actor Louis Mahoney (Louis Felix Danner Mahoney) died on June 30, aged 81. He travelled to England to train as a doctor, but joined the Royal Shakespeare Company and made his film debut in the early 1960s. Mahoney's credits include *Curse of the Voodoo* (aka *Curse of Simba*), Hammer's *The Plague of the Zombies* and *Prehistoric Women*, *The Final Conflict* and *Sheena*. On TV, he appeared in episodes of *Doctor Who*, *Urban Gothic*, *Sea of Souls*, *Being Human* and *You Me and the Apocalypse*. Mahoney also helped establish the Equity Performers Against Racism group, developed to circumvent Equity rules preventing political campaigning.

Johnny Mandel

American composer, arranger and songwriter Johnny Mandel [John Alfred Mandel] died on June 29, aged 94. Best known for writing such songs as the Oscar-winning 'The Shadow of Your Smile' and 'Suicide is Painless' (the theme from *M*A*S*H* and, as an instrumental, the subsequent TV series), he also composed the music for *Pretty Poison*, Disney's *Escape to Witch Mountain* and *Freaky Friday* (1976), *Deathtrap* (1982), *Foxfire*, *Brenda Starr* and an episode of TV's *Amazing Stories*. Mandel also contributed (uncredited) additional music to the 1960 Jerry Lewis comedy *Visit to a Small Planet* (1960).

Dr. Colin Manlove

Scottish fantasy scholar Dr. Colin [Nicholas] Manlove died after a long illness on June 1, aged 78. His books of literary criticism include *Modern Fantasy: Five Studies*, *The Impulse of Fantasy Literature*, *Science Fiction: Ten Explorations*, *C.S. Lewis: His Literary Achievement*, *Christian Fantasy: From 1200 to the Present*, *Scottish Fantasy Literature: A Critical Survey*, *The Fantasy Literature of England*, *From Alice to Harry Potter: Children's Fantasy in England*, *The Order of Harry Potter: Literary Skill in the Hogwarts Epic*, *Scotland's Forgotten Treasure: The Visionary Romances of George MacDonald* and *George MacDonald's Children's Fantasies of the Divine Creation*. Manlove also edited *An Anthology of Scottish Fantasy Literature* (1996).

Bob March

American local TV personality Bob March, who, as "Captain Satellite", hosted a weekday afternoon children's

show live on KTVU, Channel 2, in the Oakland-San Francisco area from 1958-69, died on August 7. After the show ended, he continued to make guest appearances around the San Francisco Bay Area at various events, including at SF movie openings and amusement parks. March also had small roles in *Bullitt* (1968) starring Steve McQueen and the 1973 "Dirty Harry" movie *Magnum Force* starring Clint Eastwood. He retired in 1995.

Rafael R. Marchent

Spanish director, screenwriter and actor Rafael R. (Romero) Marchent died on February 13, aged 93. He directed and co-scripted *Santo vs. Doctor Death* (1973) and directed *Curse of the Black Cat* (1977).

Vincent Marezello

British actor Vincent Marezello died of complications from dementia on March 31, aged 68. He was in the James Bond films *The Spy Who Loved Me* and *Never Say Never Again*, *Superman* (1978), *The Witches* (1990) and *A Kid in King Arthur's Court*, and voiced a number of *anime* productions. On TV, Marezello turned up in episodes of *The Tomorrow People* (1994) and the mini-series *Jack and the Beanstalk: The Real Story*.

Detto Mariano

82-year-old Italian film composer Detto Mariano (Mariano Detto) died of complications from COVID-19 on March 25. His credits include *La casa stregata*, *The Exterminators of the Year 3000*, *Miami Golem* (as "Robert Marry"), *Computron 22* and *Sherlock Holmes and the Leading Lady* (starring Christopher Lee in the title role).

Malcolm Marmorstein

American screenwriter Malcolm [Jack] Marmorstein, who scripted more than 80 episodes of the first season of ABC-TV's daily Gothic soap opera *Dark Shadows* (1966-67), died of cancer on November 21, aged 92. A former Broadway stagehand and TV stage manager, his other writing credits include *Mary Mary Bloody Mary* (with John Carradine as a vampire), Disney's *Pete's Dragon* and *Return from Witch Mountain* (with Bette Davis and Christopher Lee), *Frankenstein* (1986) and *The Witching of Ben Wagner*, along with a segment of TV's *Rod Serling's Night Gallery* ('The Flip-Side of Satan' with Artie Johnson). Marmorstein also wrote and directed the 1990 zombie comedy *Dead Men Don't Die* and the vampire comedy *Love Bites* (1993), the latter based on his own play.

Gillian Martell

British TV actress Gillian Martell died on January 16, aged 83. She appeared in the 1981 *Doctor Who* spin-off *K-9 and Company: A Girl's Best Friend* and *The Hound of the Baskervilles* (1982, with Tom Baker as Holmes).

Henry Martin

New Yorker cartoonist Henry Martin died on June 30, aged 94. Between 1956 and 1998 he contributed more than 100 cartoons to *The Magazine of Fantasy and Science Fiction*.

Philip Martin

British actor and scriptwriter Philip [Charles] Martin died on December 13, aged 83. He wrote episodes of TV's *Doctor Who* ('Vengeance on Varos' and 'The Trial of the Time Lord') and *Star Cops*. Martin also scripted and novelised the *Doctor Who* spin-off film *Sil and the Devil Seeds of Arodor*, the full cast audio drama *Doctor Who: The Lost Stories: Macros*, and the *Doctor Who* tie-in novels *Invasion of the Ormazoids*, *Vengeance on Varos*, *Mindwarp* and the unproduced *Mission to Magnus*.

Robert Martin

Robert "Uncle Bob" Martin (Robert Houston Martin), co-founder and original editor (1979–85) of *Fangoria* magazine, died on July 20, aged 71. He also edited the Sc-Fi Channel's "official" magazine *Sci Fi Entertainment* under the name "Ed Fixman" (1994–96) before acrimoniously parting ways with the publication. In 1990, Martin novelised Frank Henenlotter's movie *Brain Damage*, and went on to co-script *Frankenhooker* (1990) and *Basket Case 3* (1991) with the director. He also had bit-parts in *Geek Maggot Bingo or the Freak from Suckweasel Mountain* and *Day of the Dead* (1985), wrote for film press kits, and contributed to the online horror portal *Dread Central*.

Tom Maschler

German-born British publisher Tom Maschler, who helped create the Booker Prize for literature in 1969, died on October 15, aged 87. As the head of Jonathan Cape (and associated imprints) he published *Catch-22* by Joseph Heller, *Midnight's Children* by Salman Rushdie, and works by Gabriel García Márquez, Ian McEwan and many other authors.

Phil May

75-year-old British songwriter Phil May (Philip Arthur Dennis Wadey), co-founder and lead singer with the wild 1960s pop group The Pretty Things, died of complications from hip surgery on May 15 after falling off his bike earlier in the week. The Pretty Things appeared as the house band in the 1981 movie *The Monster Club* (Vincent Price and John Carradine), based on stories by R. Chetwynd-Hayes. May's songs can also be heard in Pete Walker's 1978 horror film *The Comeback*, along with episodes of TV's *Timeslip*, *Doomwatch*, *Doctor Who* and *Black Lightning*, and he was also the uncredited lead vocalist on the music for George A. Romero's *Dawn of the Dead*.

Helen McCabe

British romance and horror author Helen McCabe died on April 25, aged 78. Her "Piper Trilogy" (*Piper*, *The Piercing* and *The Codex*) was published in the UK by Telos.

Penny McCarthy

Penny McCarthy, who worked as an assistant auditor on the original *Star Wars* (1977), died on September 17. However, she is better known for her appearances as a "Jawa" in the Mos Eisley Cantina scene, a Cantina Band member, and the demonic-looking "Kardue'sai'Malloc", a Devaronian criminal seen on Tattooine. McCarthy was also the hand-double for Carrie Fisher's Princess Lia when she inserts the disc containing plans of the Death Star into R2-D2.

Kay McCauley

New York literary agent Kay McCauley died on November 8. She began working with her brother Kirby (who died in 2014) in the 1980s, helping him build his list of clients that

included such names as Stephen King, George R.R. Martin, Karl Edward Wagner, Dennis Etchison and many others. When her brother semi-retired because of health reasons, she continued with The Pimlico Agency and, later, as Aurous.

Martin McKenna

51-year-old British Fantasy Award-winning artist Martin McKenna committed suicide at the beginning of September. He started his career in the late 1980s, illustrating for such small-press magazines as *Fantasy Tales*, the H.P. Lovecraft-devoted *Dagon*, *Winter Chills* and *The Scream Factory*, before going on to work for Games Workshop's magazine *White Dwarf* and the company's Warhammer Fantasy

Roleplay publications, including the very first *Warhammer 40,000* book and other GW books and boardgames. He also worked on other games-related material such as the "Fighting Fantasy" series from Puffin Books/Wizard Books and cards for *Magic: The Gathering* from Wizards of the Coast. He contributed artwork to a number of books, and he did concept and production art for computer games and film and TV productions, the latter including 'The Magician of Samarkand' for the BBC's *Jackanory* and the *Gulliver's Travels* mini-series for Hallmark/Channel 4/Jim Henson Productions. His artwork was used as large-scale backdrops for live performances by The Orchestra of Scottish Opera; he wrote several books about digital art, including *Digital Fantasy Painting Workshop* and *Digital Horror Art*, and in 2007 he edited *Fantasy Art Now: The Very Best in Contemporary Fantasy Art & Illustration*.

Frank McLaughlin

American comics artist and inker Frank [X.] McLaughlin died on March 4, aged 84. He entered the comic book industry in the early 1960s, and worked on such titles as *Blue Beetle*, *Captain Atom*, *Strange Suspense Stories* and *Mysteries of Unexplored Worlds* at Charlton; *Planet of the Vampires* for Atlas/Seaboard; *Adventure Comics*, *Justice League of America* and *Ghosts* at DC Comics; *Captain Marvel*, *Chamber of Chills* and *Adventure Into Fear* for Marvel, and *Eerie* at Warren Publishing. McLaughlin also collaborated with Mike Gold on the books *How to Draw Those Bodacious Bad Babes of Comics* and *How to Draw Monsters for Comics*.

Armelia McQueen

American character actress Armelia [Audrey] McQueen died on October 4, aged 68. Best known for her role as one of Whoopi Goldberg's sisters in *Ghost* (1990), she also appeared in *Merry Christmas George Bailey* and episodes of TV's *Nightmare Classics* ('Carmilla'), Disney's *Adventures in Wonderland* (as the "Red Queen"), and *Wishful Things*.

Michael Medwin

Veteran British supporting actor and film producer Michael [Hugh] Medwin OBE died on February 26, aged 96. He made his screen debut in 1946, and his many credits include *The Queen of Spades* (1949), *Helter Skelter* (1949), Hammer's *Spaceways*, *Alice Through the Looking Box*, *Kali-Yug Goddess of Vengeance*, *Il mistero del tempio indiano*, *Night Must Fall* (1964), *Scrooge* (1970), *O Lucky Man!*, *Pogled iz potkrovlija*, *Britanna Hospital*, the James Bond film *Never Say Never Again*, *Sleepwalker*, *Alice Through the Looking Glass* (1998) and *Cinderella* (2000). Medwin produced *If. . .*, *O Lucky Man!* and *Memoirs of a Survivor* (based on the novel by Doris Lessing).

Francis Megahy

83-year-old British-born screenwriter, director and documentary filmmaker Francis Megahy died in Los Angeles on May 1 after a long battle with cancer. He co-wrote (with Bernie Cooper) and directed the *Hammer House of Horror* episode 'Carpathian Eagle', and directed 'Growing Pains' and co-scripted (again with Cooper) 'Charlie Boy' for the same 1980 TV series. Megahy was also a consulting producer on the 2016 TV movie *Cursed Angel*. During the 1960s he briefly managed singer Rod Stewart.

Andree Melly

British actress Andree Melly, best remembered as one of the vampiric "brides" in Hammer's *The Brides of Dracula* (1960), died in Spain on January 31, aged 87. She played a similarly vampish character in the same director's 1964 horror comedy *The Horror of It All*, and her other credits include an episode of TV's *Tales of Mystery* (Algernon Blackwood's 'Ancient Sorceries'). Melly was the younger sister of jazz singer George Melly.

Andree Melly (1932–2020) was prominently featured (bottom right) on this Belgium poster for Hammer's The Brides of Dracula (1960).

Jiří Menzel

Czech director Jiří Menzel, best known for his 1966 film *Closely Observed Trains*, died after a long illness on September 5, aged 82. As an actor he worked on a number of movies, starring as the mad doctor in Juraj Herz's *Ferat Vampire* (1982) and turning up in a supporting role in *The Sunken Cemetery* (2002).

Hans Meyer

South African-born German character actor Hans Meyer died in France on April 4, aged 94. A former advertising model, he appeared in *The Night of the Generals* (uncredited), *The Devil's Garden*, *Vortex*, *Red Sonja*, *Brotherhood of the Wolf*, *Cruel* and episodes of TV's *Thriller* (1974), *The Case-Book of Sherlock Holmes* and *The Young Indiana Jones Chronicles*.

Monique Mercure

French-Canadian film and theatre actress Monique Mercure died of cancer on May 17, aged 89. She appeared in the 1979 SF movie *Quintet*, David Cronenberg's *Naked Lunch*, and *Master Key*.

Norma Michaels

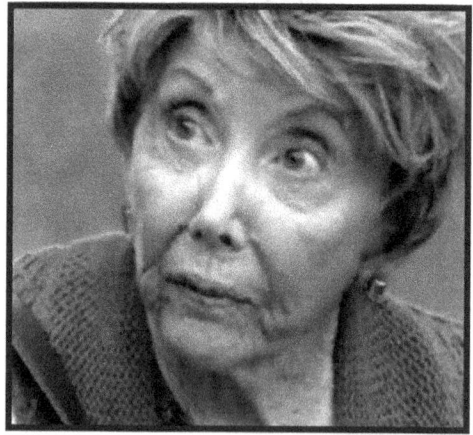

American character actress Norma Michaels died on January 11, aged 96. She appeared in *The Zodiac Killer* and episodes of TV's *Highway to Heaven*,

Buffy the Vampire Slayer, *Angel*, *Medium* and *The Booth at the End*.

Clark Middleton

63-year-old American character actor Clark Middleton, who had recurring roles in the TV series *Fringe*, *South of Hell* and *Twin Peaks* (2017), died of the mosquito-borne disease West Nile Virus on October 4. He had been afflicted with juvenile rheumatoid arthritis from the age of four. Middleton appeared in *Sin City*, *The Attic*, *Snowpiercer*, and episodes of TV's *Gotham*, *American Gods* and *Agents of S.H.I.E.L.D.*

George Mikell

Lithuanian-born Australian actor George Mikell (Jurgis Mikelaitis) died in London, England, on May 12, aged 91. Often cast as Nazis or foreign spies, he appeared in *Where the Spies Are* and *Doppelgänger* (aka *Journey to the Far Side of the Sun*), along with episodes of TV's *Sherlock Holmes and Doctor Watson* and *Hammer House of Mystery and Suspense*.

Thomas L. Miller

American sitcom writer, producer and executive Thomas L. Miller died of complications from heart disease on April 5, aged 79. He started his career as an assistant to Billy Wilder in the late 1950s, and went on to be in charge of development at 20th Century Fox and Paramount on such TV movies as *Dr. Cook's Garden* (starring Bing Crosby) and *Terror in the Sky*, along with the series *The Immortal* (1969-71). Miller also produced the 1973 TV movie *The Devil's Daughter*, featuring Shelley Winters and Jonathan Frid.

Fabrizio Mioni

Italian-born actor Fabrizio Mioni died in Los Angeles on June 8, aged 89. He appeared as "Jason" opposite Steve

Reeves in both *Hercules* (1958) and *Hercules Unchained* (1959, co-directed by Mario Bava) before moving to America, where he was in episodes of TV's *One Step Beyond*, *The Man from U.N.C.L.E.* and *The Girl from U.N.C.L.E.* Mioni also featured in *The Venetian Affair* (with Boris Karloff) before retiring from the screen in the early 1970s. From 1961 until her death in 2008, he was married to actress Maila Nurmi, better known as the 1950s TV horror-host "Vampira", who appeared in Ed Wood's infamous *Plan 9 from Outer Space* (1959).

Kurt Mitchell

American writer and illustrator Kurt [Davis] Mitchell died of a heart attack on July 1, aged 67. He worked as a video game developer (*The Tale of Orpheo's Curse*, *The Indian in the Cupboard*, etc.), and his artwork appeared in such newspapers as *The Chicago Tribune* and *The Chicago Sun-Times*. Mitchell also created the self-published comic strips/graphic novels *Oxbluud: A Gladiator's Tale*, *Cannonboy* and *The Pigeon Eater*, and his illustrated books include the novel *The Stranger Side of Red*, *Poor Ralph*, *Pen & Ink*, and the story collection *Scratched from Dreams*. For some years he had been working on a series of books using anthropomorphic animals in re-workings of classic stories. The artist's drawings grace the walls of Chicago's Horse Thief Hollow Brewing Co., and he designed the beer cans for their Spoonful Hazy IPA and Little Wing Pilsner, along with the bottle labels for Next Century Spirits.

Haruma Miura

30-year-old Japanese actor and singer Haruma Miura hanged himself in a closet on July 18. A former member of the J-pop group Brash Brats, he successfully turned to acting in the early 2000s with roles in *Negative Happy Chainsaw Edge* and *Attack on*

Titan Parts 1 and *2*. He also starred in the *manga*-based TV series *Bloody Monday* (2008–10).

Marvin Mondlin

92-year-old Marvin Mondlin, a long-time book buyer at the Strand Bookstore in New York City, died on March 6. He started in the book-selling trade in 1951 as a stock boy and worked his way up to estate book buyer for the Strand, founding the store's Rare Book Room (with then-owner Fred Bass). Mondlin was co-author of *Book Row: An Anecdotal and Pictorial History of the Antiquarian Book Trade*, chronicling the history of the city's "Book Row" district. He was a member of the Antiquarian Booksellers Association of America.

"Morgus"

American TV horror host "Morgus" (Sidney Noel Rideau, aka "Sid Noel") died on August 27, aged 90. Starting with *House of Shock* on WWL-TV, Channel 4, New Orleans, Louisiana (1959–62), Rideau played mad scientist "Dr. Momus Alexander Morgus" (with assistant Chopsley, Eric

the talking skull, landlady Alma Fetish and manager Wiley Faye) on various TV networks for more than sixty years, including WDSU, WGNU, and in national syndication with re-runs on WVUE and Cox Cable. Morgus became so popular that he inspired his own novelty record ('Morgus the Magnificent' performed by "Morgus and the Ghouls" [Frankie Ford and Mac Rebennack]) and starred in the 1962 regional movie *The Wacky World of Dr. Morgus*. In 2019 Rideu sold out a one-man show at the Orpheum Theatre in New Orleans in which he recalled his long career as Morgus, and the character was inducted into the Horror Host Hall of Fame in 2011.

Ennio Morricone

Possibly the greatest Italian film composer of all time, Ennio Morricone, died following a fall in Rome on July 6, aged 91. Best known for composing the haunting theme to his schoolmate Sergio Leone's iconic "Spaghetti Western" *The Good, the Bad and the Ugly* (1966), the Oscar-winning Morricone's prodigious and diverse list

of more than 500 credits include such films as *Nightmare Castle* (starring Barbara Steele), *The Witches* (1967), *Operation Kid Brother*, *Matchless*, Mario Bava's *Danger: Diabolique*, Dario Argento's *The Bird with the Crystal Plumage*, *The Cat o' Nine Tails*, *Four Flies on Grey Velvet* and *The Stendhal Syndrome*, *When Women Had Tails*, Lucio Fulci's *A Lizard in a Woman's Skin*, *Black Belly of the Tarantula*, *Short Night of Glass Dolls*, *When Women Lost Their Tails*, *What Have You Done to Solange?*, *The Master and Margarita*, *Bluebeard* (1972), Umberto Lenzi's *Spasmo*, *Arabian Nights* (1974), *The Antichrist*, *Autopsy*, *Last Stop on the Night Train* (aka *Night Train Murders*), *Leonor*, *Exorcist II: The Heretic*, *Orca*, *Holocaust 2000* (aka *The Chosen*), *The Humanoid*, *The Island* (1980), John Carpenter's *The Thing* (1982), *Blood Link*, *Treasure of the Four Crowns*, *Hundra*, *Red Sonja*, *Hamlet* (1990), *Wolf*, *The Phantom of the Opera* (1998) and *Mission to Mars*.

Kirby Morrow

Canadian character actor Kirby [Robert] Morrow died of substance abuse on November 19, aged 47. He had a long history of alcohol addiction. A prolific voice actor (most notably as "Michelangelo" in *Ninja Turtles: The Next Mutation*, "Cyclops"/"Scott Summers" in *X-Men: Evolution* and "Anakin Skywalker" and "General Grevous" in various *Lego Star Wars* series), Morrow also appeared in numerous TV shows, including episodes of *Viper*, *The Outer Limits* (1997-98), *Highlander: The Raven*, *Total Recall 2070*, *First Wave*, *Seven Days*, *Special Unit 2*, *Stargate SG-1*, *Stargate: Atlantis* (as regular "Capt. Dave Kleinman"), *Blood Ties*, *Stargate Universe*, *Supernatural*, *Fringe*, *Arrow*, *Ring of Fire*, *Spooksville*, *Olympus*, *The Flash*, *Van Helsing*, *Travelers*, *Legion*, *The Man in the High Castle* and *Supergirl*, along with the TV movies *Deadly Skies*, *High Moon* and *A Wish for Christmas*, and the 2014 movie reboot of *RoboCop*.

Basil Moss

British character actor and musician Basil [David] Moss, who portrayed

SHADO's resident Doctor in four episodes of ITC's *UFO* (1970–71), died on November 28, aged 85. He also turned up in the James Bond film *You Only Live Twice* (as an uncredited British Navy Officer), *Doppelgänger* (aka *Journey to the Far Side of the Sun*) and an episode of TV's *Dr. Terrible's House of Horrible* ('Lesbian Vampire Lovers of Lust').

Jean-Pierre Moumon

French writer, translator, editor and publisher Jean-Pierre Moumon (Jean-Pierre Henri Maurice Moumon, aka "Jean-Pierre Laigle", "Rémi Maure", "Rémi-Maure" and "Karlheinz Debon") died on July 1, aged 73. He founded the semi-professional SF and fantasy magazine *Antares*, which ran for forty-seven issues from 1981–96. He also wrote novels and short stories and edited the anthologies *Dimension Antarès* and *Dimension Antarès 2*.

Becky Mullen

American actress and professional wrestler Becky Mullen (Beckie Mullen) died of cancer on July 27, aged 56. A star (as "Sally the Farmer's Daughter") of *Gorgeous Ladies of Wrestling* (GLOW), she also appeared in *Cast a Deadly Spell*, *Hard Hunted* and episodes of TV's *Hard Time on Planet Earth* and *Black Scorpion*.

Jerrold Mundis

American author Jerrold [James] Mundis, who made his genre debut (as "Eric Corder") in *Bizarre! Mystery Magazine* #3 (1966), died of COVID-19 on April 5, aged 79. He also had a few short stories published in *New Worlds* in the 1960s. Under the "Corder" pseudonym Mundis edited

the anthology *Murder My Love* for Playboy Press and he published the Gothic novels *Echo in a Dark Wind* and *The Shuttered Room* (apparently a tie-in to the 1967 movie of the same name) as "Julia Withers".

Bruce Myers

British actor Bruce Myers died of complications from COVID-19 in Paris, France, on April 15, aged 78. Best known for his work with director Peter Brook on the French stage, he also appeared in the films *No Blade of Grass*, *The Awakening* (as "Dr. Khalid"), *Nostradamus* (1994) and *Let There Be Light*. On TV, Myers was featured in episodes of *The Case-Book of Sherlock Holmes* ('The Eligible Bachelor'), *Highlander* and *Relic Hunter*.

Kellye Nakahara

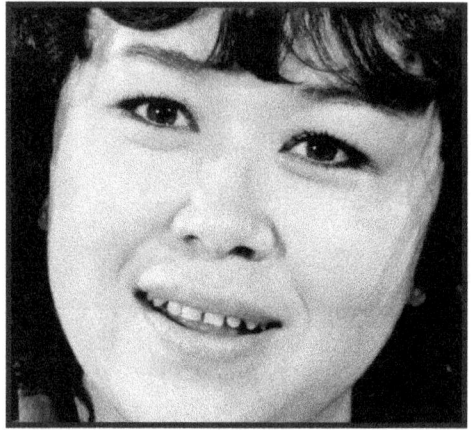

Hawaiian-born character actress Kellye Nakahara [Watson], who was a regular on TV's M*A*S*H (1973–83), died of cancer on February 16, aged 72. She appeared in *Amazon Women on the Moon* and *Doctor Dolittle* (1998), along with episodes of TV's *Kolchak: The Night Stalker*, *Otherworld* and *Sabrina the Teenage Witch*.

Lori Nelson

American actress Lori Nelson (Dixie Kay Nelson), who co-starred opposite Universal's Gill Man in the sequel *Revenge of the Creature* (1955), died of

Lori Nelson (1933–2020) co-starred with Universal's Gill Man in Revenge of the Creature (1955).

Alzheimer's disease on August 23, aged 87. A former child performer and fashion model, she was also in Roger Corman's *Day the World Ended*, *The Pied Piper of Hamelin* (with Claude Rains) and *The Naked Monster*.

Claudette Nevins

American stage and screen actress Claudette Nevins (Claudette Weintraub) died on February 20, aged 82. She co-starred in her debut movie, the 1961 3-D film *The Mask* (aka *Eyes of Hell*), and her other credits include *The Possessed* (1977), *Don't Go to Sleep*, *Child of Darkness Child of Light* and *Star Trek: Insurrection*. On TV, Nevins was in episodes of *Electra Woman and Dyna Girl* (as "Empress of Evil"), *Out of This World*, *Free Spirit*, *Picket Fences* and *Lois & Clark: The New Adventures of Superman*, and she was the voice of "Nova" in the animated series *Return to the Planet of the Apes* (1975).

Ted Newsom

American filmmaker Ted Newsom (Robert Theodore Newsom III) died after a long battle with cancer on July

7, aged 67. Newsom worked in all aspects of the industry, but is probably best known for writing and directing such documentaries as *Flesh and Blood: The Hammer Heritage of Horror* (1994, which featured the final teaming of Peter Cushing and Christopher Lee), *Monsters & Maniacs*, *Wolfman Chronicles: A Cinematic Scrapbook*, *Hollywood Dinosaurs*, *Frankenstein: A Cinematic Scrapbook*, *Dracula: A Cinematic Scrapbook*, *Vincent Price: My Life and Crimes*, *Ed Wood: Look Back in Angora*, *The Vampire Interviews*, *A Century of Science Fiction*, *The Other Dracula – The Vampire Films of John Carradine* and the 1996 TV series *100 Years of Horror*. He also wrote and directed such micro-budget movies as *Evil Spawn*, *The Alien Within*, *The Naked Monster*, *Whispers from a Shallow Grave* and *Superman and the Secret Planet*, which often featured old-time genre actors. Newsom also turned up in bit parts in such movies as *Inner Sanctum* (1991), *Attack of the 60 Foot Centerfolds*, *Deadly Tales*, *Witch House 2: Blood Coven*, *The Craven Cove Murders*, *The Naked Monster*, *Ghost in a Teeny Bikini*, *Bikini Girls from the Lost Planet*,

Bewitched Housewives, Super Ninja Doll, Blood Scarab, Bikini Frankenstein, Twilight Vamps, Housewives from Another World, Bikini Time Machine, Sexual Witchcraft and *Strippers from Another World*, along with episodes of TV's *Jason of Star Command* and *The Lair*. With John D. Brancato, in 1985 he co-scripted an unproduced script for *Spider-Man* for director Joseph Zito.

Jeremy Newson

British actor, filmmaker, singer and songwriter Jeremy Newson died of motor neurone disease on December 16, aged 73. He portrayed "Ralph Hapschatt" in *The Rocky Horror Picture Show* (1975), and was the only actor to reprise his original role in the follow-up, *Shock Treatment* (1981). He also wrote a number of songs for Lulu in *Peter Pan* at the London Palladium.

Brian Nickels

British actor-stuntman Brian "Sonny" Nickels died of cardiac arrest on

January 15, aged 54. He worked on the James Bond films *Tomorrow Never Dies, Skyfall* and *Spectre, Sleepy Hollow* (1999), *The Mummy Returns, The Phantom of the Opera* (2004), *Children of Men, The Golden Compass, Doomsday, Sherlock Holmes* (2009), *The Wolfman, Harry Potter and the Deathly Hallows: Part 1* and *Part 2, Pirates of the Caribbean: On Stranger Tides, Captain America: The First Avenger, John Carter, Wrath of the Titans, Snow White and the Huntsman, Jack the Giant Slayer, Kick-Ass 2, Thor: The Dark World, Guardians of the Galaxy, Avengers: Age of Ultron, The Legend of Tarzan* (2016), *Fantastic Beasts and Where to Find Them, Wonder Woman, Kingsman: The Golden Circle, Jurassic World: Fallen Kingdom, The Kid Who Would Be King, Fast & Furious Presents: Hobbs & Shaw* and *Dolittle*, along with episodes of TV's *Merlin* (1998 and 2010-12), *Life on Mars, Ashes to Ashes, Game of Thrones, Da Vinci's Demons*, and the mini-series *The Odyssey* and *Arabian Nights* (2000).

Daria Nicolodi

The Queen of Italian Horror, actress Daria Nicolodi, died in Rome on November 26, aged 70. The long-time

partner of writer/director Dario Argento until 1985 (their daughter is actress/director Asia Argento), she appeared in Argento's *Deep Red*, *Suspiria* (1977, which she co-scripted), *Inferno* (she came up with the original story), *Tenebrae*, *Phenomena*, *Opera* and *Mother of Tears*, along with Mario Bava and Lamberto Bava's *Shock*, Lamberto Bava's *Delirium*, Luigi Cozzi's *Paganini Horror* (which she also co-scripted) and Michele Soavi's *The Sect*. On TV, Nocolodi's credits include the series *I giochi del diavolo* and episodes of *Turno di notte* (Cozzi's 'Giallo Natale') and *Alta tensione* (Lamberto Bava's 'School of Fear'). She also narrated the movie *Sinbad of the Seven Seas* and the animated TV series *Saban's Adventures of the Little Mermaid*, and wrote the original script of what eventually became Cozzi's *The Black Cat* (1989).

Sue Nicols

Disney visual development and character designer Sue [Carol] Nicols [Maciorowski] died of breast cancer on September 1, aged 55. She worked on the original stories for *Aladdin* (1992) and *The Hunchback of Notre Dame*

(1996), was also involved in the development of *Beauty and the Beast* (1991), *The Pagemaster*, *Hercules*, *Fantasia 2000*, *Atlantis: The Lost Empire*, *Lilo & Stitch*, *Enchanted* and *The Princess and the Frog*.

Lennie Niehaus

American composer and arranger Lennie Niehaus (Leonard Niehaus), who was best known for his music for Clint Eastwood movies, died on May 28, aged 90. A former jazz alto saxophonist, he worked on such films as *Johnny Got His Gun* (1971), *The Nightcomers*, *Demon Seed*, *Pee-Wee's Big Adventure*, *Pale Rider* and *Ratboy*, along with six episodes of TV's *Faerie Tale Theatre* and one episode of *Amazing Stories*.

Daria Nicolodi (1950–2020) co-starred in her long-term partner's giallo, Deep Red (1975).

Margaret Nolan

British actress and artist Margaret Nolan, who was featured as the gold-painted model in the title sequence and poster for *Goldfinger* (1964), died October 5, aged 76. A former glamour model under the name "Vicki Kennedy", Nolan also played "Dink" in the iconic James Bond film, and her other credits include appearances in a number of "Carry On" titles, *A Hard Day's Night* (with the Beatles), *Witchfinder General* (with Vincent Price) and *Toomorrow*, along with episodes of TV's *Adam Adamant Lives!*, *Mystery and Imagination* ('Dracula', 1968) and *The Adventures of Don Quick*. Apparently her scenes were cut from Alfred Hitchcock's *Frenzy*.

Nobuhiko Ôbayashi

Japanese director, writer and editor Nobuhiko Ôbayashi died of lung cancer on April 10, aged 82. His films include *House* (1977), *The Visitor in the Eye*, *The Aimed School*, *I Am You You Am Me*, *The Little Girl who Conquered Time*, *The Drifting Classroom*, *The Discarnates*, *Ashita*, *Switching – Goodbye Me* and *Labyrinth of Cinema*. Many of his movies dealt with such themes as time-travel or body-swapping.

George Ogilvie

Australian film director and drama teacher George [Buchan] Ogilvie died of cardiac arrest on April 5, aged 89. He had suffered from emphysema for years. In 1985 Ogilvie co-directed *Mad Max Beyond Thunderdome* with George Miller.

Michael O'Hear

American character actor and filmmaker Michael O'Hear died on June 24, aged 56. At the end of May he was admitted to Niagara Falls Memorial Hospital to remove a kidney blockage, but complications followed. A GoFundMe page was set up to help with his medical expenses. O'Hear mostly worked in independent, micro-budget, direct-to-video East Coast productions, and appeared (often as the character "William Sanders") in *Frightworld* (also cinematographer), *Something Dark* (also associate producer, scriptwriter, segment director and casting director), *Red Scream Nosferatu*, *House of Horrors: The Movie*, *Gore* (also producer) and the short *Pigman vs. Gore*, Greg Lamberson's *Slime City Massacre* (also first assistant director and casting director), *The Haunted Boy: The Secret Diary of the Exorcist*, *Prisoners of the Dead*, *Abstract Messiah*, *Henry's Future* (also production assistant), *Snow Shark: Ancient Snowbeast*, *Crimson: The Motion Picture*, *House of Horrors: Gates of Hell*, *Battledogs*, *Return to Nuke 'Em High: Volume 1*, *Dry Bones* (also co-director and co-producer), *Mostly Dead*, *Wormchild 3: Darkest Destiny*, *Killer Rack*, *Alive: An Undead Survival Series Volume 2*, *Mercy*, *Model Hunger*, *The OUTLAW: The Living Comic Book 666*, *STAR [Space Traveling Alien Reject]*, *Death House* (with Tony Todd), *Johnny Gruesome*, *Fang*, *Post Apocalyptic Commando Shark*, *Grace is Gone* and *The Horrific Evil Monsters*, along with the online series *Mansion of Mystery* and *Captain Isotope & the Enemy of Space*.

Denny O'Neil

Influential American comics writer and editor Denny O'Neil (Dennis Joseph O'Neil), who started his career as one of Stan Lee's editorial assistants at Marvel in the mid-1960s and went on to reinvent (with artist Neal Adams) the character of "Batman" at DC Comics for a whole new generation during the following decade, died on June 11, aged 81. Amongst the many titles he worked on are *Strange Tales* ('Doctor Strange'), *X-Men*, *Beware the Creeper*, *Green Arrow/Green Lantern* (again with Adams), *Batman*, *Detective*

Comics, *Superman*, *Captain Marvel*, *The Shadow* (with artist Mike Kaluta), *The Amazing Spider-Man*, *Iron Man* and *Daredevil*. He also scripted some comics for Charlton under the pseudonym "Sergius O'Shaugnessy". O'Neil's short fiction was published in *Fantastic Stories*, *The Magazine of Fantasy and Science Fiction*, *Haunt of Horror*, *Unknown Worlds of Science Fiction* and anthologies edited by David Gerrold, Roger Elwood and John Varley. His novel *The Bite of Monsters* appeared from Belmont in 1971 and he wrote the novelisations of the movies *Batman Begins* and *The Dark Knight*. On TV, he scripted episodes of *Logan's Run*, *G.I. Joe: A Real American Hero*, *Superboy* and *Batman: The Animated Series*. O'Neil co-created the characters of "Ra's al Ghul" and his daughter "Talia al Ghul" in the *Batman* mythos, and he also is credited for coming up with the name for the Transformers' leader "Optimus Prime".

Ernie Orsatti

Veteran American stuntman and actor Ernie [Frank] Orsatti, who was stunt coordinator on the TV series *Charmed* (1998-2000) and *Carnivàle* (2003-05), died after suffering a haemorrhagic stroke on September 12, aged 80. Best known for his remarkable thirty-two foot fall onto a glass skylight in the 1972 disaster movie *The Poseidon Adventure*, Orsatti also worked on *The Swarm*, *The Entity*, *Phantasm II*, *Ghost Dad*, *Donor*, *Theodore Rex*, *Tremors II: Aftershocks*, *Alien: Resurrection*, *The Love Bug* (1997), *Fallen*, *Doctor Dolittle* (1998), *Pleasantville*, *My Favorite Martian* and *Black Knight*. On TV, his credits include episodes of *The Powers of Matthew Star*, *Picket Fences*, *Wild Palms* and *The Pretender*. As an actor, Orsatti also appeared in *The Car* and *Alice in Wonderland* (1985), and episodes of *Wonder Woman*, *The Incredible Hulk* and *The Greatest American Hero*.

James Otis

American character actor James Otis, who portrayed "Famine" in a 2010 episode of TV's *Supernatural* (his final role), died after a long illness on March 3, aged 71. He was also in *Henry: Portrait of a Serial Killer Part 2*, *Inhabited*,

The Prestige, *Nite Tales: The Movie* and episodes of *Star Trek: Deep Space Nine* (as "Solbor") and *The X Files*.

Ulf Ôtsuki

Swedish-Japanese character actor Ulf Ôtsuki (Ulf Georgii-Hemming) died on August 15, aged 85. He appeared in *Godzilla vs. Megalon*, *Nostradamus* (1994) and episodes of the TV series *The Space Giants*, *Johnny Sokko and His Flying Robot*, *Kamen Rider Stronger*, *Space Ironmen Kyodain*, *Brain 17*, *Kamen Rider Super-1*, *Dennou Keisatsu Cybercop* and *Kamen Rider Drive*.

Geoffrey Palmer

Lugubrious British character actor Geoffrey [Dyson] Palmer OBE, who was often cast as policemen, doctors or politicians, died on November 6, aged 93. Probably best known for his appearance in the 1997 James Bond film *Tomorrow Never Dies*, his other credits include *O Lucky Man!*, *A Midsummer Night's Dream* (1981), *Alice Through the Looking Glass* (1998), *Peter Pan* (2003) and *Paddington*. Palmer began his busy career in television in the mid-1950s, and he was in episodes of *The Avengers*, *Mystery and Imagination*, *Out of the Unknown*, *Doctor Who* ('Doctor Who and the Silurians' and 'Voyage of the Damned'), *Doomwatch*, *Whoops Apocalypse*, *Stig of the Dump* (2002), *Ashes to Ashes* and *Grandpa in my Pocket!*.

Alan Parker

British scriptwriter and director Sir Alan [William] Parker died after a long illness on July 31, aged 76. His credits include the 1974 short film *Footsteps*, *Pink Floyd: The Wall* and *Angel Heart*, although he is better known for some of his other movies.

Ulf Ôtsuki (1934–2020) was featured in Godzilla vs. Megalon (1973).

Nicholas Parsons

British TV and radio personality [Christopher] Nicholas Parsons CBE died after a short illness on January 28, aged 96. He made his screen debut in 1946, and his film credits include *The Ghost Goes Gear* (1966). On TV, Parsons was the voice of "Sheriff Tex Tucker" in Gerry Anderson's puppet series *Four Feather Falls* and "Dagon, Lord of the Files" in *Good Omens*, and he appeared in the 1989 *Doctor Who* serial 'The Curse of Fenric'. On the stage, he was featured in the original London cast of the Stephen Sondheim musical *Into the Woods* at the Phoenix Theatre in 1990 and he took the role of "Narrator" in the 1994 revival of *The Rocky Horror Show*, touring with the production for the next two years.

Martin Pasko

Canadian-born comics writer and TV scriptwriter and story editor Martin [Joseph "Marty"] Pasko (Jean-Claude Rochefort, aka "Kyle Christopher") died in Los Angeles on May 10, aged 65. He wrote or co-scripted episodes of *Buck Rogers in the 25th Century*, *The Incredible Hulk*, *Fantasy Island*, *The Twilight Zone* (1985-86), *Max Headroom* and *Free Spirit*, along with such cartoon shows as *Blackstar*, *Thundarr the Barbarian* (1980-81), *Beauty and the Beast* (1983), *G.I. Joe*, *Superman* (1988), *Teenage Mutant Ninja Turtles* (1988-90), *The Legend of Prince Valiant*, *Batman: The Animated Series* (for which he won a 1993 Daytime Emmy® Award), *Cadillacs and Dinosaurs*, *Batman: Mask of the Phantasm* (1993) and *The Tick*. Nicknamed "Pesky Pasko" by DC comics editor Julius Schwartz, for whom he wrote for many years, he also worked for other comics publishers, including Warren (*Vampirella*, *Creepy*), Seaboard (*Weird Tales of the Macabre*), Marvel (*Monsters Unleashed*, *Star Trek*, *Gargoyles*) and DC (*Saga of the Swamp Thing*). Pasko was best-known for writing DC's Superman in various media – including TV animation, newspaper syndication, webisodes, comics, illustrated books and *The Essential Superman Encyclopedia* – and he co-created (with artist Walt Simonson) the 1975 revamp of "Dr. Fate", which became the basis of the character's current incarnation.

Ivan Passer

Czechoslovakian-born American scriptwriter and director Ivan Passer died on January 9, aged 86. His credits include *Creator*, *Haunted Summer*, *The Wishing Tree* and an episode of TV's *Faerie Tale Theatre*.

Alan Pattillo

British editor, scriptwriter and director Alan [Hutchinson] Pattillo died on January 16, aged 90. He directed such Gerry Anderson TV puppet productions as *Four Feather Falls*, *Supercar*, *Fireball XL5*, *Stingray*, *Thunderbirds* and *Terrahawks*. Pattillo also scripted episodes of *Thunderbirds*, *The Avengers*, *Captain Scarlet and the Mysterons* and *UFO*, and he edited *The Fiend* (aka *Beware My Brethren*), *Straight on Till Morning*, *Chimera*, *Cyborg Cop* and an episode of *Space: 1999*.

Pilar Pellicer

Mexican actress Pilar Pellicer died of complications from COVID-19 on May 16, aged 82. She made her screen debut in the mid-1950s, and her credits include *Las visitaciones del diablo*, *The World of the Dead* (co-starring with Santo and Blue Demon) and *Dulce espiritu*.

Krzysztof Penderecki

Polish music composer and conductor Krzysztof [Eugeniusz] Penderecki died after a long illness on March 29, aged 86. He composed the music for such films as *The Saragossa Manuscript* and *Demon* (2015). Penderecki's music was also heard in *The Exorcist*, *The Shining* (1980), *Wild at Heart*, *The People Under the Stairs*, *Children of Men*, *Shutter Island*, *Ready Player One* and episodes of TV's *Twin Peaks* (2017) and *Black Mirror*.

Regis Philbin

American talk-show host, game-show host, singer and TV personality Regis [Francis Xavier] Philbin died on July 24, aged 88. He appeared (often playing a version of himself) in *Everything You Always Wanted to Know About Sex* *But Were Afraid to Ask*, *SST: Death Flight*, *Little Nicky* and episodes of TV's *Get Smart*, *Lucan*, *Fantasy Island*, *Kung Fu: The Legend Continues* and *Honey I Shrunk the Kids: The TV Show*. More recently, Philbin did voice work for *Pinocchio* (2002), *Shrek the Third*, *Shrek Forever After* and TV's *Hercules* (1998), *The Simpsons* ('Treehouse of Horror IX') and *Lilo & Stitch: The Series*.

Michel Piccoli

Leading French actor [Jacques Daniel] Michel Piccoli died on May 12, aged 94. He appeared as the monster in the

Frankenstein-inspired short *Torticola contre Frankensberg* (1952), and his other credits include *The Crucible* (1957), *Amazons of Rome*, *The Creatures* (1966), Mario Bava's *Danger: Diabolik*, Luis Buñuel's surreal *The Discreet Charm of the Bourgeoisie* and *The Phantom of Liberty*, *Themroc*, *La Grande Bouffe*, *The Infernal Trio* and the SF short *The Timekeeper* (as "Jules Verne").

Hayford Pierce

78-year-old American science fiction and mystery writer Hayford Pierce died in hospital from a self-inflicted gunshot wound on November 19 after Arizona sheriff's deputies visited his home and found his wife, 51-year-old Wanda Zhang, dead in a possible murder-suicide. Pierce's light-hearted short stories appeared in *Analog*, *Galaxy*, *Omni*, *Alfred Hitchcock's Mystery*

Magazine and *Ellery Queen's Mystery Magazine* and were collected in *Aliens, With a Bang and Other Forbidden Delights* and *Elephant's Graveyard and Other Science Fiction Stories* (with David Alexander). He also published the novels *Napoleon Disseminated, The Thirteenth Majestral* (aka *Dinosaur Park*), *Phylum Monsters, Flickerman, The Spark of Life, Black Hole Planet, The 13th Death of Yuri Gellaski* and *In the Flames of the Flickerman*. Pierce's uncle was the prominent painter Waldo Pierce.

Tom Pollock

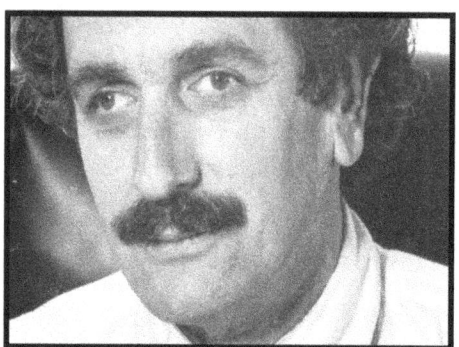

Tom Pollock, the former chairman of Universal Pictures and the American Film Institute, died of a heart attack on August 1, aged 77. In 1970, he co-founded the entertainment law firm Pollock, Rigrod, and Bloom, where George Lucas was one of his first clients. Pollock negotiated the deal that secured Lucas the merchandising and sequel rights to *Star Wars*. He was also involved in the negotiations for the *Indiana Jones* and *Superman* franchises. Pollock left his firm in 1986 to become executive vice president of MCA Inc. and chairman of its Motion Picture Group, Universal Pictures. As such, he oversaw production of *Jurassic Park*, the *Back to the Future* trilogy, *Field of Dreams* and many others movies. In 1996, he resigned from his position and became AFI's chairman of the board, teaming up two years later with Ivan Reitman to form The Montecito Picture Company, where he received executive producer credits on *Evolution* (and its TV spin-off), *Disturbia, The Uninvited* (2009), *Hitchcock*, the 2016 reboot of *Ghostbusters* and *A Babysitter's Guide to Monster Hunting*.

Wu Pong-fong

Taiwanese actor Wu Pong-fong (Pong Fong Wu) died of a stroke on May 25, aged 55. He made his movie debut in the late 1990s, and his credits include the horror films *The Ghost Tales* (2012) and *Soul* (2013).

Leslie A. Pope

Oscar-nominated American set decorator Leslie A. (Anne) Pope died on May 6, aged 65. She had been recovering from heart surgery. Pope worked on the movies *Angel Heart, The*

Astronaut's Wife, *S1m0ne*, *Spider-Man 3*, *The Amazing Spider-Man*, *Captain America: The Winter Soldier*, *Ant-Man*, *Ghostbusters* (2016), *Avengers: Infinity War* and *Avengers: Endgame*.

Peggy Pope

American character actress Peggy Pope, who played the tipsy office secretary in the comedy *9 to 5* (1980), died on May 27, aged 91. She made her TV debut in the mid-1960s, and her credits include the movies *Oh God!*, *The Last Starfighter* and *Once Bitten*, along with episodes of *Bewitched*, *Mork & Mindy*, *Twilight Zone* (1986) and *Highway to Heaven*. Pope also appeared on Broadway in a 1970 revival of *Harvey* with James Stewart.

Lovelady Powell

American singer and actress Lovelady Powell (Lovelady Hedges) died on February 2, aged 89. Her few screen credits include *The Possession of Joel Delaney*, *The Happy Hooker* and a 1967 episode of TV's *Dark Shadows*.

Taryn Power

Taryn [Stephanie] Power, the actress daughter of Tyrone Power and Linda Christian, died of leukaemia on June 26, aged 66. Best known for her role as "Dione" alongside Patrick Wayne's swashbuckling hero and Ray Harryhausen's special effects in *Sinbad*

and the Eye of the Tiger (1977), her other credits include *The Sea Serpent* (with Ray Milland) and an episode of TV's *The Hardy Boys/Nancy Drew Mysteries* ('The Mystery of King Tut's Tomb').

Kelly Preston

American actress Kelly Preston (Kelly Kamalelehua Smith) died after a two-year battle with breast cancer on July 12, aged 57. She appeared in *Metalstorm: The Destruction of Jared-Syn*, *Christine* (based on the novel by Stephen King), *Spacecamp*, *Love at Stake*, *Amazon Women on the Moon*, *Spellbinder*, *From Dusk Till Dawn*, *Jack Frost*, *Battlefield Earth* (with her husband John Travolta), *The Cat in the Hat* and *Sky High*. On TV Preston had a recurring role in *Medium* and appeared in episodes of TV's *Blue Thunder* and *Tales from the Crypt*.

Dave Prowse

British actor and bodybuilder Dave Prowse MBE (David Charles Prowse) died of complications from COVID-19 on November 28, aged 85. Although best known for playing the body of

"Darth Vader" in the original trilogy of *Star Wars* movies (*Star Wars*, *The Empire Strikes Back* and *Return of the Jedi*), James Earl Jones overdubbed his broad Bristol accent. Prowse also portrayed Frankenstein's Monster in three films – *Casino Royale* (1967) and Hammer's *The Horror of Frankenstein* and *Frankenstein and the Monster from Hell*, and his other credits include *A Clockwork Orange*, Hammer's *Vampire Circus*, *Jabberwocky*, *Gulliver's Travels* (1977) and Amicus' *The People That Time Forgot*. On TV Prowse appeared in episodes of *The Champions*, *Ace of Wands*, *Doctor Who* (as the Minotaur in 'The Time Monster'), *The Tomorrow People* ('The Medusa Strain'), *Omnibus* ('The Need for Nightmare' – as the shadow of the Frankenstein Monster), *Space: 1999*, *The Hitchhiker's Guide to the Galaxy* and as the "Green Cross Code Man" in a series of Government road safety advertisements during the 1970s and '80s. In his autobiography, *Straight from the Force's Mouth* (2011), he details how he trained Christopher Reeve for his role in *Superman* (1978) and the feud with Lucasfilm which led

Dave Prowse (1929–2020) was prominently featured on this Spanish poster for Hammer's The Horror of Frankenstein *(1970).*

to him being banned from all official *Star Wars* events.

André Ptaszynski

André Ptaszynski, British theatre producer and chief executive of the Really Useful group, died on July 29, aged 67. His fifty-year stage credits include Bob Carlton's *Return to the Forbidden Planet* (1990), *Love Never Dies* (the sequel to *Phantom of the Opera*) and the 2016 production of *Groundhog Day* at the Old Vic.

Joseph S. Pulver, Sr.

American horror author, poet and editor Joseph S. Pulver, Sr. died after a long illness on April 24, aged 64. He lived in Germany for many years and was heavily influenced by the works of H.P. Lovecraft and, especially, Robert W. Chambers (notably *The King in Yellow*). Pulver published the novels *Nightmare's Disciple* and *The Orphan Palace*, and his short fiction was collected by Hippocampus Press in *Blood Will Have Its Season*, *Sin & Ashes*, *Portraits of Ruin* and *A House of Hollow Wounds*. He edited the anthologies *Aklonomicon* (with Ivan McCann), *A Season in Carcosa*, the Shirley Jackson Award-winning *The Grimscribe's Puppets*, *Cassilda's Song: Tales Inspired by Robert W. Chambers' King in Yellow Mythos*, *The Doom That Came to Providence*, *The Madness of Dr. Caligari*, *Walk on the Weird Side* and *Darker Companions* (with Scott David Aniolowski). Pulver also guest-edited such magazines as *Midnight Shambler*, *Crypt of Cthulhu*, *Phantasmagorium* and *Lovecraft eZine*.

Tommy Rall

Veteran American acrobatic dancer Tommy Rall (Thomas Edward Rall) died of congestive heart failure on

October 6, aged 90. Although best known for his roles on Broadway and in such movie musicals as *Kiss me Kate* (1953), *Seven Brides for Seven Brothers* (1954) and *Funny Girl* (1968), Rall made his film debut as a member of the tap-dance group "The Jivin' Jacks and Jills" in six 1942-43 Universal movies, and his final screen role was as "The Werewolf" in *Saturday the 14th Strikes Back* (1988).

Rebecca Ramsey

American visual effects producer Rebecca Ramsey died on March 7, aged 53. She worked on *The Nightmare Before Christmas*, *Wolf*, *Mortal Kombat*, *Se7en*, *Mortal Kombat: Annihilation*, *Queen of the Damned*, *The Matrix Revolutions*, *The Cat in the Hat*, *Hellboy*, *I Robot*, *Elektra*, *A Sound of Thunder*, *Pirates of the Caribbean: Dead Man's Chest*, *Superman II: The Richard Donner Cut*, *Spider-Man 3*, *Next*, *The Invasion*, *The Mist*, *Speed Racer*, *Get Smart* (2008), *Mirrors* (2008), *Legion*, *Harry Potter and the Deathly Hallows: Part 2*, *Conan the Barbarian* (2011), *Dream House*, *Immortals*, *Project Almanac*, *Monster Hunt* and *Kin*.

James Randi

Canadian magician and escapologist James "The Amazing" Randi (Randall James Hamilton Zwinge), who became famous for debunking paranormal and pseudoscientific claims, died in Florida on October 20, aged 92. He had short stories published in *Omni* and the SF anthology *Destinies*, and his books include *Flim Flam!: The Truth About Unicorns, Parapsychology, and Other Delusions* (1980) and *An Encyclopedia of Claims, Frauds, and Hoaxes of the Occult and Supernatural* (1994). The James Randi Educational Foundation offers $1 million to anyone who can show evidence of any paranormal, supernatural, or occult power or event.

Elsa Raven

American character actress Elsa Raven (Elsa Rabinowitz), who played the "Clocktower Lady" in *Back to the Future* (1985), died on November 3, aged 91. Her other credits include *The Honeymoon Killers*, *The Amityville Horror* (1979), *Twilight Zone: The Movie* and *Creator*. On TV, Raven was in episodes of *Highway to Heaven*, *Freddy's Nightmares* and *3rd Rock from the Sun*.

Marguerite Ray

American TV character actress Marguerite Ray died on November 18, aged 89. Her credits include episodes of *The Wild Wild West*, *Bewitched* and *The Flash* (1990).

Helen Reddy

Australian singer and actress Helen [Maxine Lamond] Reddy, best known for her #1 song 'I am Woman' — an anthem for the radical feminist movement during the 1970s — died of complications from dementia on September 29, aged 78. She co-starred in Walt Disney's *Pete's Dragon* (1977) and turned up in *Sgt. Pepper's Lonely Hearts Club Band* and episodes of TV's *Fantasy Island* and *BeastMaster*.

Marge Redmond

American character actress Marge Redmond (Marjorie A. Redmond) died on February 10, aged 95. Her credits in *Carousel* (1967), *Johnny Got His Gun* and Alfred Hitchcock's *Family Plot*. On TV, Redmond co-starred as "Sister Jacqueline" in the ABC-TV sit-com *The Flying Nun* (1967–70), and she also appeared in episodes of *The Twilight Zone*, *My Favorite Martian*, *The Munsters*, *My Mother the Car*, *The Sixth Sense* and *The Six Million Dollar Man*. In 1979 she took over the role of "Mrs. Lovett" in the original Broadway production of Stephen Sondheim's *Sweeney Todd* when Angela Lansbury went on vacation. From 1950–90, Redmond was married to actor Jack Weston.

Joel M. Reed

American independent exploitation director Joel M. (Melvin) Reed died of complications from COVID-19 on April 12, aged 86, His credits include *Blood Bath* (1975), *The Incredible Torture Show* (aka *Bloodsucking Freaks*) and *Night of the Zombies*. Reed also turned up as an actor in the latter movie, plus such low budget, direct-to-video releases as *Dead Eye*, *I Spill Your Guts*, *Supernaturalz: Weird Creepy & Random*, *Trashtastic*, *Vault of Terror II: The Undead*, *The Fappening*, *Killer Waves* and *Freak in the Basement*.

Carl Reiner

American comedy legend Carl Reiner died on June 29, aged 98. He directed *Oh God*, *The Man with Two Brains* (which he also co-scripted) and *All of Me*. On TV Reiner executive-produced and starred as "Mr. Angel" in the short-lived fantasy-comedy series *Good Heavens* (1976), and he appeared in *Oh God*, *The Spirit of '76* (directed by his son Lucas), *The Adventures of Rocky & Bullwinkle* (2000) and episodes of *Rod Serling's Night Gallery* (the Lovecraft-inspired spoof 'Professor Peabody's Last Lecture') and *Faerie Tale Theatre*. He also did voice work for a number of animated projects, including *Toy Story 4* and TV's *Justice League Action*.

Barbara Remington

American artist and illustrator Barbara Remington (aka "BRem"), who created the cover art for the first Ballantine Books paperbacks of J.R.R. Tolkien's *The Hobbit* and *The Lord of the Rings* and E.R. Eddison's *The Worm Ouroboros*, died on January 23, aged 90. Her work was also used on the 1965 Tolkien-related poster *A Map of Middle-Earth*.

Bloodsucking Freaks (aka The Incredible Torture Show, 1976) was written and directed by Joel M. Reed (1933–2020).

Mike Resnick

Prolific Hugo and Nebula Award-winning American science fiction and fantasy author and editor Mike Resnick (Michael Diamond Resnick) died of lymphoma on January 9, aged 77. Perhaps best known for his "Chronicles of Lucifer Jones" series (*Adventures, Exploits, Encounters, Hazards* and *Voyages*) and the "John Justin Mallory" series (*Stalking the Unicorn, Stalking the Vampire, Stalking the Dragon* and *Stalking the Zombie*), his other books include the novels *Readbeard, The Branch, The Cassandra Project* (with Jack McDevitt) and *The Gods of Sagittarius* (with Eric Flint). Resnick also edited the magazines *Jim Baen's Universe* (2007–10, with Flint) and *Galaxy's Edge* (2013–20), and amongst his many anthologies (often in collaboration with Martin H. Greenberg) are *Shaggy B.E.M. Stories, Aladdin: Master of the Lamp, Christmas Ghosts, Dinosaur Fantastic, Witch Fantastic, Deals with the Devil* (with Loren D. Estleman), *Sherlock Holmes in Orbit, Girls for the Slime God, Return of the Dinosaurs, Women Writing Science Fiction as Men, Dirty Rotten Aliens, Alien Crimes* and *Worlds of Edgar Rice Burroughs* (with Robert T. Garcia). His short fiction is collected in *Unauthorized Autobiographies and Other Curiosities, Pink Elephants and Hairy Toads, Will the Last Person to Leave the Planet Please Shut Off the Sun?, In Space No One Can Hear You Laugh, The Incarceration of Captain Nebula and Other Lost Futures, Resnick's Menagerie, First Person Peculiar* and many other titles.

Ramon Revilla

Filipino actor and producer Ramon Revilla [Sr.] (Jose Acuña Bautista) died of heart failure on June 26, aged 93. He began his movie career in the early 1950s and starred in the 1983 horror film *The Killing of Satan*. Rivella reportedly fathered seventy-two children with sixteen different women and later became a politician.

Gene Reynolds

American TV scriptwriter, producer and director Gene Reynolds (Eugene Reynolds Blumenthal), best known for executive-producing the hit TV series M*A*S*H (1972–77), died of heart failure on February 3, aged 96. The six-

time Emmy Award-winner's other credits include episodes of *Alfred Hitchcock Presents*, *The Munsters*, *Captain Nice*, *The Ghost & Mrs. Muir*, *Lois & Clark: The New Adventures of Superman* and *Touched by an Angel*. Reynolds began his career as a child actor, appearing in *Babes in Toyland* (aka *March of the Wooden Soldiers*, with Laurel & Hardy), *The Blue Bird* (1940) and the "Dead End Kids" serial *Junior G-Men of the Air* (with Lionel Atwill).

Allan Rich

American character actor and art expert Allan Rich (Benjamin Norman Schultz), who was blacklisted during the McCarthy era, died of complications from Alzheimer's disease on August 22, aged 94. Often cast as cops, judges or doctors, he appeared in *The Archer: Fugitive from the Empire*, *Eating Raoul*, *The Entity*, *J.O.E. and the Colonel* (aka *Humanoid Defender*), *Highlander II: The Quickening* and *Rise: Blood Hunter*, along with episodes of TV's *The Incredible Hulk*, *Hero at Large*, *Misfits of Science* and *Beyond Belief: Fact or Fiction*.

Diana Rigg

Tony and Emmy Award-winning British stage and screen actress Dame Diana Rigg (Enid Diana Elizabeth Rigg), best known for her portrayal as the iconic "Mrs. Emma Peel" in more than fifty episodes of *The Avengers* (1965–68), died of cancer on September 10, aged 82. Her other credits include *A Midsummer Night's Dream* (1959 and 1968 versions), *On Her Majesty's Secret Service* (opposite George Lazenby as "James Bond"), *Theatre of Blood* (with Vincent Price), *The Great Muppet Caper*, *The Worst Witch* (1986), *Snow White* (1987), *The Haunting of Helen Walker* (based on 'Turn of the Screw' by Henry James), *A Christmas Carol Goes Wrong* and *Last Night in Soho*. On TV Diana Rigg appeared as "Mrs. Danvers" in a two-part mini-series of Daphne Du Maurier's *Rebecca* (1997), *Doctor Who* ('The Crimson Horror' alongside her actress daughter, Rachael Stirling), *You Me and the Apocalypse*, George R.R. Martin's *Game of Thrones* (as the wily "Olenna Tyrell") and the 2020 BBC mini-series of *Black Narcissus*. However, she will always be remembered as the lithe, butt-kicking partner of Patrick Macnee's "John Steed", who would leap into action any time she heard the words: "Mrs. Peel, we're needed."

Naya Rivera

33-year-old American actress and singer Naya [Marie] Rivera, who portrayed "Santana Lopez" on the TV series *Glee* (2009–15), drowned while swimming in a lake with her four-year-old son on July 8. She appeared in the movies *Frankenhood* and *At the Devil's Door*.

Maurice Roëves

British character actor Maurice Roëves, who was often cast as police detectives, died on July 15, aged 83. He began his screen career in the mid-1960s and appeared in *Outland*, *Judge Dredd* (1995), *The Sight*, *The Dark* (2005), Dave McKean's *Luna*, and *Macbeth* (2015),

along with episodes of TV's *Doomwatch*, *Out of the Unknown*, *The Nightmare Man*, *Doctor Who* ('The Caves of Androzani') and *Star Trek: The Next Generation*.

Joel Rogosin

Veteran American TV producer and scriptwriter Joel Rogosin died of complications from COVID-19 on April 21, aged 87. He was the fifth resident at the Motion Picture & Television Country House facility in Woodland Hills, California, to die from the virus. After starting out in Hollywood in 1957 as a messenger at Columbia Pictures, the Emmy Award-nominated Rogosin produced such shows as *Circle of Fear*, *Mr. Merlin* and the original *Knight Rider*.

"Ronald"

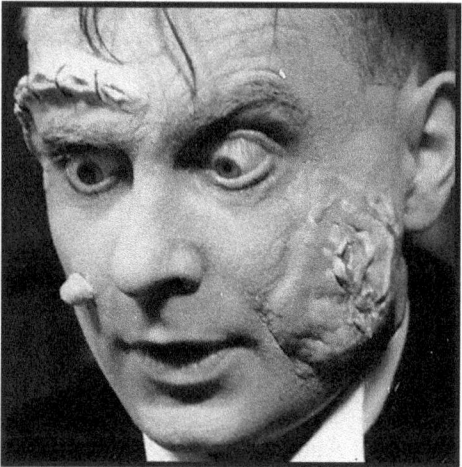

American regional horror host "Ronald" the ghoul (Jerry Sandford), who hosted the *Shock Theater* movie package on WVEC Channel 13, Norfolk-Hampton, Virginia, on Friday nights from 1959-64, died on February 11, aged 88. Halloween specials with Ronald continued to be aired until 1968, and Sandford also portrayed "Bungles the Clown" on a live afternoon show for the same station.

Suzanne Roquette

German-born actress Suzanne Roquette died in London, England, on May 28, aged 77. Her credits include *The Hunchback of Soho*, *The Vengeance of Fu Manchu* (with Christopher Lee), *The College Girl Murders* and *Indiana Jones and the Last Crusade*. On TV she played (uncredited) "Tanya Aleksandr" in twenty-two episodes of *Space: 1999* (1975-76) and two compilation movies (*Journey Through the Black Sun* and *Alien Attack*).

Elyse Rosenstein

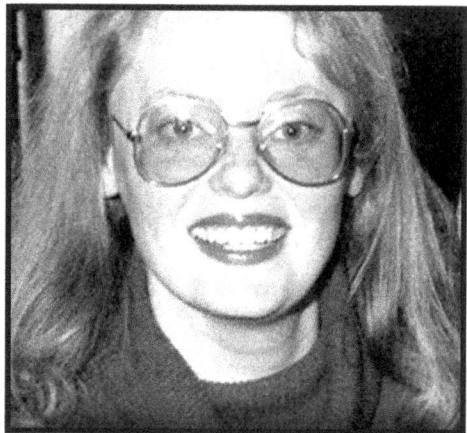

American fan and science teacher Elyse Rosenstein, who co-conceived and co-organised the first *Star Trek* convention (in New York City, January 1972), died on February 20, aged 69. She had been undergoing rehabilitation after suffering a broken leg. Rosenstein, together with her then-husband, also ran Nova Enterprises, which sold *Star Trek*-related merchandise.

Annie Ross

British-born actress and jazz singer Annie Ross (Annabelle McCauley Allan Short, aka "Annabelle Logan") died of emphysema and heart disease

in New York City on July 21, aged 86. She made her film debut in 1937 in an *Our Gang* short and was also in Hammer's *Straight on Till Morning*, *Superman III*, *Witchery*, *Basket Case 2* and *Basket Case 3*. Ross dubbed Britt Ekland in *The Wicker Man*, Marlene Clark in *The Beast Must Die* and Sarah Douglas in *Superman* III, along with various voices in *Bluebeard* (1972). She also turned up in the 1978 children's TV series *The Ghosts of Motley Hall*.

D.J. Rowe

British SF fan D.J. Rowe, who used to run Michael Moorcock's first fan club, Nomads of the Time Streams: The International Michael Moorcock Appreciation Society, died on or around April 19, aged 83. With Maureen Davey, John Davey and Ian Covell, Rowe co-edited the society's newsletter *The Time Centre Times: A Publication of the Nomads of the Time Streams* from 1993-2011.

Joe Ruby

American writer and producer Joe Ruby (Joseph Clemens Ruby), who co-created *Scooby-Doo* with Ken Spears (who died in November), died on August 26, aged 87. He began his career as a writer and editor in the early 1960s at Hanna-Barbera, before also becoming a music editor on such TV shows as *Lost in Space* and *The Time Tunnel*. As a writer and story consultant, his credits include such cartoon series as *The Herculoids*, *Space Ghost*, *The Adventures of Gulliver*, *Scooby-Doo Where Are You!*, *The Funky*

Phantom, *Planet of the Apes* and *Captain Caveman and the Teen Angels* (again created by Ruby and Spears). With Spears he also co-created the live-action series *Electra Woman and Dyna Girl* (1976) and *Bigfoot and Wild Boy* (1977). Ruby executive-produced such cartoon shows as *Fangface and Fangpuss*, *The Plastic Man Comedy/Adventure Show*, *Thundarr the Barbarian*, *Centurions*, *Sectaurs* and *Skysurfer Strike Force*, and wrote and produced the 1995 horror movie *Rumpelstiltskin*. In the 1980s Ruby hired veteran comic book artist Jack Kirby to create hundred of characters for more than two dozen projects for Ruby-Spears Productions. The intellectual property rights to those characters, artwork and projects were offered for sale after Ruby's death by his family.

Osvaldo Ruggieri

Italian actor Osvaldo Ruggieri died on October 10, aged 92. He appeared in *Planets Around Us*, *Liliom* (1968) and *Werewolf Woman*.

Barbara Rütting

German actress and children's book author Barbara Rütting (Waltraut Irmgard Goltz), who co-starred in Bryan Edgar Wallace adaptations *The Phantom of Soho* (1964) and Jesús Franco's *Der Todesrächer von Soho* (1972), died on March 29, aged 92. Her other *krimis* credits include *The Squeaker* and *Again the Ringer*. She mostly retired from the screen in 1984 to become an environmental and animal welfare activist.

José Montalbán Saiz

José Montalbán Saiz, the last of the great Spanish movie-poster artists, died on October 25, aged 94. A self-taught painter, draftsman, animator and cartoonist, his career in film poster design began in the 1950s in the workshop of Francisco Fernández Zarza Jano (1922-92). Together with Macario Gómez Mac (1926-2018), Jano and Montalbán formed a triumvirate of Spanish cinema poster artists that lasted for many decades. Perhaps best remembered for his poster for *Pánico en*

Barbara Rütting (1927–2020) co-starred in Jesús Franco's krimis, Der Todesrächer von Soho (1972).

el transiberiano (aka *Horror Express*, 1972), he created numerous posters for such Spanish distributors as Procines, Bengala Films, Castilla Films and Pelimex.

Evelyn Sakash

American production designer Evelyn Sakash, whose credits include the 1995 TV mini-series of *The Langoliers*, based on the novel by Stephen King, died in October. However, her remains were not found until March 2021, when workers cleaning out her home in Queens, New York City, discovered Sakash's mummified body on the kitchen floor beneath piles of hoarded rubbish.

Richard Sala

American comics artist Richard Sala died on May 9, aged 61. He published his first comic, *Night Drive*, in 1984 at the age of 25, and contributed to Art Spiegelman's *RAW* anthology. Sala also worked in animation and horror-themed webcomics, including such titles as *The Hidden*, *The Bloody Cardinal*, *Violent Girls*, *Violenzia and Other Deadly Amusements*, *In a Glass Grotesquely*, *Peculia*, *Mad Night*, *The Chuckling Whatsit*, *The Grave Robber's Daughter* and *Hypnotic Tales*.

Robert Sampson

Spanish poster art by José Montalbán Saiz (1925–2020) for Horror Express *(1972).*

American supporting actor Robert [Leroy] Sampson died on January 18, aged 86. He appeared in *Fear No Evil*, Lucio Fulci's *City of the Living Dead*, *Re-Animator*, *Robot Jox*, *The Dark Side of the Moon*, *The Arrival*, *Netherworld* and the SF short *Take Out the Beast*. On TV, Sampson turned up in episodes of *One Step Beyond*, *The Twilight Zone* (Richard Matheson's 'Little Girl Lost'), *Thriller* (Robert Bloch's 'Man of Mystery'), *The Alfred Hitchcock Hour*, *The Outer Limits*, *Voyage to the Bottom of the Sea*, *Star Trek*, *The Immortal*, *Good Heavens*, *The Hardy Boys/Nancy Drew Mysteries*, *Wonder Woman*, *ABC Weekend Specials* ('The Ghost of Thomas Kempe', introduced by Vincent Price), *Knight Rider*, *The Powers of Matthew Star* and *Automan*.

Reni Santoni

American character actor Reni Santoni (Reni Sands) died of throat and lung cancer on August 1, aged 81. He played "Lt. Riva" on the 1983 TV series *Manimal*, and his other credits include the movie *Radioactive Dreams* and a two-part episode of *Quantum Leap*.

Charles R. Saunders

73-year-old African-American fantasy author Charles R. (Robert) Saunders died in Canada in early May, although his passing didn't become widely known until September. He had been suffering from diabetes. Best known for his pioneering 1981 novel *Imaro* – a "sword and soul" adventure that combined sword-and-sorcery with African history, culture and mythology – Saunders followed it with the sequels *The Quest for Cush*, *The Trail of Bohu* and *The Naama War*. His other books included *Dossouye* and the sequel *Dossouye: The Dancers of Mulukau*, *Damballa* and *Abengoni: First Calling*, while some of his short fiction was collected in *Nyumbani Tales*. Saunders also edited the anthologies *Griots: A Sword and Soul Anthology* and *Griots: Sisters of the Spear* (both with Milton J. Davis), along with issues of the magazines *Stardock* (1977-78) and *Dragonbane/Dragonfields* (1978-83, latterly with Charles de Lint). From 1989 he worked as a copyeditor and writer for *The Daily News* of Halifax, until that newspaper ceased publication in 2008. Saunders was initially buried in an unmarked grave by the office of the Public Trustee of Nova Scotia until a GoFundMe page raised enough money for a headstone and a memorial stone depicting his character Imaro.

Nancy Saunders

1940s American supporting actress Nancy Saunders (Nancy Lou Sanders), who doubled Rita Hayworth in *The Lady from Shanghai* and *The Loves of Carmen*, died of leukaemia on June 13, aged 94. She appeared in The Three Stooges' shorts *I'm a Monkey's Uncle* and *The Ghost Talks*, along with a couple of Columbia's "Whistler" mysteries (*The Secret of the Whistler* and *The Thirteenth Hour*). When her career began to falter in the early 1950s, Saunders became a tour-booking agent with Air Cal Airlines. She made a return to acting in the late 1990s, and appeared in an episode of TV's *American Gothic*.

John Saxon

Hollywood leading man John Saxon (Carmine Orrico) died of complications from pneumonia on July 25, aged 83. He made his movie debut in the mid-1950s and appeared in Mario Bava's *The Evil Eye*, *The Night Caller* (aka *Blood Beast from Outer Space*), Curtis Harrington's *Queen of Blood* (with Basil Rathbone), the Gene Roddenberry pilot *Planet Earth*, *Black Christmas* (1974), *Strange New World*, *The Bees* (1978, with John Carradine), *Beyond Evil*, Antonio Margheriti's *Cannibals in the Streets*, *Battle Beyond the Stars*, *Blood Beach*, Sergio Martino's *The Scorpion with Two Tales*, Dario Argento's *Tenebrae*, *Prisoners of the Lost Universe*, *A Nightmare on Elm Street* (1984), *Hands of Steel*, *A Nightmare on Elm Street 3: Dream Warriors*, *Death House* (which was also his only directing credit), *My Mom's a Werewolf*, *Nightmare Beach*, *Aftershock*, *Blood Salvage*, *The Arrival*, *Hellmaster*, Wes Craven's *New Nightmare*, *From Dusk Till Dawn* and *Lancelot: Guardian of Time*. On TV, Saxon guest-starred in numerous shows, including episodes of *The Time Tunnel*, *The Sixth Sense*, Rod Serling's *Night Gallery*, *Kung Fu* (1972), *The Six Million Dollar Man*, *The Bionic Woman*, *Starsky and Hutch* ('The Vampire'), *Wonder Woman*, *The Fantastic Journey*, *Fantasy Island*, *Alfred Hitchcock Presents* (Stanley Ellin's 'The Specialty of the House', 1987), *The Ray*

John Saxon (1936–2020) starred in the British film The Night Caller (*aka* Blood Beast from Outer Space, *1965*).

Bradbury Theater, *Monsters* and *Masters of Horror* (Dario Argento's version of F. Paul Wilson's 'Pelts').

Tony Scannell

Irish actor Tony Scannell (Thomas Anthony Scannell), best known for playing "Detective Sergeant Ted Roach" in the ITV series *The Bill* from 1984-2000, died on May 27, aged 74. He also appeared as Ming's Officer in the 1980 film *Flash Gordon* and starred in the gangster-horror movie *Evil Never Dies* (2014).

Joel Schumacher

American movie writer and director Joel Schumacher died of cancer on June 22, aged 80. He worked as a designer and store window dresser for one of New York's fashionable stores before getting into films as a costume designer in the early 1970s on such titles as Woody Allen's *Sleeper*. He was the production designer on the TV movie *Killer Bees* (1974), going on to direct such films as *The Incredible Shrinking Woman*, *The Lost Boys*,

Flatliners, the controversial sequels *Batman Forever* and *Batman & Robin*, *8mm*, *The Phantom of the Opera* (2004), *The Number 23* and *Blood Creek*. Schumacher also scripted *The Wiz* (1978).

Ronald L. Schwary

Oscar-winning Hollywood producer Ronald L. (Louis) Schwary, who worked on six movies with Sydney Pollack, died July 2, aged 76. He was forced to retire in 2015 after struggling with a rare neurological autonomic disorder. Schwary's credits include *Shadow of the Hawk*, **Batteries Not Included* and *Meet Joe Black*. He was also a unit production manager on the additional scenes for *Close Encounters of the Third Kind* and executive produced the TV series *Now and Again* (1999-2000) and *Medium* (2005-09), directing episodes of both.

Esther Scott

American character actress Esther Scott died of a heart attack on February 14, aged 66. She appeared in *Encino Man*, *Species*, *The Craft* (1996), *Austin Powers in Goldmember*, *Serial Killing 4 Dummies* and *Transformers*. Scott was also the voice of "Shodu" in the animated TV series Ewoks (1986), and she was also in episodes of *Brimstone* and *Extant*.

Jacqueline Scott

Dependable American leading lady Jacqueline [Sue] Scott died of lung cancer on July 23, aged 89. After appearing on Broadway with Paul Muni, she was brought to Hollywood by producer/director William Castle, who cast her as the nurse in *Macabre* (1958), the movie on which she met her future husband, screenwriter Gene Lesser. Scott's many other credits include Steven Spielberg's *Duel* and Bert I. Gordon's *Empire of the Ants*, along with episodes of TV's *Matinee*

Theatre ('It Came from Out of Town'), *The Twilight Zone*, *The Alfred Hitchcock Hour* (Leigh Brackett's adaptation of 'Terror at Northfield'), *The Outer Limits* ('The Galaxy Being'), *The Immortal*, *Planet of the Apes* and *Salvage 1*.

Carol Serling

Carol Serling (Carolyn Louise Kramer), the widow of Rod Serling, died on January 9, aged 90. Following her husband's premature death in 1975, she continued his legacy with *Twilight Zone: The Movie*, *Twilight Zone: Rod Serling's Lost Classics* and the 2019-2020 revival series *The Twilight Zone*. Serling also edited the anthologies *Journeys to the Twilight Zone*, *Return to the Twilight Zone*, *Adventures in the Twilight Zone*, *Twilight Zone: 19 Original*

Stories on the 50th Anniversary, *More Stories from the Twilight Zone* and *Rod Serling's Night Gallery Reader* (with Martin H. Greenberg and Charles G. Waugh), and she co-wrote the non-fiction volume *Rod Serling and The Twilight Zone: The 50th Anniversary Tribute* with Douglas Brode.

John Sessions

Scottish comedian, character actor and impersonator John Sessions (John Gibb Marshall) died of a heart attack on November 2, aged 67. He made his film debut in Roger Christian's *The Sender* (1982) and also appeared in *Whoops Apocalypse*, *The Adventures of Pinocchio* (1996), *A Midsummer Night's Dream* (1999), *Around the World in 80 Days* (1999), *Five Children and It* (2004) and *Mr. Holmes* (as "Mycroft Holmes"), along with episodes of TV's *Gormenghast*, *Murder Rooms: The Dark Beginnings of Sherlock Holmes* (Stephen Gallagher's 'The Kingdom of Bones'), *Randall & Hopkirk [Deceased]* (2001), *Sherlock*, *Moone Boy*, *Outlander*, *Jonathan Strange & Mr Norrell* and the animated series *Doctor Who: Death Comes to Time*.

Lynn Shelton

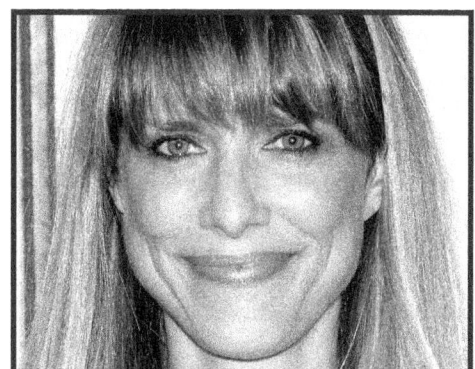

American indie director and actress Lynn Shelton died of a blood disorder on May 15, aged 54. She directed one episode each of the TV shows *The Good Place*, *Santa Clara Diet* and *Ghosted*.

Keith Short

British art department sculptor and modeller Keith Short died on September 11, aged 79. He worked on the films *Alien*, *Monty Python's Life of Brian*, *Saturn 3*, *Flash Gordon* (1980), *Raiders of the Lost Ark*, *The Dark Crystal*, *Return of the Jedi*, *Greystoke: The Legend of Tarzan*, *Indiana Jones and the Temple of Doom*, *Young Sherlock Holmes*, *Brazil*, *Highlander*, *Little Shop of Horrors* (1986),

The Princess Bride, *Willow*, *High Spirits*, *The Adventures of Baron Munchausen*, *Batman* (1989), *Judge Dredd* (1995), *Mortal Combat*, *The Wind in the Willows* (aka *Mr. Toad's Wild Ride*), *The Fifth Element*, *Star Wars Episode 1 – The Phantom Menace*, *The Mummy* (1999), *Sleepy Hollow* (1999), *The Mummy Returns*, *Harry Potter and the Prisoner of Azkaban*, *Hugo*, *Prometheus* and the James Bond films *GoldenEye*, *Die Another Day* and *Quantum of Solace*, along with the TV mini-series *The Odyssey*, *Gulliver's Travels* (1996), *Arabian Nights* (1999), *Jason and the Argonauts* (2000) and *Jack and the Beanstalk: The Real Story*. From 1989-91 Short was the supervising sculptor at Disneyland, Paris.

John Shrapnel

Velvet-voiced British stage and screen actor John [Morley] Shrapnel died of lung cancer on February 14, aged 77. His many credits include *How to Get Ahead in Advertising*, *Fatherland*, *101 Dalmatians* (1996), *Alien Autopsy*, *Mirrors* (2008), *The Awakening* (2011), *Macbeth* (2013) and *Hamlet* (2015). On TV, Shrapnel appeared in episodes of *Space: 1999*, *The Woman in White* (1982), *Invasion: Earth*, *Jonathan Creek* ('The Omega Man'), *The 10th Kingdom*, *Spine Chillers*, *Apparitions* and *Merlin* (2012).

Geno Silva

American character actor Geno Silva, best remembered as the silent assassin who kills Al Pacino's "Tony Montana" during the bloody climax of *Scarface* (1983), died on May 9, aged 72. For the past fifteen years he had been suffering from a form of dementia known as "frontotemporal degeneration". He also appeared in *My Mom's a Werewolf*, *The Lost World: Jurassic Park* and David Lynch's *Mulholland Dr./Mulholland Drive*, and on TV in episodes of *Fantasy Island*, *Monsters*, *The Sentinel* and *Star Trek: Enterprise*.

Fred Silverman

Independent American producer Fred Silverman who, while an executive at CBS, ABC and NBC controversially cancelled a number of popular shows

at each of the three major TV networks, died of cancer on January 30, aged 82. His credits include *Special Report: Journey to Mars* and such series as *Supertrain* (1979), *Father Dowling Mysteries* (1989–91, including 'The Mummy's Curse Mystery'), *Bone Chillers* (1996), *Diagnosis Murder* (1993–2001, including 'The Bela Lugosi Blues') and the "Perry Mason" TV movies (including *Perry Mason: The Case of the Sinister Spirit*). Reportedly, the character of "Fred 'Freddie' Jones" in *Scooby Doo, Where Are You!* (1969–70) was named after Silverman.

Lisa Simone

French-born actress Lisa Simone (Liliane Czajka) died in Rome, Italy, on May 2, aged 85. She was the nominal female lead in *The Giant Gila Monster* (1959) and played one of the "Moon Girls" in *Missile to the Moon* the year before. Simone retired from acting in the early 1960s.

Joe Sinnott

Legendary American comics artist "Joltin'" Joe Sinnott (Joseph Leonard Sinnott) died on June 25, aged 93. He joined Stan Lee at Atlas Comics in 1951, working on such titles as *Adventures Into Terror, Astonishing, Marvel Tales, Menace, Journey Into Mystery, Strange Tales* and *Uncanny Tales*. Sinnott would move between Atlas, Charlton Comics and various other companies before going to Marvel in 1965, where he forged a long partnership with Jack Kirby. Sinnott's inking work helped establish and define many of the company's biggest characters, including the Fantastic Four, Thor, Silver Surfer, Captain America, The Defenders and The Avengers through to the 1980s. He continued to work sporadically up

Susan Sizemore

New York Times best-selling paranormal romance writer Susan Sizemore died on July 20, aged 69. Best known for her "Children of the Rock", "Laws of the Blood", "Living Dead Girl" and "Primes" series, her other novels include the Golden Heart Award-winning *Wings of the Storm*, *In My Dreams*, *One of These Nights*, the TV tie-in *Forever Knight: A Stirring of Dust*, *Gates of Hell*, *Walking on the Moon* and *A Kind of Magic* and *Memory of Morning*. Sizemore's short fiction is collected in *Stardates: Infinite Celebrations* (with Julie D'Arcy and Jody Lynn Nye), *A Little Death* and *Dancing with the Star*. With Catherine Anderson and Christina Dodd she co-edited *Tall, Dark, and Dangerous*, and her other anthologies include *The Shadows of Christmas Past* (with Christine Feehan), *Moon Fever* (with Lori Handeland, Caridad Piñeiro and Maggie Shayne) and *First Blood* (with Meljean Brook, Chris Marie Green and Erin McCarthy).

Jan Skopecek

Veteran Czech actor Jan Skopecek died on July 27, aged 94. His credits include *Who Wants to Kill Jessie?*, *The Phantom of Morrisville*, *Záhada červeného pudru* (The Mystery of the Red Powder, as "Sherlock Holmes"), *Sen noci svatojánské* (Midsummer Night's Dream, 1973), *The Mysterious Castle in the Carpathians*, *Horror Story* and *The Rain Fairy*. Skopecek also appeared in episodes of the TV series *České pohádky* (Czech Fairy Tales), *The Visitors* and *Nexus 2.431*.

Guy N. Smith

Prolific British pulp horror novelist Guy N. (Newman) Smith died of complications from COVID-19 on December 24, aged 81. Best known for his cult series of "Killer Crabs" novels (*Night of the Crabs*, *Killer Crabs*, *The Origin of the Crabs*, *Crabs on the Rampage*, *Crabs' Moon*, *Crabs: The Human Sacrifice*, *Killer Crabs: The Return* and *The Charnel Caves*), Smith also wrote such books as *The Sucking Pit*, *The Ghoul*, *Night of the Werewolf*, *Bats Out of Hell*, *Locusts*, *Satan's Snowdrop*, *Manitou Doll*, *Entombed*, *Accursed*,

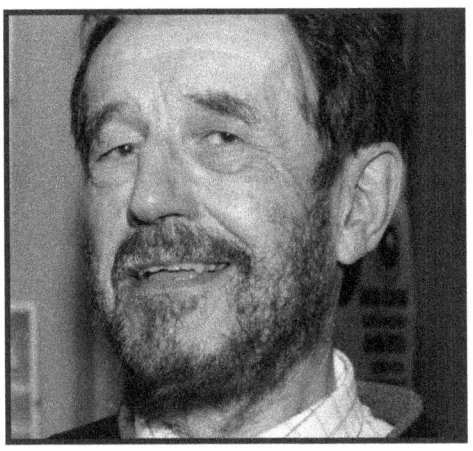

Cannibals, Abomination, Snakes, Alligators, Fiend, The Festering, Phobia, The Unseen, Carnivore, The Plague Chronicles and numerous other titles (in various genres), including the "Werewolf" trilogy and "Sabat" series. Under his Black Hill Books imprint, he self-published the 2014 collection Hangman's Hotel and Other Stories.

Lance Smith

American screenwriter and novelist Lance Smith died Alzheimer's disease in Hawaii on March 3, aged 59. He scripted Munchies, Wizards of the Lost Kingdom II (with Charles B. Griffith) and Barbarian Queen II: The Empress Strikes Back (with Howard R. Cohen).

Herbert F. Solow

Veteran American TV producer Herbert F. (Franklin) Solow died on November 19, aged 88. Best remembered as the executive in charge of production on the original *Star Trek* series (1966-68) as vice-president and head of Desilu Studios, his other credits include *The Girl from U.N.C.L.E.* and *Man from Atlantis*. Solow also adapted and produced the 1974 TV movie *Killdozer* (co-written by Theodore Sturgeon) and produced Dennis Potter's *Brimstone & Treacle* (1982) starring Sting. He wrote the books *Inside Star Trek: The Real Story* (1996) and *The Star Trek Sketchbook* (1997).

Phyllis Somerville

Night of the Crabs (*New English Library, 1976*) by
Guy N. Smith (1939–2020).

American actress and Broadway veteran Phyllis Somerville died on July 16, aged 76. She appeared in *Messengers*, *The Curious Case of Benjamin Button*, *Stoker* and *The Double*, along with episodes of TV's *Life on Mars*, *Fringe*, *Elementary*, *Daredevil* and *Castle Rock*.

Ken Spears

American TV producer and writer Ken

Spears (Charles Kenneth Spears), best known for co-creating *Scooby-Doo* with Joe Ruby (who died in August), died of complications from Lewy body dementia on November 6, aged 82. Spears' other credits include *Space Ghost*, *Fangface*, *Thundarr the Barbarian*, *Centurions* and many other animated shows, along with the live-action *Planet of the Apes* (1974) and *Bigfoot and Wildboy* (1977-79) series.

Norm Spencer

Canadian voice actor Norm (Norman) Spencer died on August 31, aged 62. He is best remembered for portraying "Cyclops"/"Scott Summers" in the animated TV series *X-Men: The*

Animated Series, *Spider-Man: The Animated Series* and various video game spin-offs. Spencer also had bit parts in the TV movie *Trilogy of Terror II* and episodes of *Forever Knight*, *Earth: Final Conflict* and *Relic Hunter*.

Jackie Stallone

American reality star and celebrity astrologer Jackie Stallone (Jacqueline Labofish), the mother of actors Sylvester and Frank Stallone and the first contestant to be voted off the UK's *Celebrity Big Brother* in 2001, died on September 21, aged 98. As "Jacqueline Stallone" she co-starred in David DeCoteau's 1993 SF-comedy *Beach Babes from Beyond*.

Sirry Steffen

Icelandic actress Sirry Steffen (Sigríður Geirsdóttir) died after a short illness on February 1, aged 81. The former Miss Iceland 1959 appeared in the low budget horror movie *The Crawling Hand* (1963).

Monica Stephens

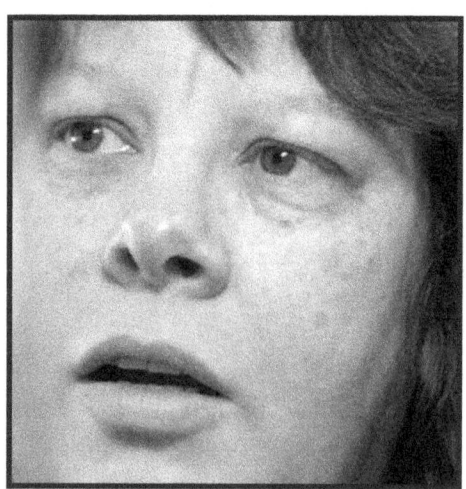

Monica Stephens, Steve Jackson's companion for more than thirty years and an employee of Steve Jackson Games for almost as long doing typography, editing, production and much more, died June 18 of congestive heart failure as a side effect of chemotherapy. She was 59.

Steve Stiles

Hugo Award-winning American fan and underground comix artist and cartoonist Steve Stiles (Stephen Willis Stiles) died of lung cancer on January 11, aged 76. He only announced his terminal diagnosis three days earlier. Stiles began publishing cartoons in the early 1960s, and amongst the many magazines and fanzines he contributed to are *Amra*, *Algol*, *Locus*, *Ansible*, *File 770* and *Xero*. With Richard A. Lupoff he created the graphic novel *The Adventures of Professor Thintwhistle and His Incredible Aether Flyer*, which was initially serialised in *Heavy Metal* in 1980 and published by Fantagraphics Books in 1991 with an Introduction by Neil Gaiman.

Jerry Stiller

American comedy actor Jerry Stiller (Gerald Isaac Stiller), the father of actors Ben and Amy Stiller, died on May 11, aged 92. A regular on *The Ed Sullivan Show* in the 1950s and '60s with his wife Anne Meara (who died in 2015), his credits include the movies *Highway to Hell* and *Secret of the Andes*, along with episodes of TV's *Time Express* (starring Vincent Price), *Tales*

from the Darkside (the George A. Romero-scripted 'The Devil's Advocate'), Monsters and Touched by an Angel.

Anton Strout

American urban fantasy author Anton Strout died on December 30, aged 50. A long-time sales manager for Penguin Random House, he published the "Simon Canderous" series (*Dead to Me*, *Deader Still*, *Dead Matter* and *Dead Waters*) and "The Spellmason Chronicles" (*Alchemystic*, *Stonecast* and *Incarnate*). Some of Stout's short fiction was published in the Martin H. Greenberg anthologies *Spells of the City*, *A Girl's Guide to Guns and Monsters*, *Boondocks Fantasy*, *Human for a Day* and

Westward Weird. He was also the host of the *Once and Future Podcast*, where he interviewed authors over more than 200 episodes.

Héctor Suárez

Mexican comedian and actor Héctor Suárez died on June 2, aged 81. In a career that spanned nearly six decades he appeared in many movies and TV series, including *Neutron Traps the Invisible Killers*, *Doña macabra* and *Mi fantasma y yo*.

Ann Sullivan

American animation ink-and-paint artist Ann Sullivan died of complications from COVID-19 at her

retirement community on April 13. She had turned 91 three days earlier. Sullivan began working in the animation paint laboratory at The Walt Disney Company in the early 1950s on such titles as *Peter Pan*. Following a stint at Filmation Hanna-Barbera during the 1970s and '80s, she returned to Disney, where she contributed to such movies as *The Little Mermaid*, *The Lion King* (1994), *The Hunchback of Notre Dame* (1996), *Hercules* (1997), *Fantasia 2000*, *Atlantis: The Lost Empire*, *Lilo & Stich*, *Treasure Planet* and the 1995 Mickey Mouse mad scientist short *Runaway Brain*. Her other credits include *Cool World* and *The Pagemaster*.

"Superhost"

American regional TV horror host Marty Sullivan, who appeared as "Superhost" on *Saturday Afternoon Mad Theater* (1969-87) on WUAB-TV, Channel 43 Cleveland, Ohio, died on February 21, aged 87. Sullivan, who was also a floor director and staff announcer for the station, recreated the character on *Supe's On!* (1969-88) and *Supe's on with the Three Stooges* (1988-89).

Carol Sutton

American character actress Carol Sutton (Carol Dickerson) died of complications from COVID-19 on December 11, aged 87. She made her acting debut in the late 1960s and her credits include *The Savage Bees*, *Mirrors*, *Candyman: Farewell to the Flesh*, *Eve's Bayou*, *Rag and Bone* (based on a story by Anne Rice), *The Dead Will Tell*, *Deja Vu*, *The Last Exorcism*, *This is the End*, *Dawn of the Planet of the Apes*, *Cold Moon* (based on a novel by Michael McDowell), *Abattoir*, *Camera Obscura* and *Gothic Harvest*. On TV, Sutton appeared in episodes of *American Horror Story: Coven*, *True Detective*, *Scream Queens*, *Scream: the TV Series* and *Lovecraft Country*.

Yûko Takeuchi

40-year-old actress Yûko Takeuchi, who had a recurring role in the ABC-TV series *Flashforward* (2009-10), was

found dead at her home in Tokyo on September 27. She was one of a number of Japanese actors to have taken their own lives in 2020. Takeuchi's credits include the original *Ringu* (1998), *Be with You*, *Kidan Piece of Darkness* and *Creepy*. She also starred as eccentric police consultant "Sara Shelly 'Sherlock' Futaba" in the Hulu TV series *Miss Sherlock* (2018).

Tony Tanner

British-born actor Tony Tanner, best known as the Tony Award-nominated director and choreographer of the 1982 Broadway production of Andrew Lloyd Webber's stage musical *Joseph and His Amazing Technicolor Dreamcoat*, died of cancer in Los Angeles on September 8, aged 88. He appeared as "Puck" alongside Benny Hill, Miles Malleson, Arthur Hewlett, Bernard Bresslaw and Alfie Bass in a 1964 ITV adaptation of A *Midsummer Night's Dream* and portrayed Burgess Meredith/"Penguin" in the TV movie *Back to the Batcave: The Misadventures of Adam and Burt* (2003).

Gianrico Tedeschi

Italian actor Gianrico Tedeschi, who starred as the titular mad scientist in *Frankenstein: Italian Style* (1975), died on July 27, aged 100. His other credits include *Dottor Jekyll e gentile signora*.

Marilyn J. Tenser

American movie producer Marilyn J. (Jacobs) Tenser died after a short illness in December, aged 89. The daughter of Crown International Pictures, Inc. founder Newton P. Jacobs, she was head of Marimark Productions, the in-house production arm of Crown International. Her credits include *Point of Terror*, *Galaxina* and *My Mom's a Werewolf*.

Dyanne Thorne

American actress Dyanne Thorne (Dorothy Ann Seib), who portrayed the sadistic death-camp warden "Ilsa" in the notorious exploitation trilogy *Ilsa: She Wolf of the SS* (1975), *Ilsa, Harem Keeper of the Oil Sheiks* (1976) and *Ilsa the Tigress of Siberia* (1977), died of pancreatic cancer on January 28, aged 83. She also played a similar role in Jesús Franco's *Greta the Wicked Warden*, while Thorne's other credits include *Pinocchio* (1971), *Point of Terror*, *Blood Sabbath*, *Wam Bam Thank You Spaceman*, *Hellhole*, *House of Forbidden Secrets*, *House of the Witchdoctor* and an episode of TV's *Star Trek* ('A Piece of the Action'). In later years, alongside her husband Howard Maurer, she served as a church-ordained, non-denominational minister in Las Vegas, Nevada.

Patrick Tilley

British SF author Patrick Tilley died after a short illness on May 25, aged 91. Best known for his "The Amtrak Wars"/"The Talisman Prophecies" post-holocaust sequence — *Cloud Warrior*, *First Family*, *Iron Master*, *Blood River*, *Death-Bringer* and *Earth-Thunder*, along with the associational volume *Dark Visions: An Illustrated Guide to the Amtrak Wars* (with Fernando Fernandez) — Tilly's other novels include *Fade-Out*, *Mission*, *Xan* and *Star Wartz: Tales of Adventure from the Rimworld*.

Ann E. Todd

Dyanne Thorne (1936–2020) starred as the iconic Ilsa: She Wolf of the SS (1975).

Former Hollywood child actress Ann E. Todd (Ann Todd Phillips) died of dementia on February 7, aged 88. She appeared (uncredited) as the "Princess" in Universal's *Tower of London* (1939), alongside Basil Rathbone, Boris Karloff and Vincent Price, and her other credits include a supporting role in *The Blue Bird* (1940) before she retired from the screen in the early 1950s

Christopher Tolkien

Christopher [John Reuel] Tolkien died in France on January 16, aged 95. The third son of author J.R.R. Tolkien, he drew the original maps for *The Lord of the Rings*. As literary executor, Tolkien also compiled and edited much of his father's posthumous work, including *The Silmarillion, Unfinished Tales*, the twelve-volume *The History of Middle-Earth* and *The Children of Húron*. His novel *The Saga of King Heidrek the Wise* was published in 1960, and he collected his father's translations of three epic narrative poems from the Middle-Ages in *Sir Gawain and the Green Knight, Pearl* and *Sir Orfeo*.

Nicholas Tucci

American actor Nicholas Tucci died of cancer on March 3, aged 38. He was in *You're Next, Chilling Visions: 5 Senses of Fear, The Ranger, Ten Minutes to Midnight* and *Father of Flies*, along with episodes of TV's *Daredevil* and *Channel Zero*.

Marshall B. Tymn

American academic and science fiction scholar Marshall B. (Benton) Tymn died of pneumonia on May 24, aged 82. A car accident in 1989 left him with traumatic brain injury. He won a Pilgrim Award for lifetime contributions from the Science Fiction Research Association in 1990, and his books include *A Directory of Science*

Fiction and Fantasy Publishing Houses and Book Dealers, *A Research Guide to Science Fiction Studies* (with L.W. Currey and Roger C. Schlobin), *Index to Stories in Thematic Anthologies of Science Fiction, Fantasy Literature* (with Robert H. Boyer and Kenneth J. Zahorski), *The Year's Scholarship in Science Fiction and Fantasy: 1972-1975* (with Roger C. Schlobin), *American Fantasy and Science Fiction: Toward a Bibliography of Works Published in the United States 1948-1973*, *A Teacher's Guide to Science Fiction, Horror Literature: A Core Collection and Reference Guide, The Science Fiction Reference Book, A Teacher's Guide to Fantastic Literature Revised Edition, The Year's Scholarship in Science Fiction and Fantasy: 1976-1979* (with Roger C. Schlobin), *The Year's Scholarship in Science Fiction Fantasy and Horror Literature: 1980, The Year's Scholarship in Science Fiction Fantasy and Horror Literature: 1981, Science Fiction Fantasy and Weird Fiction Magazines* (with Mike Ashley) and *The Year's Scholarship in Science Fiction Fantasy and Horror Literature: 1982*.

Albert Uderzo

French comics artist Albert [Aleandro] Uderzo, who created "Asterix the Gaul" with writer René Goscinny in 1959 for the new children's magazine *Pilote*, died in his sleep of a heart attack on March 24. He was 92. Asterix is one of the best-loved characters in French popular culture, with more than 370 million books sold worldwide, eleven films, and even an Asterix theme park. Uderzo retired in 2011, having sold the

rights to the character to Hachette Livre four years earlier. In 1985 he was awarded the Knight of the Legion of Honour, France's highest civil order of merit.

Shôzô Uehara

Japanese scriptwriter Shôzô Uehara died on January 2, aged 82. He worked on various *Ultraman* TV series, along with episodes of *Horror Theater Unbalance*, the Japanese *Spider Man* series (1978-79), *Kamen Rider Black* and numerous *anime* titles.

Manuel "Loco" Valdés

Mexican comedy legend Manuel "Loco" Valdés (Manuel Gómez Valdés Castillo), known for his bushy

eyebrows, died of cancer on August 28, aged 89. He began his movie career in the late 1940s and appeared in *Trip to the Moon* (1958), *Dos fantasmas y una muchacha*, *The Super He-Man*, *La caperucita roja*, *The Phantom of the Operetta* (1960, uncredited), *Caperucita y sus tres amigos*, *Locura de terror*, *Frankestein el vampiro y compañía*, *Caperucita y Pulgarcito contra los monstruos*, *Los fantasmas burlones* and *Las mujeres panteras*.

Dan van Husen

German-born supporting actor Dan van Husen died of complications from COVID-19 in Somerset, England, on May 31, aged 75. He appeared in numerous Euro Westerns and thrillers, along with *Der Todesrächer von soho*, Jesús Franco's *Night of the Skull* and *Killer Barbys vs. Dracula*, Werner Herzog's *Nosferatu the Vampyre* (1979), *Dracula Blows His Cool*, *Warum die UFOs unseren Salat klauen*, Johannes Roberts' *Darkhunters* and *Forest of the Damned*, *Chain Reaction* (aka *House of Blood*), *The Man Who Sold the World* and *Killing All the Flies*. Van Husen had a rare starring role in *Zombie Massacre 2: Reich of the Dead*.

Monique van Vooren

Belgium-born American actress Monique van Vooren (Monique Bronz) died of cancer on January 25, aged 92. A former champion skater and beauty queen, she appeared in *Tarzan and the She-Devil* (1953, as "Lyra, the She-Devil"), *Fearless Frank*, *Flesh for Frankenstein* (aka *Andy Warhol's Frankenstein*) and *Greystone Park*, along with a two-part episode of TV's *Batman* (1968). The actress also co-starred (as "Venus") in the flop Broadway musical fantasy *Man on the Moon*, which closed after just two days in 1975, despite

Manuel "Loco" Valdés (1931–2020) co-starred with his brother ("Tin-Tan", aka Germán Valdés) in Locura de terror (1961).

being produced by Andy Warhol. In 1983, a federal grand jury ordered Van Vooren to get psychiatric help and perform 500 hours of community service as part of a suspended sentence for stealing her dead mother's Social Security payments.

Max von Sydow

Swedish-born actor Max von Sydow (Carl Adolf von Sydow) died in France on March 8, aged 90. His early collaborations with director Ingmar Bergman – notably *The Seventh Seal* (1957) and *Hour of the Wolf* (1968) – made him an international star, and he went on to appear in *The Night Visitor*, *The Exorcist* and *Exorcist II: The Heretic* (both as "Father Merrin"), *Steppenwolf*, *The Ultimate Warrior*, *Death Watch*, *Flash Gordon* (as "Emperor Ming", 1980), *Conan the Barbarian* (1982), *Strange Brew*, the James Bond film *Never Say Never Again* (as "Blofeld"), *The Ice Pirates* (uncredited), *Dreamscape*, *Dune* (1984), *Until the End of the World*, Stephen King's *Needful Things*, *Citizen X*, *Judge Dredd* (1995), Richard Matheson's *What Dreams May Come*, *Minority Report*, *Night of the Living Dorks* (uncredited), *Sword of Xanten* (aka *Curse of the Ring*), *Solomon Kane*, *The Wolfman* (only in the director's cut), *Shutter Island* and *Star Wars Episode VII: The Force Awakens*. Von Sydow was also the voice of the evil "Vigo" in *Ghostbusters II* and the 2009 video game *Ghostbusters*. On TV, he played Sigmund Freud in an episode of *The Young Indiana Jones Chronicles* and turned up as the "Three-Eyed Raven" in the sixth season of HBO's *Game of Thrones*.

Philip Voss

British character actor Philip [James] Voss died of complications from COVID-19 on November 13, aged 84. He had been suffering with cancer. Although probably better known as a stage actor, Voss appeared in Hammer's *Frankenstein and the Monster from Hell*, the James Bond film *Octopussy*, and *About Time*, along with episodes of TV's *Out of the Unknown* (William Tenn's 'Time in Advance'), *Doctor Who* and *Dinotopia*. He was also the voice of "Lord of the Nazgûl" in BBC Radio's epic adaptation of *The Lord of the Rings*.

Lyle Waggoner

American leading man Lyle [Wesley] Waggoner, who portrayed "Major Steve Trevor" and his son, "Steve Trevor, Jr." on the ABC and CBS *Wonder Woman* TV series (1975-79), died of cancer on March 17, aged 84. His movie credits include *Journey to the Center of Time*, *Love Me Deadly*, *Dream a Little Evil* and *Wizards of the Demon Sword*. On TV he appeared in episodes of *Lost in Space*, *Supertrain*, *Time Express* (with Vincent Price), *Mork & Mindy* and *Fantasy Island*. Wagner tested for the title role in the 1960s *Batman* TV series, but lost out to Adam West. In 1979 he founded Star Waggons, Inc., the largest supplier of location rental trailers in the entertainment business.

Kent L. Wakeford

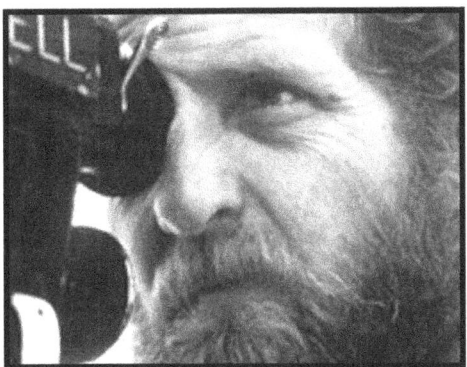

American fashion photographer turned cinematographer Kent L. Wakeford died on October 10, aged 92. Although perhaps best known for Martin Scorsese's *Mean Streets* (1973), Wakeford was also director of photography on *Doctor Death: Seeker of Souls*, *Ghost Brigade* (aka *Grey Knight*), *Last Lives* and *Halfway Home*.

Lee Wallace

American character actor Lee Wallace (Leo Melis), who played the Mayor of Gotham City in Tim Burton's *Batman* (1989), died on December 20, aged 90. He was also in the 1982 TV mini-series *World War III*.

Ron Weighell

British supernatural author Ron Weighell died on Christmas Eve, aged 70. He had suffered a major stroke in November and never recovered. Weighell's stories first started appearing in the late 1980s in such small press magazines as *Ghosts & Scholars*, *Nocturne*, *Dark Dreams* and *All Hallows*, and he had stories reprinted in Karl Edward Wagner's *The Year's Best Horror Stories: XX* and Stephen Jones' *Best New Horror #26* and *#27*.

His short fiction is collected in *The White Road: The Collected Supernatural Stories of Ron Weighell* (Ghost Story Press), *Tarshishim*, *Summonings*, *The Irregular Casebook of Sherlock Holmes* and the chapbook *The Greater Arcana*. Weighell also contributed novellas to Sarob Press' *Pagan Triptych* and *Romances of the White Day*, along with John Howard and Mark Valentine.

Dawn Wells

American actress Dawn [Elberta] Wells, who portrayed castaway "Mary Ann Summers" in the CBS-TV sitcom *Gilligan's Island* (1964–67) and spin-off movies, died of complications from COVID-19 on December 30, aged 82. She also appeared in *The Town That Dreaded Sunset* (1976), *Return to Boggy Creek*, *Soulmates*, *Silent But Deadly* and episodes of *The Invaders*, *The Wild Wild West*, *Fantasy Island*, *ALF* and *Meego*. In 2003 Wells co-executive produced the TV movie *Return to the Batcave: The Misadventures of Adam and Burt*.

Tim White

British artist Tim White (Timothy Thomas Anthony White), perhaps best known for his covers on the three volumes of *The H.P. Lovecraft Omnibus* from Grafton in 1985, died after a long illness on April 5, the day after his 68th birthday. From the mid-1970s until the late 1990s, White was a prolific artist, turning out numerous fantasy, science fiction and horror covers for such books as *The Fog* by James Herbert, *'Salem's Lot* by Stephen King, *A Scent of New-Mown Hay* by John Blackburn, *Croc* by David James, *Gather Darkness!* by Fritz Leiber, *Weaveworld* by Clive Barker, *The Mask*

of Cthulhu and The Trail of Cthulhu by August Derleth, and many other titles. His artwork was collected in *The Science Fiction and Fantasy World of Tim White* (1981), *Chiaroscuro* (1988), *TW* (1994) and *Mirror of Dreams* (1994).

Stuart Whitman

American leading man Stuart [Maxwell] Whitman, who played the doomed Sam in the "Humgoo" episode of *The Monster Club* (1981), died of skin cancer on March 16, aged 92. He made his uncredited screen debut in 1951 in *When Worlds Collide*, and his other movies include *Shock Treatment* (1964), *City Beneath the Sea*, *Night of the Lepus*, Robert Bloch's *The Cat Creature*, *Welcome to Arrow Beach*, *Eaten Alive* (1976), *The White Buffalo*, *Ruby*, *Demonoid*, *Horror Safari* (aka *Invaders of the Lost Gold*), *Vultures*, *Deadly Intruder*, *Deadly Reactor*, *Omega Cop* and *Sandman*, along with episodes of TV's *The Adventures of Fu Manchu*, *Cimarron Strip* (Harlan Ellison's Jack the Ripper episode 'Knife in the Darkness'), *Circle of Fear*, Rod Serling's *Night Gallery*, *Tales of the Unexpected*, *Knight Rider*, *Fantasy Island*, *Tales from the Darkside*, *Superboy* (as "Jonathan Kent"), *Time Trax* and *The Adventures of Brisco County Jr.*

David Whorf

American child actor turned first assistant director David Whorf died on January 5, aged 85. The son of Hollywood character actor Richard Whorf, he made his movie debut in 1948 and appeared in episodes of TV's *One Step Beyond* and *Thriller* (Robert E. Howard's 'Pigeons from Hell' and Hugh Walpole's 'Flowers of Evil'). Whorf also worked as a first assistant director on *Island Claws*, *Firestarter* (1984), *The Heavenly Kid*, the pilot for *The Immortal*, and such TV shows as *Batman* (1966–68) and *Land of the Giants*.

Fred Willard

American actor Fred Willard died on May 15, aged 85. Best known for his light comedy roles, he appeared in *Space Force*, *Salem's Lot* (1979), *The Perfect Woman*, *Prehysteria! 3*, *Idle Hands*,

Austin Powers: The Spy Who Shagged Me, I'll Believe in You, Re-Animated, My Future Boyfriend and 12 Wishes of Christmas, along with episodes of TV's Get Smart, Tabitha, Out of this World, My Secret Identity, Harry and the Hendersons, Lois & Clark: The New Adventures of Superman, Sabrina the Teenage Witch, Good vs Evil, Stargate SG-1, Pushing Daises and Wizards of Waverly Place. Willard also did voice work for many cartoons and animated movies, including Monster House, Disney/Pixar's Wall-E, and Scooby-Doo! Legend of the Phantosaur.

Logan Williams

Canadian TV actor Logan [Karl] Williams, best known for portraying the young Barry Allen in The CW's The Flash, died of a fentanyl overdose on March 2, aged 16. Williams, who had battled opioid addiction for three years, also appeared in episodes of The Whisperers and Supernatural.

Mark S. Williams

American author Mark S. Williams, who co-wrote the 2014 tie-in novel Transformers: Retribution (with David J. Williams) died on September 3, aged 48. With Williams he also contributed back-up stories to Chuck Wendig's Star Wars: Aftermath: Life Debt and Star Wars: Aftermath: Empire's End.

Barbara Ker Wilson

British-born author and children's publisher Barbara Ker Wilson died in Australia on September 10, aged 90. Her short fiction was collected in Scottish Folk-Tales and Legends (aka Stories from Scotland, 1954) and Tales Told to Kabbarli: Aboriginal Legends (with Daisy Bates, 1972), and she edited the 1976 paperback anthology A Handful of Ghosts. While working as a children's

book editor at Collins in the 1950s, she read a manuscript submitted by television cameraman Michael Bond and recommended that the publisher take it. Collins took Wilson's advice, and *A Bear Called Paddington* was published in 1958. Wilson was asked in 1985 to create a young adult fiction list for the University of Queensland Press – the first in Australia – and in 2004 she was made a Member of the Order of Australia.

Barbara Windsor

British character actress and comedy legend Dame Barbara Windsor (Barbara-Ann Deeks) died of Alzheimer's disease on December 10, aged 83. She made her film debut as an uncredited schoolgirl in *The Belles of St. Trinian's* (1954), but is best known for her association with the *Carry On* series, beginning with the sci-spy entry *Carry on Spying* in 1964. She appeared with Christopher Lee in the crime film *Too Hot to Handle* (aka *Playgirl After Dark*), and her other credits include the Sherlock Holmes vs. Jack the Ripper thriller *A Study in Terror* (as victim "Annie Chapman"), *Chitty Chitty Bang Bang*, the Pet Shop Boys' *It Couldn't Happen Here*, *Pussy in Boots* and Tim Burton's *Alice in Wonderland* (2010). On TV, Windsor portrayed pub landlady "Peggy Mitchell" in more than 1,500 episodes of the BBC's soap opera *Eastenders*, a role she recreated in a 2006 episode of *Doctor Who* ('Army of Ghosts'). She was also in the special *Carry on Christmas* (1969), and episodes of *Worzel Gummidge* (1980, as "Saucy Nancy") and *Super Gran*.

Frank Windsor

British actor Frank Windsor (Frank W. Higgins) – best known for starring as Detective Sergeant (later Detective Chief Superintendent) "John Watt" in the BBC police procedural *Z Cars* (1962-65), spin-off shows *Softly Softly* (1966-69), *Softly Softly: Task Force* (1969-76) and *Second Verdict* (1976) and, perhaps most oddly, the 1973 docu-drama series *Jack the Ripper* – died on October 2, aged 92. Windsor's other credits include *Barry McKenzie Holds His Own* and episodes of TV's *A for Andromeda*, *The Avengers*, the pilot for *Randall and Hopkirk (Deceased)*, *Into the Labyrinth* and *Doctor Who* ('The

Barbara Windsor (1937–2020) ended up as a victim of Jack the Ripper in
A Study in Terror (1965).

King's Demons' and 'Ghost Light'). In 1991, he also appeared in a touring stage production of Susan Hill's *The Woman in Black*.

Mel Winkler

American character actor Mel Winkler (Melvin R. Winkler) died on June 11, aged 78. He not only played "Inspector Bill Henderson" in the pilot for *Lois & Clark: The New Adventures of Superman* (1993) but also voiced the character (now "Commissioner") on *Superman: The Animated Series* three years later. Winkler's other credits include R.C. Matheson's *Full Eclipse*, *Maniacts*, and episodes of TV's *Star Trek: Voyager*, *Touched by an Angel*, *Babylon 5*, *Brimstone* and *The Invisible Man* (2001). He also did voice work for *The New Batman Adventures* and *Oswald*.

Jimmy Winston

British musician and actor Jimmy Winston (James Edward Winston Langwith) died on September 26, aged 75. The original keyboard player of the iconic 1960s band Small Faces, before he was replaced by Ian McLagan, Winston appeared in small roles in *No Blade of Grass* and Roddy McDowall's *The Ballad of Tam Lin* (aka *Tam Lim*), along with episodes of TV's *UFO* and *Doctor Who* ('Day of the Daleks').

David Wise

American TV writer and story editor David Wise died of lung cancer on March 3, aged 65. He worked on such cartoon series as *Star Trek: The Animated Series*, *The Space Sentinels*, *Tarzan Lord of the Jungle*, *Godzilla*, *He-Man and the Masters of the Universe*, *The Mighty Orbots*, *Defenders of the Earth*, *The Transformers*, *James Bond Jr.*,

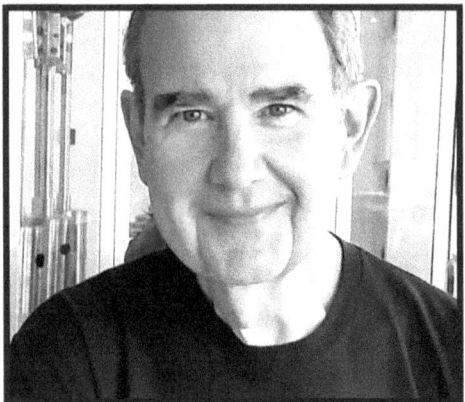

Batman: The Animated Series, Cadillacs and Dinosaurs, Speed Racer, Conan and the Young Warriors and *Teenage Mutant Ninja Turtles*, along with episodes of the live-action shows *The Secrets of Isis*, *Wonder Woman* and *Buck Rogers in the 25th Century* ('Space Vampire'). Wise also wrote and co-produced *Beastmaster III: The Eye of Braxus* (1996).

Charles Wood

Guernsey-born playwright and scriptwriter Charles [Gerald] Wood died in England on February 1, aged 87. He co-wrote The Beatles' *Help!* (1965) and adapted *The Bed Sitting Room* (1969), both for director Richard Lester.

Arthur Wooster

British second-unit cinematographer and assistant director Arthur Wooster died on September 1, aged 91. He worked as a second unit cinematographer on *Warlords of Atlantis* and *Arabian Adventure*, before combining the role with assistant director for the James Bond films *For Your Eyes Only*, *Octopussy* and *A View to a Kill*, plus *Highlander II: The Quickening*, *Split Second* (1992), *The Avengers* (1998), *Ravenous*, *Back to the Secret Garden*, *From Hell* and the TV mini-series *The Odyssey* and *Merlin* (1998). Wooster also contributed additional photography to *The Haunting of Helen Walker* (based on *The Turn of the Screw* by Henry James) and he shot and directed the opening sequence of *Snow White: A Tale of Terror*.

Ned Wynn

American bit-actor Ned Wynn (Edmond Keenan Wynn), the elder son of veteran character actor Keenan Wynn and the stepson of actor Van Johnson, died of Parkinson's disease on December 20, aged 79. He appeared in Disney's *The Absent Minded Professor* (1961) and *Son of Flubber*, along with several entries in AIP's "Beach Party" series (*Bikini Beach*, *Pajama Party*, *Beach Blanket Bingo* and *How to Stuff a Wild Bikini*). Wynn also scripted the 1982 TV horror movie, *Don't Go to Sleep*.

Merritt Yohnka

American stuntman Merritt Yohnka, who was the stunt co-ordinator for TV's *Lucifer* (2017-19), died of cancer on September 16, aged 62. His other credits include the movies *House II*, John Carpenter's *They Live*, *Wizards of the Lost Kingdom II*, *Time Trackers*, *Transylvania Twist* (1989), *Monster High*, *Leatherface: The Texas Chainsaw Massacre III*, Adam Simon's *Brain Dead*, *Peacemaker*, *Street Asylum*, *Maniac Cop 2*, *Slumber Party Massacre III*, *Syngenor*, *The Guyver*, *Future Kick*, John

Landis' *Innocent Blood*, *The Fantastic Four* (1994 and 2005 versions), *Tank Girl*, *Temptress*, *Mighty Morphin Power Rangers: The Movie*, *It Came from Outer Space II*, *Night Hunter*, *The Silencers* (1996), *Carnosaur 3: Primal Species*, *Mars*, *The Sender*, *Inspector Gadget*, *Contagion* (2002), *Storm Watch*, *Minority Report*, *Hulk*, *The League of Extraordinary Gentlemen*, *The Island*, Rob Zombie's *The Devil's Rejects*, *The Creature of the Sunny Side Up Trailer Park*, *Transformers* (2007), *Legion*, *A Nightmare on Elm Street* (2010), *Captain America: The First Avenger*, *Beneath* and *Earth to Echo*, along with episodes of TV's *Lost* and *True Blood*.

Carlos Ruiz Zafón

Spanish YA author Carlos Ruiz Zafón died of colon cancer in Los Angeles on June 19, aged 55. He made his debut in 1993 with his novel *The Prince of the Mist*, but it was his 2001 fantasy *The Shadow of the Wind* — the first in the "Cemetery of Lost Books" series — that made him an international best-seller ("*Shadow* is the real deal, a novel full of

cheesy splendour and creaking trapdoors, a novel where even the sub-plots have sub-plots," said Stephen King). Zafón followed it with the sequels *The Angel's Game*, *The Prisoner of Heaven* and *The Labyrinth of Spirits*, while his other books include *The Midnight Place*, *The Watcher in the Shadows* and *Marina*. His books sold more than 38 million copies worldwide, were translated into over forty languages, and won multiple awards.

Nazzareno Zamperla

Italian stuntman and bit-actor Nazzareno Zamperla (aka "Nino Zamperia") died on March 19, aged 82. Born into a circus family, he performed uncredited stunts in *Ulysses* (1954), *Hercules* (1958), *Hercules Unchained*, *Hercules and the Captive Women* and other "peplums", before becoming the stunt co-ordinator on such films as *Samson and the Slave Queen*, *When Women Had Tails*, *Treasure of the Four Crowns*, *Tex and the Lord of the Deep*, *Demons 2*, *Night of the Sharks*, *The Spider Labyrinth*, *Cyber Eden*, *Cemetery Man* and Antonio Margheriti's 1987 TV mini-series *Treasure Island in Outer Space*.

Jerry Zeitman

American film and TV producer Jerry Zeitman (Jerome M. Zeitman) died on September 17, aged 90. The former talent agent's credits include *Damnation Alley* (based on the novel by Roger Zelazny), Curtis Harrington's *Devil Dog: The Hound of Hell* and the 1973–74 TV series *The Starlost* (created by Harlan Ellison). As an agent, his clients included Shirley MacLaine, Fred Astaire, Frank Sinatra, Gene Kelly, Tony Curtis, Carol Channing, Rod Serling, Ron Howard, Kristy McNichol, Jerry Lewis and George Burns and Gracie Allen.

An uncredited Nazzareno Zamperla (1937–2020) had a fight scene in the Italian peplum, Hercules and the Captive Women (*aka* Hercules Conquers Atlantis).

Terri Zimmern

Macau-born Terri Zimmern (Therese Zimmern Silva), whose only screen credit is as "Tara", the assistant of the mad scientist, in the 1959/1962 Japanese-American horror movie *The Manster* (aka *The Split*), died on April 13, aged 89. Zimmern was married to the film's co-director, Kenneth G. Crane (who died in 1995).

The Manster (aka The Split, *1959/1962) was the only screen credit for Terri Zimmern (1930–2020).*

Index by Date

January

2 Shôzô Uehara
3 Derek Acorah
   Robert Blanche
4 Jerome Guardino
5 Gerry Lewis
   David Whorf
7 Silvio Horta
8 Edd Byrnes
   Buck Henry
9 Ivan Passer
   Mike Resnick
   Carol Serling
10 Charles Alverson
   Brice Armstrong
   Neda Arnerić
   Alex Beaton
   Michael Greene
   Patrick Jordan
11 Stan Kirsch
   Norma Michaels
   Steve Stiles
12 William Bogert
14 George Dugdale
   Jack Kehoe
15 Brian Nickels
16 Gillian Martell
   Alan Pattillo
   Christopher Tolkien
17 Derek Fowlds
18 Robert Sampson
21 Terry Jones
22 John Karlen
23 Robert Harper
   Barbara Remington
25 Alan Harris
   Monique van Vooren
27 Dick Balduzzi
   Jack Burns
28 Marj Dusay
   Nicholas Parsons
   Dyanne Thorne
30 Chanin Hale
   Fred Silverman
31 Mary Higgins Clark
   Andree Melly

February

1 Steven Cagan
   Sirry Steffen
   Charles Wood
2 Lovelady Powell
3 John Grant
   Douglas Knapp
   Gene Reynolds
4 Terry Hands
5 Kevin Conway
   Kirk Douglas
   Sandy Holt
6 Raphaël Coleman

7	Orson Bean	2	Logan Williams
	Ann E. Todd	3	Roscoe Born
8	Robert Conrad		James Otis
	Victor Gorelick		Lance Smith
	Paula Kelly		Nicholas Tucci
10	Marge Redmond		David Wise
11	Ron Haddrick	4	Frank McLaughlin
	Charles Lanyer	6	Marvin Mondlin
	"Ronald"	7	Rebecca Ramsey
12	Cheryl Wheeler Duncan	8	Max von Sydow
13	Rafael R. Marchent	9	Gary B. Kibbe
14	Esther Scott	15	Roy Hudd
	John Shrapnel	16	Stuart Whitman
16	Frances Cuka	17	Lyle Waggoner
	Kellye Nakahara	19	Nazzareno Zamperla
19	Robert Cobert	23	Lucia Bosè
20	Claudette Nevins		David Collings
	Elyse Rosenstein	24	Melinda Fee
21	Nick Cuti		Stuart Gordon
	Hisashi Katsuda		Albert Uderzo
	"Superhost"	25	Detto Mariano
24	Baby Peggy	28	John Callahan
	Ben Cooper	29	Krzysztof Penderecki
	Clive Cussler		Barbara Rütting
25	Nikki Fritz	30	Thomas Gianni
	Graydon Gould	31	Julie Bennett
26	Michael Medwin		Brian Blume
27	Thomas "Doc" Boguski		Andrew Jack
	R.D. Call		Vincent Marezello
28	Joyce Gordon		
29	Earl Kemp		
	Dieter Laser		

March

1 Robert Lesser

April

1 Hy Fleishman
2 Juan Giménez
3 Dorothy Dells
  Hilary Dwyer

4	Jay Benedict	18	Kaye Dowd
	Forrest Compton	19	Hector Garrido
	Dale Crain		D.J. Rowe
	Hans Meyer	21	Matteo De Cosmo
5	Shirley Douglas		Dimitri Diatchenko
	Lee Fierro		Joel Rogosin
	Thomas L. Miller	22	Mort Fallick
	Jerrold Mundis		Samantha Fox
	George Ogilvie		Shirley Knight
	Tim White	23	Bruce Allpress
6	Honor Blackman	24	Rob Gibbs
	James Drury		Eizo Kaimai
7	Merv Binns		Joseph S. Pulver, Sr.
	Allen Garfield	25	Helen McCabe
9	Malcolm Dixon	26	Aarón Hernán
	Mort Drucker		Peter H. Hunt
10	Nobuhiko Ôbayashi	27	Cis Corman
11	Keith Ferrell		Gene Dynarski
	Margot Hartman	28	Jill Gascoine
12	Tim Brooke-Taylor	29	Irrfan Khan
	Pat Brymer		John Lafia
	Danny Goldman	30	Wally K. Daly
	Joel M. Reed		Michael P. Keenan
13	Ann Sullivan		
	Terri Zimmern		**May**
14	Pip Baker		Charles R. Saunders
	Mario Donatone	1	Silvia Legrand
15	Sean Arnold		Sam Lloyd
	Allen Daviau	2	Lisa Simone
	Brian Dennehy	3	John Ericson
	Bruce Myers		Francis Megahy
16	Joseph Adler	6	Leslie A. Pope
	Gene Deitch	9	Arthur Dignam
	Andrew J. Fenady		Little Richard
17	Sergio Fantoni		Richard Sala

	Geno Silva
10	Martin Pasko
11	Jerry Stiller
12	Frank W. Bolle
	George Mikell
	Michel Piccoli
13	Gregory Tyree Boyce
15	Phil May
	Lynn Shelton
	Fred Willard
16	Pilar Pellicer
17	Monique Mercure
18	John Mahon
20	Charles M. Lippincott
22	Heather Chasen
	Denise Cronenberg
24	Marshall B. Tymn
25	Wu Pong-fong
	Patrick Tilley
26	Cindy Butler
	Richard Herd
	Anthony James
27	Peggy Pope
	Tony Scannell
28	Lennie Niehaus
	Suzanne Roquette
29	Mark Glamack
30	Michael Angelis
31	Dan van Husen

June

1	Dr. Colin Manlove
2	Mary Pat Gleason
	Héctor Suárez
3	Bruce Jay Friedman
8	Fabrizio Mioni
10	William Hale
	Anita Linda
11	Denny O'Neil
	Mel Winkler
13	Nancy Saunders
16	John Benfield
18	Harry Clein
	James Henerson
	Monica Stephens
19	Ian Holm
	Carlos Ruiz Zafón
20	Philip Latham
21	Dean Ing
22	Steve Bing
	Joel Schumacher
23	Harry Basch
	Charly Bravo
	Wendy Cooling
24	Michael O'Hear
25	Joe Sinnott
26	Kelly Asbury
	Stuart Cornfeld
	Milton Glaser
	Taryn Power
	Ramon Revilla
27	Linda Cristal
	Julian Curry
28	Jim Holloway
29	Johnny Mandel
	Carl Reiner
30	Danny Hicks
	Louis Mahoney
	Henry Martin

July

	Richard Bright
1	Kurt Mitchell
	Jean-Pierre Moumon
2	Ronald L. Schwary
3	Earl Cameron
5	Nick Cordero
	Terence Greer
6	Ennio Morricone
7	Ted Newsom
8	Naya Rivera
9	Gary William Crawford
10	Paul Hammond
11	James Keast
12	Raymundo Capetillo
	Kelly Preston
13	Carl Gafford
	Grant Imahara
14	Galyn Görg
15	Maurice Roëves
16	Phyllis Somerville
17	Lewis John Carlino
18	Moonyeenn Lee
	Haruma Miura
19	Jason Scott Campbell
	Sonia Darrin
20	Elisa Cabrera
	Robert Martin
	Susan Sizemore
21	Annie Ross
23	Brian N. Ball
	Ronald Bergan
	Jacqueline Scott
24	Regis Philbin
25	Olivia de Havilland
	John Saxon
26	Alison Fiske
27	Becky Mullen
	Jan Skopecek
	Gianrico Tedeschi
29	André Ptaszynski
31	Alan Parker

August

1	Wilford Brimley
	Susan Ellison
	Tom Pollock
	Reni Santoni
3	Billy Goldenberg
4	Brent Carver
	Daisy Coleman
7	Nando Angelini
	Bob March
10	Raymond Allen
	P.M. Griffin
13	Giancarlo Ferrando
15	Ulf Ôtsuki
16	Paul Knight
18	Ben Cross
22	John Bangsund
	Allan Rich
23	Leslie Hamilton Gearren
	Lori Nelson
25	Rolf Gohs
26	Joe Ruby
27	"Morgus"
28	Chadwick Boseman
	David S. Cass
	Shirô Kishibe
	Manuel "Loco" Valdés

30	Ann Lynn	29	Robert Eighteen-Bisang
31	Norm Spencer		Helen Reddy

September

	Martin McKenna		Janet Freer
1	Jim Janes		Evelyn Sakash
	Sue Nicols	2	Edward S. Feldman
	Arthur Wooster		Frank Windsor
5	Jiří Menzel	4	Armelia McQueen
6	Vasilis Dimitriou		Clark Middleton
	Bob Fujitani	5	Chris Carnel
7	Kevin Dobson		Margaret Nolan
8	Ronald Harwood	6	Tommy Rall
	Tony Tanner	10	Osvaldo Ruggieri
9	Stevie Lee		Kent L. Wakeford
10	Diana Rigg	11	Ronald Forfar
	Barbara Ker Wilson	12	Conchata Ferrell
12	Barbara Jefford		Gerald Gardner
	Ernie Orsatti	14	Rhonda Fleming
11	Keith Short		David Geiser
14	Sei Ashina	15	Ed Benguiat
	Al Kasha		Tom Maschler
16	Merritt Yohnka	18	Dana Baratta
17	Terry Goodkind		Richard De Croce
	Penny McCarthy	19	Gianni Dei
	Jerry Zeitman	20	James Randi
20	Michael Chapman	21	Marge Champion
21	Ron Cobb		Dee Hartford
	Michael Lonsdale		Pamela Kosh
	Jackie Stallone	22	William Blinn
22	Xavier Loyá		Arv Greywal
23	Juliette Gréco	23	Len Lakofka
26	Jimmy Winston		Richard A. Lupoff
27	Kevin Burns	25	Johnny Leeze
	Yûko Takeuchi		José Montalbán Saiz

October

31	Sean Connery		Dave Prowse
	Debra Doyle	29	Ben Bova

November

1 Rachel Caine
  Charles Gordon
  Eddie Hassell
  Joe Kane
2 John Sessions
3 Elsa Raven
4 Johnny Kevorkian
6 Ken Jones
  Geoffrey Palmer
  Ken Spears
7 John Fraser
8 Kay McCauley
9 Joseph Altairac
12 Michael Z. Hobson
13 Janet Ann Gallow
   Philip Voss
14 M.A. Foster
16 David Hemblen
17 Jael
18 Marguerite Ray
19 Kirby Morrow
   Hayford Pierce
   Herbert F. Solow
21 Dena Dietrich
   Robert Garland
   Jery Hewitt
   Malcolm Marmorstein
23 Abby Dalton
25 Chuck Bail
26 Daria Nicolodi
28 Basil Moss

December

  Marilyn J. Tenser
1 Hugh Keays-Byrne
2 Warren Berlinger
  Richard Corben
  Rafer Johnson
  David Larkin
3 Alison Lurie
4 Cliff Green
  David Lander
7 Phyllis Eisenstein
  Walter Hooper
10 Tommy "Tiny" Lister
   Barbara Windsor
11 Carol Sutton
12 David Galanter
13 Tsugunobu Kotani
   Philip Martin
15 Parnell Hall
16 Jeremy Newson
17 David Ashford
   Jeremy Bulloch
   Doug Crane
18 Peter Lamont
19 David Giler
   Rosalind Knight
20 Lee Wallace
   Ned Wynn
23 James E. Gunn
   Rebecca Luker
24 Guy N. Smith
   Ron Weighell

27	William Link		Anton Strout
29	Claude Bolling		Dawn Wells
	David Britton	31	Robert Hossein
	Pierre Cardin		G. Howard Klar
30	Mike Fenton		

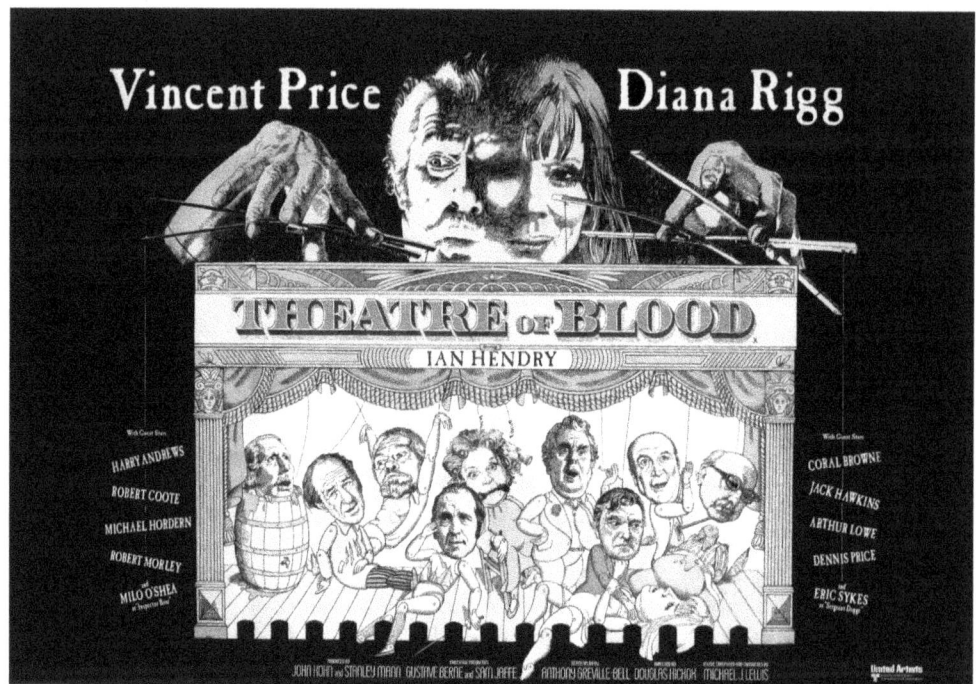

Diana Rigg (1938–2020) co-starred with Vincent Price and the cream of British character actors in Theatre of Blood *(1973).*

About the Author

Stephen Jones

British writer and editor Stephen Jones lives in London, England. A Hugo Award nominee, he is the winner of four World Fantasy Awards, three International Horror Guild Awards, five Bram Stoker Awards, twenty-one British Fantasy Awards and a Lifetime Achievement Award from the Horror Writers Association. One of Britain's most acclaimed horror and dark fantasy writers and editors, he has more than 160 books to his credit, including the illustrated histories, *The Art of Horror*, *The Art of Horror Movies* and *The Art of Pulp Horror*; the film books of Neil Gaiman's *Coraline* and *Stardust*, *The Illustrated Monster Movie Guide* and *The Hellraiser Chronicles*; the non-fiction studies *Horror: 100 Best Books* and *Horror: Another 100 Best Books* (both with Kim Newman); the single-author collections *Necronomicon* and *Eldritch Tales* by H.P. Lovecraft, *The Complete Chronicles of Conan* and *Conan's Brethren* by Robert E. Howard, and *Curious Warnings: The Great Ghost Stories of M.R. James*; plus such anthologies as *Terrifying Tales to Tell at Night: 10 Scary Stories to Give You Nightmares!*, *The Mammoth Book of Folk Horror*, *The Mammoth Book of Halloween Stories*, *The Lovecraft Squad* and *Zombie Apocalypse!* series, and thirty volumes of *Best New Horror*. You can visit his web site at www.stephenjoneseditor.com or follow him on Facebook at "Stephen Jones-Editor."

Coming in 2022...

www.ingramcontent.com/pod-product-compliance
Lightning Source LLC
Chambersburg PA
CBHW080448170426
43196CB00016B/2727